BEYOND OIL

BEYOND OIL
The Threat to Food and Fuel in the Coming Decades

JOHN GEVER
ROBERT KAUFMANN
DAVID SKOLE
CHARLES VÖRÖSMARTY

Complex Systems Research Center
University of New Hampshire

A Project of CARRYING CAPACITY, INC.

Ballinger Publishing Company • Cambridge, Massachusetts
A Subsidiary of Harper & Row, Publishers, Inc.

International Standard Book Number; 0-88730-074-X(CL)
0-88730-075-8(PB)

Library of Congress Catalog Card Number: 85-20007

Third Printing 1987

Printed in the United States of America

Library of Congress Cataloging-in-Publication Data
Main entry under title:

Beyond oil.

   "A project of Carrying Capacity, Inc."
   Bibliography: p.
   Includes index.
   1. Power resources—United States.   I. Gever, John.
TJ 163.25.U6B44   1985   33.79'0973   85-20007
ISBN 0-88730-074-X
ISBN 0-88730-075-8 (pbk.)

To my mother, father, and brother, who
encouraged my curiosity in all things alive;

To Charlie Hall, Berrien Moore, and
F. Harvey Pough, who brought this curiosity
to fruition;

and to Shauna Tannenbaum, who provided
the joy needed to do the work.

Love,

R.K.

To my son Daniel, for whom our findings
hold the greatest challenge.

C.V.

To Stanford Gibson, Robert Peffley, and
my parents, who taught me to think.

J.G.

To my parents and my son, Jordan;
for humanism and hope.

D.S.

CONTENTS

LIST OF FIGURES

LIST OF TABLES

ACKNOWLEDGMENTS

No work of this scope could ever be published without the efforts of many more people than the authors alone.

First and foremost, we extend heartfelt thanks to the director of the Complex Systems Research Center, Berrien Moore III, without whom this work would literally not have existed. It was Berrien who involved us in this project; it was Berrien who showed us the way out of numerous dark alleys and tight corners; it was Berrien who ran interference for us among various bureaucracies; it was Berrien who revived our sometimes flagging spirits during the three years it took to complete this book.

We are also in debt to our benefactors at Carrying Capacity, Inc.: Jay Harris, Gary Imhoff, and Ed Passerini. Jay first conceived this project, and his unceasing support saw us through the many dead ends, unexpected turns, and rough spots to its conclusion. Gary patiently slogged through countless drafts of the manuscript, politely weeding out dozens of our rhetorical excesses and correcting hundreds of verbal laxities. Moreover, he made so many substantive suggestions that he should really be considered a fifth author. Ed constantly challenged us to do better: to support this argument with more data, to consider that opposing argument, to explain and justify the counterintuitive, to be more rigorous in general.

Because today's science is a cooperative endeavor, we also wish to thank Charles A.S. Hall and Cutler J. Cleveland. With them we developed ways to use Howard Odum's theories to examine economic activity. Their watchful eyes caught most of the inaccuracies that inevitably arise during any transfer of information.

We thank the many academic and government experts who reviewed the manuscript at various stages, sometimes savagely but always usefully: Sandra Batie, Lynton Caldwell, John M. Corliss, Jr., Pierre Crosson, Otto Doering III, Medard Gabel, Edward Goldsmith, David Goldstein, Joan Gussow, Alex Haynes, Earl O. Heady, Robert Healy, Gary Heichel, Robert Herendeen, Nurel Islam, Wes Jackson, G. McCleary, Dennis Meadows, David Norse, Walter Parham, David Pimentel, John Richardson, Richard Rowberg, Vernon Ruttan, Abraham Sirkin, Malcolm Slesser, Thomas Stoel, Maryla Webb, Garth Youngberg, and James Zucchetto. Warm thanks also to Peter Haas, Amy Miller, and Fay Rubin for their critical comments on the general logic, rigor, and readability of the manuscript.

Our gratitude extends to Denise Clement for her hours of tedium in the library and at the computer plotter, to Irene Bartholomew, John Kelly, Cordelia Shea, Judy Spiller, and Steven Wolf for their work on an early version of the study, and to Laurie Badger and Diana Voyles for deciphering handwriting that would have baffled a roomful of cryptographers. Thanks also to Laurie, Clara Kustra and Mal Merrill for making flawless travel plans, arranging for reimbursements, and otherwise shielding us from local ugly realities while we concentrated on global ugly realities. Finally, we owe our wives and children an incalculable debt for tolerating the many weekend skull sessions and feverish late-night pushes to meet deadlines.

Oh yes—we also thank Federal Express and its clones, without which this work would probably have taken six years instead of three.

John Gever
Robert Kaufmann
David Skole
Charles Vörösmarty

Durham, New Hampshire
August 1985

INTRODUCTION

Consider the quality of American life in the near future:

- Around the turn of the new century we will use more energy exploring for oil than we gain from it.
- By the second decade of the new century U.S. farmers—already experiencing serious difficulty—could find energy so unaffordable that we would cease being a net exporter of agricultural products.
- A long-term slide in U.S. per capita GNP will begin in the 1990s, reflecting declining stores of oil and gas.
- The polluted skies that clouded the beginning of the Industrial Revolution could return in the form of acid rain and altered weather patterns as the United States reverts to coal.

Some of these gloomy scenarios are avoidable, but only through proper planning now. To believe that unfailing Yankee inventiveness or cure-all new technologies will solve our energy crisis is to foolishly deceive ourselves. For despite the current decline in the power of the OPEC cartel and the prevailing U.S. farm surpluses, few people would dispute the inevitability of declining energy resources, a decrease that will threaten the quality of life, the economy, the environment, and food production. Concerted action by government, business, and the American public must be taken to maintain the high living standards that we know.

The genius of the United States throughout its first two centuries has been in recognizing no limits, in believing that everything is possible. Ironically, to continue to stay wealthy we must now acknowledge limits to our resources and learn to be creative in making the most of them. Where we have been liberal and even radical in our use of resources, now we must be conservative. In fact, conservation is one key to a workable future. We must plan a future within the "carrying capacity" of our resources.

"Carrying capacity" is a useful planning concept. It means the number of plants, animals, or people that an area's resources can support indefinitely, that is, without impoverishing the environment.

Our organization, Carrying Capacity, Inc., was formed to analyze the carrying capacity of U.S. resources and how to move toward a permanently sustainable way of life in the United States and, over time, the world. We explore the policy implications of:

- the interplay among population, consumption, and environmental degradation in the United States;
- the social and economic consequences of a smaller, less consuming American society; and
- appropriate population and consumption levels for our nation, and how to reach those levels.

We chose to concentrate initially on the United States for one major reason: While many persons might agree that over the next few decades human populations will strain against natural resources in Asia or Africa, the prevailing view is still that the United States is a cornucopia country—a land of plenty, exempt from the problems of carrying capacity. Accordingly, the determination of how natural systems place limits on the population of a country as prosperous as the United States holds dramatic implications for the entire world.

In 1982 we asked the Complex Systems Research Center (CSRC) at the University of New Hampshire to model the energy future of the United States and, having done that, to project its effects on the nation's agricultural system. This book summarizes that intensive study.

The CSRC investigates problems stemming from interactions between humans and their environment. Rather than breaking down natural and global problems into isolated pieces and studying each piece separately, the Center uses mathematical modeling and policy analysis to study them as systems. Societies and national economies, inappropriate subjects for controlled experiments and physical testing, are best studied through computer-based mathematical modeling. This is CSRC's specialty.

Although we have long concurred with many of the conclusions and policy recommendations from previous energy studies, we believe the CSRC study—by reason of its rigor, extent, and longer time frame—more persuasively supports those conclusions. Potential critics will also find the study's premises and methodology open to their scrutiny. It is therefore a substantial advance beyond previous work and a very useful basis for policy initiatives.

The CSRC study concludes clearly that:

- Although the United States imports less than than one third of its oil today, it is likely to import over two thirds *only ten years from now*, putting the major OPEC nations permanently back in control.
- Over three fourths of all the oil that can be extracted from the lower 48 states has *already been extracted and used.*
- U.S. oil production, which has been falling slowly for over a decade, is *poised on the edge of a sharp drop-off.*
- The United States will be virtually out of oil by 2020, and the world will be out by 2040.
- In the 1950s, we discovered about 50 barrels of oil for every barrel invested in drilling and pumping. Today, the figure is only *five* for one. Sometime between 1994 and 2005 that figure becomes *one to one.* In other words, perhaps as early as 1994, it will generally become uneconomical to search for any oil for energy in the United States.
- The faster we drill for oil, the more oil we waste and the sooner we run out.
- The United States, which depends heavily on oil in its agriculture and is currently the only major exporter of food, *may be*

unable to export food much beyond the year 2000. Our soils are deteriorating rapidly, making a major transformation to a sustainable agriculture system imperative.

- Some kinds of conservation of energy may be much more difficult than previously believed.
- The U.S. Gross National Product is likely to enter a *significant long-term decline* before the turn of the century because of the emerging scarcity of oil.
- The sooner we stabilize our population, the higher our per capita income will be.

Carrying Capacity, Inc. believes that within a few decades there will be major energy shortages as well as food shortages in the world—conceivably extending to the United States—accompanied by an economic retrenchment created partly by the diversion of energy to agriculture from other economic sectors.

Modern industrial agriculture is inextricably tied to oil; it has flourished and it will decline in step with oil production. The CSRC study warns that we must move rapidly away from industrial agriculture to more sustainable forms of food production based on maximum use of the renewable energy of sunlight.

Technology has enabled us to get more out of the Earth faster and thus support five billion people—temporarily—although there are already major signs of stress in many areas of the world, particularly in desertified regions such as Ethiopia and the Sahel. But we have achieved this plenitude by mining the nonrenewable geologic deposits of fuel, phosphates, underground water, and other minerals. Technology enables us to farm our land so that we erode and degrade it faster than did any previous civilization. When our nonrenewable stocks run short, the Earth's carrying capacity will drop unless we can massively tap into sustainable sources of food and energy.

Can technology help us make the switch? The evidence to date is not encouraging. Technology seems to help us take resources from the past and future to increase present consumption. Most technologies are consumers of energy rather than producers or conservers. But perhaps this can be changed.

The matter before us is not just a question of new technologies but a question of the best technologies and directions for the long term. If we can learn to choose the right technologies, perhaps we can preserve and even increase our carrying capacity. If we choose exploitive technologies (whether existing or yet-to-be-invented), we will erode that capacity.

It is ironic that the environmental and alternative energy movements have been identified with a liberal political agenda in recent decades. In reality, conservation and energy development are conservative issues. Although government can set an example, private industry needs to assure itself of sufficient energy sources and will likely provide the entrepreneurial drive to create new sources while protecting existing supplies and ensuring jobs. Carrying Capacity, Inc. hopes that the publication of the CSRC study will help to politically depolarize the energy debate. We hope to work in concert with public policy organizations from left to right to identify viable solutions that maintain the long-term standards of living we associate with the "American way of life." In the Afterword to this book we add some positive comments on new energy saving techniques which were not included in the "soft path" calculations. We also propose a number of public policy initiatives which we believe are crucial, particularly with oil selling below twenty dollars a barrel. Although the CSRC study supports many of these initiatives, they represent solely the point of view of Carrying Capacity, Inc.

We hope that this study, the first comprehensive computer analysis of U.S. energy and agricultural resources that extends beyond the year 2000, will lead to a great many more long-range interdisciplinary studies and that government and private decisionmakers can use the CSRC model (a version will soon be available from our office with disk and written user instructions for either IBM PC [and compatibles] or Apple MacIntosh) to evaluate alternative policies. Inquiries about the research and model should be addressed directly to the Complex Systems Research Center, University of New Hampshire, Durham, New Hampshire, 03824. Inquiries about the implications of the study should be addressed to Carrying Capacity, Inc., 1325 G Street, N.W., Suite 1003, Washington, D.C., 20005.

Dr. Edward Passerini, Chair
John A. Harris IV, Secretary-Treasurer
Carrying Capacity, Inc.

February 1987

BEYOND OIL

1 CARRYING CAPACITY AND HUMAN SYSTEMS

Carrying capacity The population an area will support without undergoing deterioration.
—*Webster's New Collegiate Dictionary*

During the last 20,000 years, an eyeblink in geologic time, the human population has expanded from a few million sociologically uniform hunter-gatherers to a highly diverse population of nearly five billion. In fact, much of this growth has occurred only in the last 200 years. Our physical, chemical, and electromagnetic fingerprints are detectable everywhere, even in space. We have suddenly become earth's preeminent lifeform, just as dinosaurs were 60 million years ago.

But the success of the dinosaurs directly paralleled their biological evolution. Their numbers grew as their bodies evolved to become increasingly suited to their environment. Humans, on the other hand, haven't changed much physiologically in the last 20,000 years. The man of 20,000 years ago, dressed in a business suit, could pass unnoticed in any city in the world. It is our social organization, powered by our ingenuity and plentiful resources, that has evolved enormously during this period and that has been responsible for our biological success.

This social organization has enabled us to do more than merely multiply. In most places, our lives are now safer and more comfortable. Death from predators is now a remarkable occurrence—a man-bites-dog story, so to speak. The so-called natural death, death from old age, is actually most unnatural,

1

being almost entirely limited to humans and their pets. In the United States and other industrial nations, famine and epidemics are almost forgotten and the average life expectancy is now over seventy years, nearly double that of the poorest countries, which have infant mortality rates nearly twenty times higher. Although malnutrition and disease in the United States have not been stamped out, most of us have access to goods and services that are not needed for simple survival—for example, 99 of every 100 households have a television set.

We wanted to fly, so we invented flying machines; our bodies could not defend us against certain microbes and viruses, so we developed various chemical aids that could; we wanted to do more work than we could with our muscles, so we learned how to make domestic animals, falling water, wood, coal, oil, and uranium work for us. This seeming mastery of our environment has led many people to believe that nothing can contain the momentum of human progress, that not even the supply of natural resources should limit the size of our population or our material standard of living. If we run short of a particular natural resource, it is thought, our technology will find more of it or a substitute for it, or discover how to prosper without it at all. Confident of our technological capability to overcome limits, many people think that we can consume without regard to the future: "The present generation may give future generations fewer natural resources, but it will give future generations a higher level of technology and more capital."[1]

In short, many believe *Homo sapiens* has escaped the original limits on population size and standard of living imposed by the relatively meager flow of materials and energy available before the discovery of fire and the domestication of animals. We have become *Homo economicus*, rational consumers trying to maximize the happiness we can draw from the glittering array of consumer goods created by our ingenuity.

The boundlessness of human progress has not had a better showcase than the United States. In 350 years North America has been converted from a virtual wilderness to a huge industrial complex. Since 1850 the output of the U.S. economy has grown forty-three-fold in real dollars and the population has grown fivefold. Our scientists have tripled the amount of corn grown on an acre of farmland, enabled us to talk instantly to practically anyone, anywhere, at the touch of a few buttons, and put astronauts on the moon. These successes have been written into our national psyche almost as a law: increasing material wealth is an American birthright.

But the milk of past successes has begun to curdle. The U.S. economy now is in turbulence. Periodic recessions, far from being abolished, have continued to occur, and have become more severe with each recurrence in the last twenty years. The intervening inflations have become progressively steeper: the 3.1 percent average annual rise in prices between 1960 and 1972 was replaced by a 7.6 percent average annual rise from 1973 to 1984. Today we celebrate an unemployment rate of 7 percent, which ten years ago was considered disastrous.

Not only has the economy sputtered, but it seems beyond the control of the human ingenuity that built it. According to Keynesian and monetarist economic theories, which have guided policymakers for the last forty years, many of the recent signs of turbulence should not occur simultaneously. Double-digit inflation and 20 percent interest rates are supposed to be symptoms of an overheated economy, while high unemployment and low growth in gross national product (GNP) are indicators of a recession. Nevertheless, in 1981 the economy suffered all these at once.

A number of groups have been identified as potential villains in this state of affairs: free-spending politicians, tight-fisted bankers, greedy unions, OPEC. These groups may have exacerbated the nation's economic problems, but there is another force that may be ultimately responsible for creating those problems: the supply of natural resources.

Economic troubles, widespread environmental alteration and pollution, and dissatisfaction with the policies and traditions that produced them have rekindled an age-old debate concerning the place of humans in nature and the optimum population size. The important question is whether the same laws that limit the size of plant and animal populations also limit the size of human populations, or whether human intellect frees us from these constraints. Is any level of population, any level of resource consumption, too large? And, if so, have we reached or surpassed it already?

Populations of some plant and animal species seem to oscillate about a certain level that ecologists term the *carrying capacity*. Carrying capacity is defined as the number of individuals of a given species that a given area can support indefinitely. This sustainable population size is set by the amount of resources available and the rate at which individuals use them. These resources can take several forms: food, water, hiding places, territory, and so on. Since individual needs change very slowly, the carrying capacity for a plant or animal population can be estimated straightforwardly from the total supply of resources and per capita needs.

The "law" of perpetual progress and the powers of human intellect would seem to exempt human populations from the same constraints that set the carrying capacity for plant and animal populations. Technology has enabled humans to redefine the types of materials they consider resources, to transport resources to places where they don't normally exist, and to use resources deposited over millions of years in previously inaccessible locations. It is therefore extremely difficult to calculate a long-term carrying capacity for human populations because we can't know what will or will not be a resource in two hundred years, nor can we predict the level of per capita demand.

Some people, often called *cornucopians* or *resource optimists*, believe that our carrying capacity is essentially boundless. Natural resources of any type should not limit human carrying capacity because our ingenuity can make even ordinary seawater a useful resource. They see current economic problems as a transition to a new period of increased affluence. Do we have an energy shortage? Not in the long run, they believe, since our ingenuity will come up with plentiful new sources: Herman Kahn wrote, "[Humans are] now prepared to utilize the best tools from the most recent technology in the development and exploitation of several new alternatives that are known to constitute essentially *eternal* sources."[2] Is there a population problem? If there is, say the resource optimists, it is a problem of having too few people to bring sufficient brain power to bear: according to Julian Simon, "[Since] improvements—their invention and their adoption—come from people, it seems reasonable to assume that the amount of improvements depends on the number of people available to use their minds."[3] Our present difficulties are little more than growing pains that will appear as we enter an age of unprecedented affluence.

But many others argue that humans are not so different from plant and animal populations and that the size and material affluence of human populations is limited by the amount of natural resources available. Humans depend ultimately on the environment for all the materials needed to survive, even though the materials needed may change from time to time. Since the earth is finite, its carrying capacity must be, too. Such a view of human carrying capacity was central to the argument of Thomas Malthus, who argued that human numbers are limited by their food supply:

> Population, when unchecked, increases in a geometrical ratio. Subsistence increases only in an arithmetical ratio. A slight acquaintance with numbers will show the immensity of the first power in comparison of the second.

Adherents to the modern version of this view, the neo-Malthusians, see the current economic turbulence and confusion as symptoms that humans are approaching, if not exceeding, their carrying capacity (though, in contrast to Malthus, they do not generally view this situation as preordained or as better than all alternatives). Are we running out of resources? We certainly are, says David Brobst: "Geological exhaustion is not imaginary. It happens."[4] Do we have a population problem? We certainly do, according to researchers at the Worldwatch Institute: "Growing numbers of consumers are using up the world's finite energy resources more and more rapidly."[5] According to this view, it is only a matter of time until the growing individual demands of an expanding population catch and surpass the earth's ability to supply these resources, causing population contraction, reduced individual consumption, or both.

The debate between the cornucopians and the neo-Malthusians is not merely academic, for both national priorities and guidelines for individual actions over the coming decades depend on who prevails. If human intellect has freed us from natural constraints, we as individuals and as a society can consume fuels and other resources as we always have. On the other hand, if the human population is approaching or exceeding its carrying capacity, we had better discover what these limits are and formulate responsible strategies to keep ourselves within them.

THE TWO COMPONENTS OF PROGRESS

At some level, certainly, human actions are constrained by the same physical, chemical, and biological principles that limit the actions of other life forms. Such principles define rules that humans must obey. Humans cannot repeal the laws of gravity or annul the laws of thermodynamics. These physical laws set the operating conditions to which the strategies of all creatures, including humans, must conform. We did not suspend the laws of gravity when we learned to fly; rather, we learned how to shape a wing so that aerodynamic forces balanced the force of gravity. We did not repeal the laws of thermodynamics when we learned to make hydrogen bombs; rather, we learned how to create conditions like those inside the sun and other stars, at least for a few picoseconds.

Among the most important physical laws limiting our actions are the laws of thermodynamics. These laws state that energy can be neither annihilated nor created from nothing, and that the universe moves spontaneously toward greater disorder. Opposing this tendency by imposing order on a group of disordered objects takes work, and performing work requires using—disordering—some energy. In fact, enough energy must be "used" so that the net amount of disorder, which is called *entropy* and which can be measured, of the objects plus the energy is increased. Plants, animals, and people represent highly ordered agglomerations of atoms into organic molecules, molecules into cells, cells into tissues, tissues into organs, and organs into systems that function together as living creatures. To achieve this "unnatural" order, all living creatures have developed strategies for capturing highly ordered energy and using it to build and maintain their organic structure. Plants are able to capture energy from the sunlight that falls on them (which is highly ordered compared to most of the radiation originating here on earth); and animals, including humans, capture their energy from plants or other animals linked in the food chain to plants.

But humans in industrial societies need more than just food energy to support themselves. We now depend on inanimate capital structures that have far greater energy requirements than individual humans. These structures have enabled our population to grow well beyond that supportable by a hunter-gatherer lifestyle, to the point that now we *need* this capital—farm equipment, factories, roads, and the fuel to build and maintain them—to keep all of us alive. Human survival, except in the most primitive societies, is now contingent on the ability to obtain energy for our nonliving support systems. The best way to estimate the bounds on what people can and cannot do—that is, the carrying capacity for humans—is to examine the amount of energy available to human populations and the ways in which that energy is used.

We have achieved technological success, historically, by understanding the physical constraints on human activity and devising ways to finesse or circumvent these limits. Since most useful activity goes against the universe's general tendency toward increasing disorder, for the most part this technology has involved harnessing nonfood energy to do work. As we shall describe in Chapter 3, much of the increased productivity of today's worker has been achieved by finding new ways to increase the rate at which humans can direct energy for their own purposes.

Particularly during the past 200 years, control over bur-geoning flows of nonfood energy has enabled us to support more people at higher material standards of living. Human ingenuity developed the theory behind the internal combustion engine, and our technology enabled us to mold such a device from metals obtained from rocks. The environment also provided us with a fuel, petroleum, to power both the production and operation of the engine. This advance allowed farmers to trade their horse-drawn plows for tractors, which in turn enabled each farmer to produce more food from an acre of land with fewer hours of work. Many people left their farms to work in cities producing other goods. Thus, increasing technological knowhow increased the amount of usable material at our disposal and helped us shape it into useful goods by subsidizing our meager muscle power with the energy from other living and nonliving sources of energy. Technology boosted our carrying capacity.

The rate at which technological advances allow human populations to grow and to raise their material standard of living depends on the two components of technical progress and economic growth: the technological capabilities of people to find ways to use energy and other natural resources, and the supply of energy and other natural resources available to implement this knowledge. As a practical matter, either human knowledge or resource supply will lag behind the other, so that the economy can grow only as quickly as the less developed or available component. This idea of a limiting factor for the rate of economic growth parallels the biological concept of the "Liebigian limiting nutrient." Justus Liebig, a nineteenth-century German chemist, found that the rate at which a plant or animal can grow depends on the supply of the nutrient that is least available relative to other nutrients. For example, if a plant needs 10 units of nitrogen and 100 units of carbon to synthesize one unit of new leaf, and has 10 units of nitrogen but only 50 units of carbon, it can synthesize only half a unit of new leaf because it has only enough carbon to combine with half the nitrogen it has available. Carbon, in this case, is the limiting nutrient.

Similarly, technological knowledge was the limiting factor for economic growth in North America until recently. When Europeans first reached the New World, large deposits of timber, fuels, metals, and other natural resources lay waiting. Some of these materials were immediately useful to the newcomers based on what they already knew or learned from the native population. However, other resources went unrecognized or undiscovered. Although tremendous deposits of hematite iron ore lay in the new land, it was not until the Bessemer steelmaking process was introduced in 1865 that they became useful as a source of iron. Therefore, the exponential rise in iron mining did not start until the latter half of the nineteenth century. Similarly, the first oil well was drilled in 1859, but gasoline was not an important source of energy until Henry Ford made automobiles affordable to the masses.

During this period of relatively immature technology, people in the United States acquired a "frontier mentality." We believed that we could always get as much of anything as we wanted if only we wanted it badly enough—that there were no limits to the resource base. Progress was identified with the construction of capital structures, like railroad, mines, and steel mills, which enabled us to exploit resources at ever-increasing rates. This point of view took for granted the supply of fuels and other natural resources fed into these capital structures and used to build them in the first place. It was a useful assumption, insofar as its brash confidence helped the United States become the industrial giant it is today.

But simply because resources have always been abundant in the past does not mean that they always must be in the future. Assuming perpetual plenty blinds us to important changes in the resource base that are already having a significant impact on our economy. Technology has finally caught up with the supply of resources—the economy has matured.

Over the last fifty years, we have made serious inroads into the supply of many of our high-quality fuels and other natural resources. As a result, perhaps the most important hypothesis of this book is this: *the supply of fuels and other natural resources is becoming the limiting factor constraining the rate of economic growth.*

The history of oil production in Louisiana is a microcosm of this reversal. According to energy analysts Robert Costanza and Cutler Cleveland, the amount of effort needed to pump a barrel of oil can be explained by two factors: the rate of technological advance and the rate of resource depletion.[6] At first, our knowledge of how to remove oil from the ground in Louisiana increased much faster than the actual resource extraction, allowing us to produce more oil at less expense. Eventually, however, the rate of increase in technological knowhow began to slacken and the pace of oil withdrawal sped up. At the end, which we are fast approaching, we know a great deal about oil drilling, but it becomes so expensive and energy-intensive to pump any more that we stop trying. At some point in the middle, resource supply replaced technology as the limiting factor to oil production—and resource supply will eventually become the limiting factor to all resource extraction.

The U.S. economy is now reaching that crossover point, and examples abound. The technology exists for putting moving sidewalks in cities or building extremely lightweight but sturdy cars from exotic alloys, but society has decided that the energy and materials needed to implement this technical knowhow are needed elsewhere. We simply don't have the resources to do everything we know how to do or would like to do. It would make Robert Browning happy to know that our reach still exceeds our grasp.

SEEING INTO THE FUTURE

Every attempt at seeing into the future, including this one, involves the extrapolation of past trends. Past trends are the only tool available for this: we are sure that the moon won't explode tomorrow because the mechanisms underlying its physics and chemistry have never before led to explosions. But we may not get an accurate picture of what lies ahead if we extrapolate superficial trains of events rather than mechanisms: until May 18, 1980, Mount St. Helens had a very long history of not exploding.

Thus, we must be careful to choose the *mechanisms* to extrapolate, both in volcano monitoring and in economic forecasting. The latter case is particularly treacherous because many recent events resulted from the combination of an immature technical base and a high-quality resource base, conditions that no longer apply. Failure to understand these changed conditions can lead to very dangerous conclusions. For example, Julian Simon, probably the best known cornucopian, predicts that most metals will become less scarce in the future.[7] His argument is based on the observation that amount of metal produced per worker-hour or purchased by an hour's wage has increased in the past, a trend that he simply assumes will continue in the future. But he does not consider the mechanisms behind the extraction technology that made this past trend possible. Although the physical quality of these ores has declined, we have found ways to use plentiful, high-quality fossil fuels to extract increasing amounts of metal from poorer ores. In the future, as the supply of high-quality fuels shrinks, we will no longer have enough energy to compensate for declining resource quality, and the amount of metal produced per hour or purchased with an hour's wage will diminish. Because of progress's dependence on resource quality and human knowledge, it is important to look beyond surface trends and understand how these two components of technology led to past trends and what the future behavior of these components portends. To sketch the future of a resource-limited world, we need to perform an inventory of our resources, examine how rapidly we are degrading or depleting them, and assess the ability of our technology to slow or stop these trends.

During the last 100 years, we have changed our natural resource base in two important ways. First, we have "used" many materials faster than they are replenished. That is, we have built these materials into our buildings, sewers, roads, and the rest of our infrastructure or thrown them away irretrievably. This "drawdown" applies to both the so-called nonrenewable and renewable resources. We are now using copper faster than the earth's biogeochemical cycles create new ores and faster than our economy recycles copper scrap. Similarly, we have killed whales faster than they reproduce, driving several species to the brink of extinction. These trends are occurring to some degree for almost every resource we use.

Second, we have exhausted many of our highest-quality deposits of resources and have been forced to recover them from progressively lower-quality deposits. The hematite ores of the Mesabi range in Minnesota contained 60 percent iron, but we have depleted them and we now must use lower-quality taconite ores that have an iron content of about 25 percent. Again, this trend is occurring for almost every resource. As a result, we must work harder to get the same amount of material out of the ground.

Alone, neither of these trends would be too disturbing. We may currently be using our copper faster than we find new deposits or recycle it, but in the future why couldn't we mine it from seawater and mount a major recycling effort? The quality of our ores may be declining, but why couldn't we build better machines to squeeze resources from these poorer ores? Certainly such strategies worked in the past, and they are the cornerstone of Simon's and Kahn's cornucopian vision of the future.

The problem is that it takes energy to mine seawater, to run a recycling network, and to refine ores. And, as with other resources, the United States and the world is using its major energy resources much faster than they are being replenished by natural processes. The world uses oil and gas at least 10,000 times faster than the earth's geological processes are replacing it. To make matters worse, we are depleting the best fuel stocks and are having to use progressively poorer deposits. The average energy content of a pound of coal dug in the United States has dropped 14 percent since 1955, and the amount of energy needed to drill an average foot of oil well has tripled since 1945 as we drill deeper in more hostile environments. And, contrary to a commonly held belief, rising fuel prices will not create new supplies of fuel. They haven't so far, anyway: despite quadrupled prices for oil and gas products, the "moral equivalent of war," and a 280 percent increase in drilling, the United States is producing less oil today than it did in 1973.

If our economy and our lifestyles were not at stake, the struggle between our increasing technological sophistication and the accelerating decline in resource quality and fuel supplies would make an entertaining spectacle. Will substitutes and more efficient technologies be found in time to offset this decline, or will we undergo a period of economic contraction? This book attempts to answer this question for the United States. Although the problems and trends discussed are global, we focus on the United States for several reasons: It is the largest industrial nation, so that a change in its resource consumption will have worldwide implications; its citizens enjoy one of the highest standards of living, and it has long been considered a land of plenty in a world of want; much of the world depends on the United States for food; and statistics going back several decades are easily available. (Our analysis is based primarily on U.S. government data and other sources of conservative—that is, standardized and relatively noncontroversial—statistics.)

Of course, there is a drawback to looking only at the United States. The United States already depends on foreign suppliers for many important resources. Moreover, if domestic resources are becoming poorer, it is possible to supplement or replace them with imports as Japan and many European nations have done.

However, significant expansion in the percentage of U.S. resource consumption coming from foreign sources would carry tremendous but unpredictable costs. First, in order to assure that supplies of strategic resources would not be cut off abruptly, the United States would have to adopt a Japanese-style friend-to-all foreign policy, and/or expand its global military presence even more. The political history of the United States suggests that either would meet with fierce opposition. The former would require us to give up the option of refusing to deal with nations, like Iran, whose governments we don't like; the latter would entail sacrificing, not just a lot of money and energy, but also our self-image (realistic or not) as a nation that leads by moral instead of military force.

Second, for the United States to expand the already considerable fraction of world resources that it uses, the rest of the world would have to consent to permanent status as an economic colony of the United States: they supply the resources we need to maintain our affluent lifestyles, in return for a few scraps. Resources consumed in the United States are no longer available to developing economies; therefore, expansion in U.S. imports further impedes economic growth in the Third World. Having to outbid other nations for resources could have ramifications, like higher prices, here at home as well. We certainly don't rule out an increased role for imported resources in the U.S. economy, but it is fair to say that the consequences would not go down well with the rest of the world. The forms that their displeasure might take, however, can't be predicted or quantified. And, anyway, even if imports did let the United States circumvent the limits imposed by its domestic resources, it would only be temporary as long as resource use remains unsustainable. Thus, we have just looked at what could happen in the absence of massive imports. The conclusions of this analysis should be interpreted in this light: per capita production of material wealth could be higher than our limited investigation suggests, but there would be substantial tradeoffs.

The time scale chosen in such an analysis is critical in intepreting the results. The rate at which we're depleting our oil supplies doesn't matter if we are only interested in the next five years. At the same time, the ability of technology to change our definition of resources—today's useless rock is tomorrow's valuable resource—makes it impossible to say whether our society is sustainable for the next 500 years. Because of these difficulties, human carrying capacity must be examined in a limited scope and in a limited period. Our analysis primarily addresses the next forty years. During this period we will be forced to make the transition away from oil and gas, which today make up 75 percent of the U.S. energy budget, to some yet-to-be-determined alternative fuels.

What we have found is sobering: absent a technological miracle, the United States won't be able to develop new sources of fuel or to improve the economy's energy efficiency fast enough to avert a decline in economic output stemming from the deterioration of the resource base. The projected decline is not steep nor necessarily permanent—but neither does it appear that it *must* be moderate and temporary. If we don't begin now to plan a smooth transition away from oil and gas, the decline could be much more precipitous and unpleasant. The future is not already determined, and we still have much room to maneuver, for better or for worse.

These conclusions regarding the U.S. economy as a whole apply with at least equal force to the agriculture system. The production of food has become almost totally dependent on oil and gas, not only to provide the chemicals and machinery now used on our farms, but also to process and distribute farm products. At the same time, and partly as a result of industrial farming methods, the land base has been degraded by soil erosion, chemical pollution, and water depletion. For the last few decades, the impact of this degradation on crop production has been more than offset by the intensification and refinement of industrial agriculture, including (but not limited to) the development of hybrid crop varieties. But over the last few decades, the amount of energy needed to produce a unit of food in the United States has risen steadily. Moreover, yearly increases in agricultural productivity attributable to improved technology have become smaller in the last fifteen years, and some agronomists are warning that the well of agricultural technology may be running dry. The rising dollar costs of modern farming techniques, combined with low food prices, are driving many farmers into bankruptcy.

The future of U.S. agriculture is murky indeed. Land degradation could be controlled if farmers were to adopt soil-conserving practices; on the other hand, too many farmers may refuse to adopt them because they're worried about the drops in crop production that are widely thought to accompany such practices. Genetic engineering could breathe new life into agricultural research; on the other hand, it may turn out to be another Comet Kohoutek. Thus, any effort at prognostication must take this tremendous uncertainty into account. But one thing is clear: today the quality of the agricultural resource base is deteriorating. Therefore, as fossil fuel supplies dwindle and as population grows, it will be increasingly difficult for the agriculture system to match its past successes.

Based on a projection of a decline in economic and agricultural output, it could be said that we exceeded our carrying capacity once we began to use resources faster than they are created or when we began to deplete high-quality stocks. In the strictest sense this may be true—such use is by definition unsustainable, and if it is unsustainable then the long-term carrying capacity is being exceeded—but it is misleading. Most of us wouldn't care if our use of resources were unsustainable for the next five hundred years; this time scale is too large to affect today's decisions. The problem is that current patterns of resource use, including the ways in which we respond to perceived scarcities, are not sustainable even for the next forty or fifty years.

We're not Luddites condemning all unsustainable use of resources. Many important human accomplishments have been achieved by depleting resources. What kind of society would we have today if nonrenewable veins of coal had never been mined?

The key to reconciling the use of nonrenewable resources with the concept of carrying capacity lies in the rapid adaptability of humans. We would say that *a population, human or otherwise, is exceeding its carrying capacity if severe hardships and/or population contraction become inevitable*. Other species are not very flexible in the short term with regard to important resources. They generally can't find replacements for important resources; if they use a resource much faster than it is replenished, a population collapse usually ensues. But history is full of examples in which humans adjusted quickly to the absence of a particular resource by finding substitutes and averted substantial hardship.

In short, simply because we are using certain resources faster than they are replenished does not necessarily mean that we are exceeding our carrying capacity and have doomed ourselves to a population collapse. But, on the other hand, the longer we use resources unsustainably, the closer we come to the edge of our carrying capacity and the more difficult it will be to back away from it.

Many people are aware of our resource supply-versus-consumption problem but, sometimes unconsciously, dismiss it by assuming that a technological breakthrough will solve it in the nick of time. This is really no different from the *deus ex machina* (literally, "god from a machine") of classical drama, a clumsy and contrived way to resolve a complicated plot. Although we do consider the steady, incremental development of technology in this book, we don't assume either that technological quantum leaps are possible or that they are impossible, and therefore we disregard them. As a result, our projections are necessarily open to the "what if" criticism: "What if there is a big breakthrough in oil drilling or fusion power? What if photovoltaic cell technology develops faster than expected? What if a new steelmaking process is developed that needs only one-third the energy of the best current technique? Wouldn't such discoveries greatly alleviate the problems you describe?" The short answer, of course, is that such breakthroughs can't be ruled out and that they would indeed help reduce our resource problems. But no single breakthrough would solve them, and the probability that several could be achieved is vanishingly small. We would also point out that it is a matter of simple prudence, in planning for the future, to assume that we will receive no such windfalls. Therefore, we should try to prolong our dwindling stocks of high-quality fossil fuels and other resources rather than gamble our economy and our relatively comfortable lifestyles on a suite of technological breakthroughs—if not for our own sake, then for that of our children.

THE BASIC ARGUMENT

Energy, Natural Resources, and Dollars

Energy is the one natural resource that we can't do without and for which there is no substitute. The laws of thermodynamics tell us that energy is needed to create goods and services from natural resources. Our ability to create goods and services depends on the availability of energy. Energy's importance and the limits to its supply can be appreciated in several ways. Consider what would happen to the economy if all fossil fuels suddenly disappeared. Alternatively, consider what life would be like if energy were free, if we didn't have to work—to dig mines, drill wells, or build dams—to get it: we could keep everybody's homes at 72° year-round, drive cars that get 5 miles per gallon, fit all our cities with moving sidewalks, turn lead into gold, and perhaps even eliminate poverty.

But even though fuel isn't free, it has been plentiful enough to transform society. Human muscle power now supplies less than two-tenths of 1 percent of the work done in the U.S. economy. Jobs in which people are paid solely for the energy of their muscles have virtually disappeared from the economy; machines that run on fossil fuels have supplemented, and to some extent have replaced, people that run on food energy. The primary function of people in an industrial economy is to control and direct fossil fuel energy, or to manage other people who do. People still exert themselves and get tired, but the amount of physical work their bodies do is only an infinitesimal portion of the total work accomplished. Most of the work it takes a riveter to drive a thousand rivets is done by a pneumatic gun, not by the person using it: a riveter using a hammer could drive far fewer rivets in a day. Most middle-class homes are filled with "labor-saving" gadgets that really just shift the burden from human muscles to distant electric generating plants.

Because industrial societies depend on nonhuman and nonanimal forms of energy, particularly fossil fuels, we can use the energy requirements for a particular process to measure its cost. For instance, if it takes 15 barrels of oil to mine a ton of copper, the *energy cost* of a ton of that copper is 15 barrels of oil. To be complete, estimates of energy costs should include not only the fuel used directly in a process, but (where data are available) also a fraction of the energy used to produce the necessary machinery and to supply the workers with food, warm houses, and transportation. Standard accounting procedures have been developed to calculate energy costs. By comparing these costs to our total energy budget, we can gauge how much of the total work our society does that must be done merely to get the natural resources we need.

We care about the relative size of this effort because people cannot do an infinite amount of work at any given time; committing energy and resources to one activity reduces the amount of energy and resources available to do other things. Therefore, if we must work harder to obtain natural resources, we can do less work elsewhere in the economy and we can have fewer goods and services, unless we can discover how to create more useful output from the same amount of resources and energy.

Usually we think of the cost of goods or resources in terms of dollars. But the dollar price of something measures its *value*, which is determined by a great many factors. The price of copper depends on the quantity sold, the effort expended to extract the resource, the rent paid to the mine owner, the taxes paid to the government, the rate at which capital equipment can be depreciated, consumer income, the cost of alternative materials, the usefulness that the copper can provide, and so on. But the extrinsic availability of a resource, as measured by the effort needed to obtain it, is usually swamped by the large number of other factors that determine the resource's dollar value. If we want to know the cost of getting copper from the environment, only one of these factors—the effort expended to find and extract resources—is relevant. Only in the rare case in which the effort needed to extract a natural resource dominates both the supply and demand sides of the dollar valuation will changes in dollar costs accurately measure changes in its physical availability.

The energy cost straightforwardly measures the effort needed to obtain a resource, since energy cost is usually unaffected by the other factors that influence the resource's price. Given a particular technology, the total energy cost of extracting and refining a resource rises as the quality of the resource declines—that is, as the concentration of the resource in ore declines or as new sources of ore must be found deeper in the ground or in more remote or hostile environments. Of course, technological changes can alter the amount of energy required, but, as we describe in Chapter 2, this century has seen very few instances in which technological advances have been able to counterbalance the increased energy costs incurred by exploiting lower-quality deposits.

In short, while the dollar cost of a given resource is a broad measure of the value we place on it, the energy cost reflects one important component of that value: the scarcity of the resource relative to our total ability to create goods and services, a component that most economists, unfortunately, don't worry about.

In Chapter 2 we examine one of the two components of technical progress—the supply of resources needed to implement human knowledge—by looking at historical trends regarding the energy costs of resources. We see that those costs have risen consistently over the last 50 to 100 years. Metals and other geological resources are scattered through the earth's crust in deposits of varying concentration and accessibility. Naturally, we have exploited the most highly concentrated and most accessible deposits first; these deposits had the lowest energy costs. As we depleted these high-quality deposits, we had to use deposits of lower quality that required more energy to recover. The growth in energy costs has thus been an inevitable consequence of industrial expansion and rising demand for industrial output.

The energy costs of self-reproducing resources like trees, fish, and farm products have risen, too. As we have removed these resources faster than the most accessible and rich forests, fishing grounds, and croplands can replenish themselves, we have had to begin harvesting more marginal resources. Moreover, rising demand has led us to try to control these resources in order to increase the supply, raising energy costs further. In colonial times, for example, people who wanted water simply filled a bucket at the town spring or well. Today, we dam rivers and pipe the captured water hundreds of miles to many of our cities, where it is passed through sophisticated treatment plants before being used and through equally sophisticated sewage plants afterward. In many cases, this kind of resource management has failed to keep up with demand, and renewable resources have been exploited faster than they've been renewed. This has led to dwindling supplies, as in the case of water in many western states.[8]

It might not matter if the energy costs of resources kept increasing, so long as we had the fuel to pay them. But energy itself has an energy cost; it takes energy to drill oil and gas wells, to dig coal and uranium mines, and to build hydroelectric dams, windmills, and solar collectors. Since fossil fuels are nonrenewable, we should not be surprised to find that the energy costs of oil, natural gas, and coal, which supply nearly 90 percent of all energy consumed in the United States, are rising rapidly. The best projections of the energy costs of and energy returns on oil and gas exploration show, in fact, that *by 2005 it will be pointless to continue exploring for oil and gas as energy sources in the United States*: after that more energy would be used to look for these fuels than the oil and gas we found would contain. (Conceivably, exploration for gas alone could proceed for a few more years; moreover, we'll still be able to pump oil and gas from known fields at an energy profit for some time after exploration becomes fruitless.) The United States has a great deal of coal and its energy cost is lower than oil's, but solid coal is a poorer, more polluting fuel than oil and gas, and coal liquefaction and gasification have very high energy costs.

We can make a reasonably confident prediction of annual domestic and world oil and gas production for the decades ahead. In the 1950s geologist M. King Hubbert developed a method for projecting future oil production: he predicted then that U.S. oil production would peak in about 1970 and decline thereafter. Though it was scoffed at then, the Hubbert analysis has since been proved to be remarkably accurate. If we redo the analysis today for oil and gas with the most up-to-date information, we find that domestic oil and gas stores—including fields yet to be discovered as well as proven reserves—will be effectively empty by 2020. World oil and gas supplies will last perhaps three decades longer, or more if Third World economies fail to develop, as is beginning to appear likely.

Recently, oil and gas journals and the lay press have talked optimistically about the 60 percent or more of underground oil that can't be reached with conventional recovery techniques, and the possibility of exploiting at least some of it with sophisticated "enhanced oil recovery" technologies. The coal industry reminds us regularly about the magnitude of U.S. coal reserves and how they could supply all our energy needs for centuries. Barry Commoner has sung the praises of methane and ethanol in *The New Yorker*. But only rarely do these panegyrics consider the energy costs of these options, and when known these costs are usually substantial. Energy costs must be spelled out if we are to evaluate such claims realistically—if a so-called fuel source actually consumes more energy than is contained in the fuel, as is the case with some alcohol technologies, the "fuel" is actually a drain on the economy's energy supplies. The economy runs on *net energy*, the energy left over after the costs of obtaining it are subtracted, and not on gross energy.

Moreover, the energy costs of obtaining fuel and performing other tasks must include *all* energy used in the process, whether directly or indirectly. For example, the manufacture of alcohol from corn has been promoted as an alternative fuel of the future. Energy profit calculations usually include the fuel needed to run the tractors used to grow the corn. But the additional fuel needed to build the tractors or to make the pesticides and fertilizers they spread is rarely considered. When all such costs are included, analysts find that, at best, converting corn to alcohol barely turns an energy profit and may be a net loss.[9] Indirect costs can be as important, and are often more important, than direct fuel costs in the extraction of energy from the environment and indeed in all economic activities. But they are usually disregarded, even though accounting methods, which we use in this book, have been developed that include them.

We have combined a Hubbert analysis with a realistic appraisal of the energy costs of various fuels at our disposal, including coal- and solar-based "alternative" fuels. We are forced to conclude that, absent a discovery of a huge new source of low-cost fuel, the annual flow of gross energy to the U.S. economy simply can't grow very much for the next forty years. As population continues to grow, each individual's share of a static or shrinking energy pool must decline. Moreover, as rising energy costs divert an increasing amount of fuel to the tasks of obtaining raw fuel and nonfuel resources, including food, less energy will be left over to run the rest of the economy. This means less energy will be available to build TV sets and cars and all the other material accouterments of modern American life. More important, it also means less energy will be available to retool industry and to build the infrastructures needed to develop the energy sources of the future.

But does less net energy and falling resource quality necessarily mean less output of material goods? Mightn't the efficiency with which we use energy to produce goods be improved? To answer these questions, we must examine the second component of technical progress: the methods by which we convert fuels and other resources into goods. On the surface, it appears that our knowledge is already more than offsetting the effects of declining resource quality: the economy's energy efficiency, as measured by the ratio of the real gross national product (in constant dollars) to the nation's total fuel consumption (in kilocalories, BTUs, or other units of heat), rose 78 percent between 1929 and 1983, and more than half of this rise occurred after 1970. Thus, we have apparently been able to create more output with each unit of fuel, presumably through increasingly clever technology. This, at least, has been the conventional wisdom.

But the conventional wisdom overlooks two important structural changes, discussed in Chapter 3, in the way technology uses energy. One change involves the switch in our primary energy sources from bulky, solid fuels like wood and coal to more efficiently handled fuels like oil, natural gas, and electricity. The other change is that the amount of fuel used in the household sector has declined in the last ten years. (The *household sector* is that part of the economy made up of the activities of private individuals and includes automobile driving as well as activities taking place in the home *per se*. In this book, *household consumption* includes all consumption of goods and services by individuals that does not result in other goods or services for resale.) Together, these structural changes have a 96 percent correlation with the year-to-year variation in the ratio of GNP to fuel consumption since 1929. Little change is left over to attribute to replacing energy with improved machinery or to better manufacturing processes. In fact, an explicit statistical consideration of fuel prices shows that prices, except for their impact on household fuel use, have had only a small effect on the GNP/fuel ratio. We don't doubt that there has been industrial conservation, but the behavior of the GNP/fuel ratio suggests that much of this conservation has been offset by added fuel costs elsewhere in the economy.

Thus, while finding ways to replace wood and coal with electricity, oil, and gas involved an astonishing amount of technological wizardry, this is a very different sort of technology than what is often credited with improving the economy's energy efficiency. We have not, as is usually thought, been doing the same things with less energy. Instead, we have been doing different things with different fuels.

Why should the types of fuels used affect the economy's energy efficiency, either in the past or in the future? Very briefly, oil and gas create more economic value per kilocalorie (kcal) than coal does because liquids and gases make better motor and boiler fuels than solids do and are easier to transport. And, because electricity is so well suited for use in electronic equipment and small motors, a kcal of it is even more useful than a kcal of oil and gas, especially in manufacturing. As the percentage of the nation's fuel budget supplied by electricity and oil and gas has risen, GNP has risen even faster. But this trend almost certainly can't continue in the future because oil and gas production is declining and will continue to decline and because our ability to increase the production of electricity is heavily constrained. The Hubbert analysis and the increasing energy costs of oil and gas development ensure that domestic oil and gas production can't be raised for long without hastening and steepening the inevitable decline; the large-scale hydroelectric sites with the lowest energy costs of development have already been developed; for a variety of reasons, including safety and financial cost, nuclear energy is unpopular; and photovoltaic, wind, and other solar-based electric technologies, although developing rapidly, are still in their infancy. Thus, one trend underlying the increase in the economy's apparent energy efficiency—a larger measure of oil and gas and electricity—will not continue. The fuel mix will *decrease* the energy efficiency if we are forced to return to coal and wood as our primary energy sources.

Another source of increase in apparent energy efficiency, on the other hand, might well continue into the future. Historically, when household fuel use dropped, the ratio of real GNP to fuel consumption rose. This occurred because a dollar's worth of fuel bought by a household is a lot more energy than the energy used to produce a dollar's worth of other goods and services (where fuel is one of several ingredients). If you had spent a dollar on gasoline in early 1985, you would have gotten about

26,000 kcal in energy. If, on the other hand, you had spent a dollar on something besides fuel, the energy you "bought"—that is, the energy used to produce that dollar's worth of nonfuel goods—was only a fraction of 26,000 kcal. Thus, when the household sector spends more of its dollars on fuel and less on other things, it tends to depress the real GNP/fuel ratio. During World War II and after the 1973 oil price shocks, for example, household fuel use dropped, so the GNP/fuel consumption ratio rose. This is a trend that certainly could continue in the future, but it remains to be seen whether further reductions in household fuel use can be achieved without also curtailing people's living standards.

In addition to these two structural changes, fluctuations in fuel prices also have an effect on energy efficiency. However, a statistical analysis shows that, over the 1929–83 period, the effects of the fuel mix and household fuel consumption have dwarfed the impact of fuel prices, largely because fuel prices were extraordinarily stable until the 1970s. Even since 1973, rising prices seem to have influenced household fuel purchases more than energy use in manufacturing and other "intermediate" (as opposed to final demand) sectors. A statistical treatment described in Chapter 3 shows that the *energy price elasticity* of intermediate sectors (the degree to which energy purchases are reduced by a given price increase) is much smaller than previously thought. But on the other hand, the analysis suggests that if fuel prices continue to fall as they have in the last two years, both households and businesses will lose whatever incentive they now have to become more efficient.

We can quantify and project the above trends associated with the resource base and technical knowhow into the middle-term future with reasonable confidence. This allows us to construct a computer model of their interactions and see generally what sort of material future we might expect, given the assumptions we've made. Chapter 4 contains the results of this effort: We may expect per capita GNP to keep rising until the mid-1990s, when it will level off and then decline. By 2020, assuming a major effort has been made to replace dwindling stocks of oil and gas with other fuels, per capita GNP will have fallen back to a level like that of today. Moreover, this picture is improved only slightly even if a lot more oil is pumped than the Hubbert method predicts or if nuclear power plants are built at an unprecedented rate. On the other hand, the model shows that it is quite possible to choke off all economic growth and ensure a considerably worse future, even before 2025, by allowing population growth to accelerate or by falling back into energy-wasting personal habits. The only way to keep per capita GNP near our accustomed levels is to cut population growth and residential fuel use drastically and, at the very least, to maintain incentives to increase manufacturing efficiency.

We're certainly not recommending maximization of GNP as the primary goal of national policy. Per capita GNP is an imperfect indicator of living standards, and it becomes more imperfect all the time. We use it in the model because our purpose is to assess the economy's ability, given declining supplies of net energy in the future, to deliver the sorts of goods it did in the past when energy was abundant. Per capita GNP is a relatively good indicator of the kinds of goods and services we consumed in the past. But as the fraction of our economic effort devoted simply to finding fuels and other resources continues to mount, per capita GNP will no longer reflect the consumption of consumer goods: it will be bloated by the rising real cost of resources. Moreover, as we pointed out earlier, GNP can be raised substantially by diverting fuel from the household sector to manufacturing sectors. But although per capita GNP might be raised thereby, per capita "happiness" may not be: people like to use energy directly in their homes and cars. We may not enjoy a rise in per capita GNP if it means giving up home heating oil in exchange for blankets and union suits.

Furthermore, these projections should not be confused with predictions because they assume that all available energy supplies will be used each year, neglecting the likelihood that business cycles will occasionally depress fuel use below the maximum potential level. The projections are also based on the assumption that no radical changes will occur in our basic economic structure. We've assumed that industrial societies won't be shattered by revolution or nuclear war or transformed by the discovery of huge, energy cost-free sources of fuel or other technological fixes. We can't rule out these possibilities, of course. But every present alternative fuel that could conceivably be available in sufficiently large quantities to replace oil and gas either has formidable environmental or energy costs, as do coal and solar-based fuels, or is decades away from commercial application, as is controlled nuclear fusion. It's nice to hope and try for technological fixes, but it would be foolish to put ourselves in a predicament in which we *must* have them—especially if we can get along comfortably without any fixes at all.

Many of these conclusions at first glance seem to be contradicted by the current situation. Oil prices in the United States have fallen, the economy looks healthy, inflation is lower than in the early 1980s, fuel imports are far below the peaks of the 1970s. How then can we claim that the postwar period of rapid economic growth is coming to a close and that energy supplies will severely limit the economy in the future? The answers can be found in the Hubbert method and in a consideration of the Unites States' place in the world.

The prices that the United States pays in the world market for oil are declining because, thanks to the world's reaction to the price shocks of 1973–74 and 1979–80, the world's output and use of oil is growing much more slowly. In 1973 the world was using practically all its oil production capacity. But since then the drastic price rises and the consequent recessions and conservation have reduced demand for oil, while the world's capacity to produce oil has continued to increase: the Hubbert curve for world oil won't peak at least until 2000. This gap between demand and potential supply has depressed oil prices in the United States, and these depressed prices in turn have played a major role in powering the U.S. economic recovery. However, as of 1985, oil prices for most of the rest of the world were *not* declining. OPEC countries insist that oil be paid for with U.S. dollars, and the strength of the dollar meant that the price of oil in francs, lire, and most other currencies wasn't falling at all. As a result, most of the world's economies remained in the doldrums.

The forces behind these economic realities—the U.S. budget deficit, stalled Third World development, and a rising world Hubbert curve—will probably combine to keep oil prices in the United States relatively low and the economy robust (except for cyclical dips). But a few Persian Gulf nations still control a vastly disproportionate share of world oil reserves, and eventually the conditions of 1973 will be recreated. Sometime before

2010, perhaps even by 1995, the non-OPEC world will be producing at full capacity, which will allow Saudi Arabia, Kuwait, Iran, and the United Arab Emirates to cut back their production slightly and force prices up again. Oil's essential scarcity will again be felt. Thus the United States faces an extreme hazard: a "crisis of abundance." The United States is becoming dangerously complacent about energy, and efforts to wean the economy away from oil and gas are losing momentum. If the United States does nothing about its still heavy dependence on these fuels before world oil production begins its inevitable decline, the nation will find itself reliving the energy crisis of the 1970s, and this time it will last much longer.

Energy and Agriculture

The conventional wisdom about the history of agriculture is also marked by misconceptions as to the source of "progress." Typically, American ingenuity and technology are credited with making this nation the World's Breadbasket. In one sense this has been true, but Chapter 5 shows that ingenuity and technology have been implemented by funneling ever-increasing flows of fossil fuels into the agricultural system. Take away the fossil fuel subsidies—in the form of tractors, fertilizers, herbicides, insecticides, and the other paraphernalia of modern agriculture—and the agriculture system would be lacking virtually everything that makes it more productive than it was in the colonial era. True, the high-yielding crop strains of the Green Revolution have greatly increased per-acre crop yields, and in the laboratory such strains produce more food per unit of fertilizer applied; but over the last forty years in the real world, these increases have gone hand in hand with even faster increases in the use of energy-based agricultural inputs. The success of U.S. agriculture has relied, and probably will continue for some time to rely, on the heavy use of fuel.

The quality of our agricultural resource base has declined just as surely as the quality of our copper resources. Over the last fifty years, the number and size of tractors, the annual use of fertilizers and pesticides, and other fuel-based inputs to agriculture have increased much faster than farm output. That is, the energy cost of growing food has been rising. This is partly, perhaps mostly, due to a real decline in the quality of the land we cultivate. Heavy erosion, sinking water tables, pollution, and compaction of soil result from the industrialization of agriculture. Along with the conversion of farmland to urban uses, these side effects of industrial agriculture degrade the agriculture resource base. It is difficult or impossible to calculate the loss of productivity due to these effects. But we can be sure that a significant fraction of the increase in fuel-based inputs into the agriculture system has been needed to make up for resource degradation. We seem to be caught in a vicious circle: intense cultivation techniques are used to make up for the effects of agricultural degradation, but at the same time they worsen that degradation, requiring even more intense cultivation to keep food production up.

The rising domestic demand for crops can be traced both to rising population and to the relatively large proportion of the average diet, about 35 percent of its caloric content, made up of animal products. Nearly 60 percent of our meat, poultry, eggs, dairy products, and animal fats come from animals fed on crops rather than grazing land. Based on the proportions of the different kinds of animal-based foods in the average U.S. diet, each kcal of animal-based food requires about 16 kcal (a kcal is the same as a calorie, the familiar measure of food energy) of crops to produce. Not only is there far too little grazing land to accommodate the demand for animal products, but crop-fed animals (especially cattle) generally produce tenderer meat than grazed animals do. The end result is that less than one-fifth of the crops grown in the United States for domestic use are eaten directly by people; the vast bulk are fed to cattle, hogs, and chickens.

Moreover, when the agriculture system is understood to include the transportation, processing, packaging, and distribution of food, it is even more inefficient in terms of edible food energy produced per unit of fuel input and even more dependent on fuel. About three times as much energy is consumed in these off-farm activities as is used on the nation's farms. Supermarkets across the United States carry oranges, broccoli, and other fresh produce, as well as hundreds of kinds of canned and frozen prepared foods, all year long. Many foods that once were pre-

pared at home in a few simple steps now undergo heavy processing before a consumer sees them. The potatoes in Pringle's
Potato Chips, for example, are dehydrated, rehydrated,
mechanically pressed into a special shape, cooked, packed into a
brightly colored plastic, metal, and paper container, and then
shipped to stores across the country. Consumers may enjoy
these conveniences, but fossil fuels are required to provide
them.

Given the heavy dependence of the agriculture system on fossil fuels and the limits to the nation's energy supplies, we asked
whether the United States can continue to be the World's
Breadbasket. The question is particularly pertinent in light of
the importance of food in the nation's trade balance: food
exports in 1981 offset half of the dollar cost of imported oil.

Chapter 6 presents the results of the computer model we created to help answer that question. Briefly, the model shows that
current trends are not sustainable over the next forty years. We
found that the nation can continue to be a net exporter of food
only if changes are made in the ways in which food is grown.
Either the system must be made more efficient by means such
as reducing demand for meats or reversing the ongoing decline
in agricultural resource quality, or else an increasing fraction
of the nation's scarce fuel supplies will have to be diverted to
agriculture from other sectors of the economy. The latter course
is extremely perilous: not only would it squeeze manufacturing
and service sectors between the rock of agriculture and the hard
place of other resource-extraction activities, but it would also
entail a further intensification of industrialized agriculture,
hastening the long-term decline in the agricultural resource
base. Relieving the pressure on the agriculture system might
require disagreeable and unpopular sacrifices of cherished eating habits, but failure to make them would jeopardize the entire
economy and the long-term ability even to feed ourselves.

CONCLUSION

Current patterns of resource use are certainly not sustainable
indefinitely: it's absurd to think that we can continue to mine
metals without a major recycling effort or that we can use fossil

fuels forever. The real question, however, is whether it is too late to change these patterns before they bring on a serious economic disruption.

The Hubbert curve, projections of the energy costs of resources, and the interplay of the various components indicate that we have enough time to make changes. But they also indicate that we have little time to spare, that we need to begin soon the transition away from fossil fuels and use-it-once-and-throw-it-away patterns of resource consumption. In the past, such patterns were not necessarily bad: they gave us the vast reserve of technology and knowledge that we hope can be turned to finding sustainable ways to use resources. But those patterns were appropriate only as long as they didn't tangibly endanger the availability of resources to future generations. Today they do.

Soon the people of the United States must choose among their patterns of resource use and decide which to keep and which to modify or jettison. For example, the United States must choose the fuels to replace oil and gas. Solid coal, a plentiful fuel that has a high energy profit ratio but that is also ill suited for many uses, such as transportation? Synthetic fuels, which would function in the economy just like oil and gas but at the price of low energy profit ratios? Or renewable solar-based fuels—such as photovoltaics, wind power, active and passive solar thermal systems, alcohol, and the like—which are clean and will last forever but which the nation's economic structure is less prepared to assimilate?

Moreover, as the United States's total per capita fuel supply shrinks, people must also decide whether to cut back on their direct uses of fuel or on their consumption of other goods and services, which take fuel to make. Traditional economic analyses say that there is no need to choose at all—new, ultraefficient energy-using goods can save fuel and money for consumers with no reduction in the goods' usefulness—but currently most consumers refuse to buy such goods. This suggests that, regardless of the savings involved, most consumers believe that buying these goods entails some kind of unacceptable sacrifice. Plainly the traditional analyses are missing something. Chapter 7 describes how the information that the market sends to consumers must be changed if the United States wants them to buy energy-efficient appliances, homes, and cars. The alternative is to make no changes at all, to leave the current market structure as it is, which will encourage people to continue using a lot of fuel directly and will lead to fewer nonfuel goods and services.

But no matter how effective the nation is in reducing household fuel use, it is highly probable that the amount of fuel available to industry will still decline. Such a decline poses another dilemma: should the United States reduce the amount of fuel used per worker-hour, and by extension labor productivity and hourly wages, in such a way as to maintain a forty-hour work-week for 90 percent of the labor force? Or should the nation keep energy use per worker-hour (and labor productivity) near current levels and reduce the number of worker-hours instead? And again, the current market structure is pushing the economy toward one of the options: the low employment, high productivity strategy. If people in the United States prefer the other strategy, they must change the way in which decisions about production methods and employment are made.

Constraints on energy supplies (and on potential cropland area) also will impose changes on the agriculture system. Current market forces are combining, in a complex way, to reduce the overall energy efficiency of farming, despite improvements in farming technology. As energy production drops, so then will food production. However, the model in Chapter 6 suggests that deliberate acceptance of slightly lower crop yields per acre, combined with soil conservation efforts and further improvements in technology, could reverse the decline in efficiency. In fact, such a program could also solve many farmers' financial difficulties and, in the long run, lead to higher food production than would be possible by letting the existing market run its course.

Lastly, the nation should be wondering whether the current massive military buildup may be locking the United States into a prolonged economic contraction. Would we really rather spend trillions of dollars (and the scarce energy they represent) on enormous weapons systems that (we hope) will never be used, or should we spend it on an economic foundation for the future? How much security do weapons give us if to pay for them we hurt our economy and become even more dependent on foreign sources of energy? Isn't a strong, stable economy a nation's best defense?

We suspect that most people in the United States are not in favor of the strategies favored by the existing market for dealing with resource limitations. The policies suggested for changing the market structure are not radical, and in many cases reflect nothing more than what Europe and Japan have lived with for years. Nevertheless, many people in the United States would find them unpleasant, and it will take a good deal of courage and vision for a politician to advocate them in the 1980s. They will almost certainly be rejected by those who believe that, since existing systems and strategies were highly successful in the past, they must continue to be in the future, and who do not understand our changed circumstances. They overlook the fact that the successes of the past were the result of escalating withdrawals from a limited patrimony of fossil fuels, an inheritance that is nearing exhaustion. There is still enough of this one-time inheritance left for us to invest at a decent rate of return, but the decision to do so must be made *now*.

2 THE DECLINING RESOURCE BASE

The sun and the moon and the stars would have disappeared long ago . . . had they happened to be within the reach of predatory human hands.

—Havelock Ellis

THE DEMAND FOR RESOURCES

Since the Industrial Revolution came to the United States in earnest, around 1850, the demand for resources has exploded. Between 1870 and 1980 the gross national product (GNP) of the United States increased by a factor of 43 (measured in constant 1958 dollars). GNP, which also measures the total demand for goods and services, can be broken down into two components, population size and per capita demand. The U.S. population in 1980 stood at 5.7 times its 1870 level, while the 1980 level of real per capita GNP was 7.5 times higher than it was in 1870. This means that growth in per capita demand accounted for 57 percent of the increase in total demand for goods and services. Since 1940, in fact, growth in per capita GNP accounts for an even larger fraction—67 percent—of total GNP growth.

With few exceptions, we've been able to satisfy this high demand only by using our resources in unsustainable ways. We have used resources faster than we have recycled them or than they are naturally replenished, and we have decreased the rate of replenishment. Unsustainable resource use has led inexorably to exhaustion or depletion of many so-called high-quality

33

resources. As we pointed out in Chapter 1, unsustainable resource *use* is not in itself dangerous. As long as we can adjust smoothly to life without a particular resource when it runs out, unsustainable use is tolerable. What is intolerable is *dependence on*, the inability to do without, a resource that is being used unsustainably.

This notion of sustainability lies behind the familiar labels we apply to various resources: *renewable* or *nonrenewable*. Resources that are replenished after humans use them are usually considered renewable; those that aren't, we call nonrenewable. Unfortunately, these definitions are less than ideal, since it is not always clear how a resource ought to be classified. For example, groundwater is fed by rainfall and is therefore part of the renewable hydrologic cycle of water between earth, ocean, and atmosphere. Yet in parts of New Mexico groundwater is replenished at the rate of about one-fifth of an inch per year, while it is used at a rate of several feet per year. Is groundwater in New Mexico renewable? The only way to answer such questions is to define renewability so that it applies, not to the resource itself, but to the rate at which humans use it. Industrial societies are characterized by (among other things) a high rate of resource use. A renewable resource, by our definition, is one that an industrial society uses sustainably or could use sustainably, even though it may not be doing so at the moment. Most trees, fish, sunlight, and surface waters are thus renewable; fossil fuels and New Mexico groundwater are nonrenewable.

But even with this loose definition of renewability, qualitative differences appear between renewable and nonrenewable resources. Nonrenewable resources tend to be mineral in origin, formed by geological processes in large deposits. The total supply of these nonrenewable resources for the next fifty years is already in place and waiting to be exploited, so extraction can proceed as rapidly as demand warrants. Renewable resources, on the other hand, are generally biological or solar based; they are renewed much as interest accumulates on money in a savings account. This "interest" is usually much smaller in a given year than the amount of a nonrenewable substitute that we could mine.

These differences in the availability of resources have led the United States and other societies to meet burgeoning demand by using nonrenewable resources in addition to or in place of renewable counterparts. For example, the total annual demand in the United States for coal, a nonrenewable resource, is about 0.15 percent of our total coal reserve. If we tried to replace coal with wood, a renewable resource, we would need 82.7 million cubic feet of wood each year, which is about 12 percent of all U.S. forest growing stock. Our forests would quickly disappear. This is one reason why fossil fuels have replaced renewable fuels like wood in industrial economies. Fossil fuels have also been easier and cheaper to extract than their renewable counterparts, once technologies were developed to find and make use of them. They have also been better fuels: oil is cleaner and more convenient than wood. As a result, nonrenewable fuels' share of the U.S. energy budget jumped from 9 percent in 1850 to 95 percent by 1981 (Figures 2–1a and 2–1b).

The mechanisms that encouraged the substitution of nonrenewable for renewable fuels apply as well to many other types of resources. The development of synthetic rubber, for instance, allowed society to supersede the limits imposed on rubber products by the number of rubber trees and the rate at which they could be tapped. Now the supply of rubber products is limited by the rate at which we can obtain petrochemicals. While production of natural rubber increased by 3 percent a year during the 1960s and 1970s, production of its ersatz cousin rose 9 percent, so that by 1978 synthetic rubber accounted for 70 percent of the world market (Figure 2–2). Synthetic fibers like nylon have similarly begun to displace natural ones (Table 2–1). Such substitutions may improve the utility of consumer goods as well as help to boost production— many people consider polyester-cotton blend shirts superior to all-cotton ones—but they also help addict us to unsustainable patterns of resource use.

As long as demand for nonrenewable resources grows, and as long as we don't have a 100 percent efficient recycling system, no use of nonrenewable resources is sustainable indefinitely. But reliance on renewable resources is no guarantee that resources will be used sustainably. In the United States, in fact,

Figure 2–1a. Quantity of Energy Supplied by Nonrenewable Fuels Such as Oil, Gas, Coal, and Nuclear Electricity and the Amount of Energy Supplied by Renewable Sources Such as Wood, Wind, and Hydroelectricity and Food Consumed by the U.S. Population

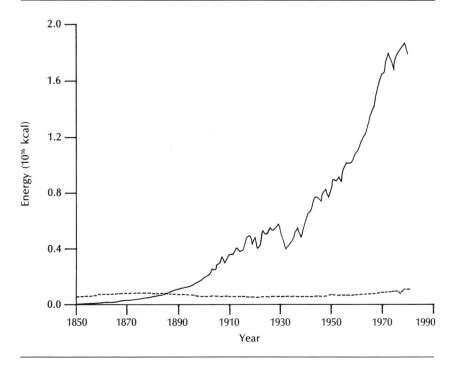

Sources: U.S. Department of Commerce, Bureau of the Census, *Historical Statistics of the United States, Colonial Times to 1970* (Washington, D.C.: USGPO, 1975); U.S. Department of Energy, *Monthly Energy Review* (Washington, D.C.: DOE, various years); U.S. Department of Energy, Energy Information Administration, *Estimates of U.S. Wood Energy Consumption from 1949 to 1981* (Washington, D.C.: USGPO, 1982).
Note: Dotted line is renewable fuels; solid line is nonrenewable fuels.

very few renewable resources are being fully renewed; most are being degraded or treated as nonrenewables in response to increased demand. For example, because of the agricultural system's extreme dependence on fossil fuels, described more fully in Chapter 5, it makes little sense anymore to talk of farm products as renewable resources. Moreover, erosion and other soil management problems are jeopardizing the fertility of as much

Figure 2–1b. Percentage of U.S. Fuel Budget Supplied by Nonrenewable Fuels

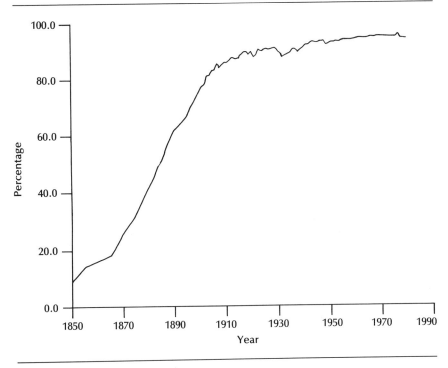

Year

Note: Solid line is nonrenewable fuels.

as one-third of U.S. farmland, according to the U.S. Department of Agriculture. Indeed, the United States has managed to "mine" some of its renewable resources to the brink of exhaustion. Giant redwoods, several whale and fish species, and the buffalo (which has made a modest comeback, thanks to government protection) are well-known examples. Production of most other renewable resources, such as trees and fish, is not keeping pace with the general growth in demand for resources. We rely increasingly on imports and on nonrenewable substitutes to make up the difference, but they are only stopgaps so long as demand for resources continues to grow. Demand for a particular resource must level off at some point, voluntarily or otherwise.

Figure 2–2.   Sources of World Rubber Supplies

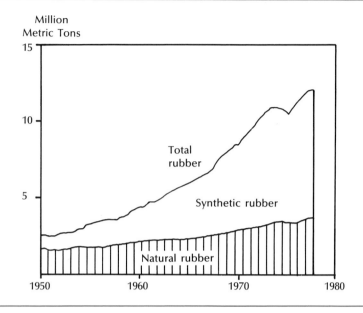

Source: C. Flavin, "The Future of Synthetic Materials: The Petroleum Connection,"
Worldwatch Paper 36 (Washington, D.C.: Worldwatch Institute, 1980).

Table 2–1.   Sources of Various Fibers Used in the World

Year	All Fibers	Cotton	Wool	Rayon	Synthetics (Polyester, Acrylics, Nylon)	Synthetics as Share of Fibers Used (percentage)
		(million metric tons)				
1951	10.8	7.8	1.1	1.8	.1	1
1955	12.5	8.8	1.2	2.3	.3	2
1960	15.2	10.4	1.5	2.6	.7	5
1965	18.1	11.3	1.5	3.3	2.1	11
1970	21.8	12.1	1.6	3.4	4.7	22
1975	24.7	13.0	1.4	3.0	7.4	30
1979	29.1	13.8	1.5	3.4	10.4	36

Source: C. Flavin, "The Future of Synthetic Materials: The Petroleum Connection,"
Worldwatch Paper 36 (Washington, D.C.: Worldwatch Institute, 1980).

THE DECLINE IN RESOURCE QUALITY

Deposits of a given resource vary in concentration and accessibility. Most metals, for example, don't lie around in 0.998 pure nuggets; they are chemically or physically bonded to other materials in ores and may occur in tiny concentrations. For example, people have mined gold ore with 0.12 ounces of metal per ton. The ores themselves may be easy to get at and bring to market, or they may lie in remote areas or deep in the earth. In fact, concentration and accessibility separate "ores" from other rocks that contain traces of some valuable metal; the earth's crust underneath the United States contains roughly 500 trillion metric tons of manganese, yet the 1982–83 U.S. Statistical Abstract lists U.S. manganese reserves as essentially zero. This crustal manganese is too dispersed and/or too deep in the earth to be considered useful as a reserve at current prices. That, in fact, is the distinction between reserves and resources: *reserves* are the known deposits that may be economically exploited with existing technology, while the term *resources* encompasses every trace in existence.[1] On paper, at least, all resources might someday become part of the reserves, but some of the reserves will still be more easily exploitable than others. We sum up this gradation in accessibility with the term *resource quality*.

Resource quality can be measured in several ways.[2] In this book, we measure it in terms of the energy required to extract the resource and refine it to a state useful to humans. This is the *energy cost* of a resource. High-quality deposits of fuels, metals, and other resources (both renewable and nonrenewable) require less energy to exploit than other deposits of the same material.

We use energy costs to measure resource quality because energy is the most fundamental ingredient of economic activity. Energy is required to perform *all* activities, including many (such as creating and supporting labor pools, capital stocks, and "entrepreneurial spirit") that are not generally associated with energy inputs. Additionally, energy cannot be created or recycled within the economic system but must always be procured fresh from "outside"—that is, from the environment.

Often, however, economists measure the quality of a resource by its dollar price, which may lead to wrong conclusions. The dollar price of a resource is really an indicator of its value to humans, which is bound up with human desires for that resource based on the utility it can provide. The quality of a resource, on the other hand, should measure the effort humans must invest to get it from the environment. Since *effort* can be equated with *work*, and *work* is equivalent to *energy*, energy costs reflect the relative effort that society must make to obtain resources from different deposits.

Resource quality is important because the additional energy needed to tap lower-quality resources is energy that is no longer available to turn raw materials into finished products. Given a set amount of energy, society can have fewer finished products if it must use lower-quality resources. (In the next chapter we discuss the possibility of offsetting lower resource quality through increased energy efficiency.)

The problem with dollars as a measure of resource quality is that they are artificial quantities that exist only in transactions between people and are therefore almost always inappropriate for evaluating transactions between people and the environment. We can't get iron ore out of the ground by giving dollars to the earth; we have to *work* for it, and the laws of physics state that work requires energy. A resource's dollar price is therefore often a very imperfect measure of the difficulty of obtaining the resource from the environment. For instance, the dollar price of silver rose from $6.50 per ounce in January 1979 to more than $50 in January 1980. Was there a sudden decline in the quality or quantity of silver ore? No: by late 1979, after several years of quiet but heavy silver purchases, Nelson Bunker Hunt and William Herbert Hunt possessed or had contracted to take delivery on almost half the world's marketable silver; their buying spree temporarily panicked the world's metal markets. The price soon fell back to nearly its original level. The Hunts didn't make it any more difficult to obtain silver from the environment: they merely made it more difficult to obtain it from other people. We don't want to imply that dollars are not needed in the extraction of resources; of course, workers and suppliers of materials must be paid, and dollars suggest how much of which resources are needed. But in addition to these interpersonal transactions conducted in dollars, the quite different interaction between people and the environment is conducted with energy, and it is this transaction that is often neglected or badly assessed by dollar costs.

This focus on energy and the distinction between a resource's value and its cost are somewhat foreign to conventional economics, which has concerned itself primarily with transactions between people and has left the interactions of people with their environment to ecologists. In the average economist's view, the economy is a closed, self-regulating, self-driven cycle of goods and services flowing between "households" and "firms." Although this simplifying assumption has allowed economists to describe and predict certain kinds of economic exchanges, it is unrealistic: the economy is not closed but requires inputs of resources, especially energy, from outside the economic system. This inaccuracy was unimportant when the amount of energy needed to obtain resources (including fuels) from the environment was small compared to the total amount of energy used in the economy. But as high levels of demand have caused us to deplete our highest-quality resources and to put increased pressure on the resource base, the model of a closed and self-regenerating economy has become further and further divorced from reality. Economic problems have arisen from changes in the relationship between the economic system and the environment, a relationship that traditional economics assumed was static and insignificant.

Conventional (more precisely known as neoclassical) economists usually don't consider the possible effects of human-caused changes in the environment on our economy. These economists assume that, if a resource is valuable enough (that is, if its dollar price is high enough), demand for it can always be fulfilled. Rarely do they consider the economywide effects of using lower-quality deposits or even whether people have the physical ability to go out and get those resources. We can therefore expect that conventional economic laws will become increasingly ineffective at explaining or providing solutions for economic problems. The increasingly severe inflation, unemployment, and interest rates of the last dozen years are signs that the laws are failing now.[3]

When resource quality is defined in terms of energy investment, the record shows clearly that quality is declining across
almost the entire spectrum of resources. Generally, people have
used high-quality deposits first, and as these deposits became
exhausted or when demand surpassed the rate at which they
could be exploited, lower-quality deposits were used.[4] An equivalent statement is that the energy cost of producing one more
unit rises as the current supply of a resource shrinks.

The production histories of individual metal deposits, entire
metal industries, and the whole extractive sector of the U.S.
economy reflect this pattern. Figure 2–3 details the silver production of the Comstock lode in Nevada. As cumulative ore
production rose, both the silver concentration and the rate of
silver production fell. Near the end, very low-quality ore and

Figure 2–3.   Production History of the Comstock Silver Lode

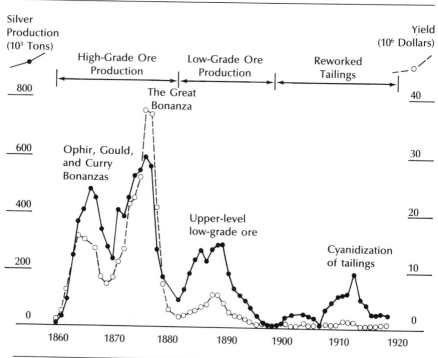

Source: E. Cook, "Limits to the Exploitation of Nonrenewable Resources," *Science* 191 (1976): 677–82. © 1976 AAAS

Figure 2–4. Ore Quality of U.S. Copper, 1906 to 1980

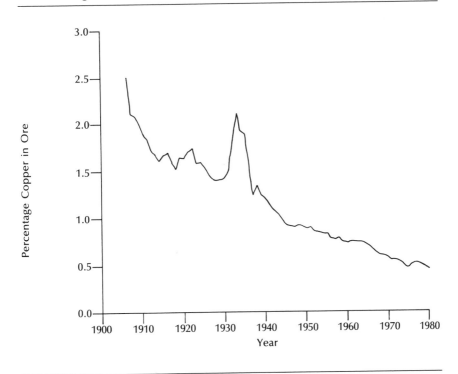

Source: U.S. Department of the Interior, Bureau of Mines, *Minerals Yearbook* (Washington, D.C.: USGPO, 1906 and subsequent years).

even mine tailings were exploited, but very little silver was obtained. Figure 2–4 shows the history of U.S. copper mining. Except for a brief rise in average quality during the 1930s, when a Depression-induced 75 percent drop in copper demand forced the closing of all but the best-quality mines, the same trend is evident.[5]

The relation between cumulative production, resource quality, and energy costs can be seen in the U.S. copper industry. In the early 1960s it used about 38 billion BTUs of energy (in fuels, electricity, and capital equipment) to refine a ton of copper. By 1977 it took 62 billion BTUs to obtain the same ton of copper. The energy cost of U.S. copper is substantially higher than for copper from other countries[6] (Figure 2–5), which may contribute as much to the price disparity between domestic and foreign copper as do the oft-cited "unfair practices" of foreign competitors. The decline in quality of U.S. metals, fuels, and minerals is widespread: the amount of output produced per unit energy has declined between 1939 and 1977 (Figure 2–6).

We have only a finite amount of energy at our disposal at any given time, and we must budget it among various activities. This trend toward lower resource quality is important because it forces us to use more of our energy budget to obtain the same quantity of resources. New finds of high-quality deposits may increase the average quality, but to our knowledge this has not occurred in the United States for nonfuel resources since the turn of the century. Moreover, as will be explained in detail later, technological improvements have only rarely reduced the amount of energy needed to exploit a resource. The best, and perhaps only, example of such an improvement was developed in the 1950s: the pelletization method for obtaining iron from

Figure 2–5.   Quantity of Energy Required to Extract a Ton of Copper from Different Quality Deposits

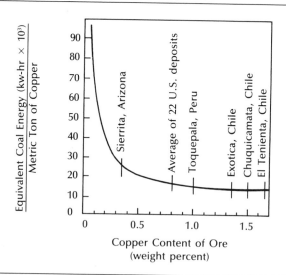

Source: E. Cook, "Limits to the Exploitation of Nonrenewable Resources," Science 191 (1976): 677–82. © 1976 AAAS

Figure 2–6. Index of Mineral Output per kcal of Energy Used to Extract It, 1939 to 1977

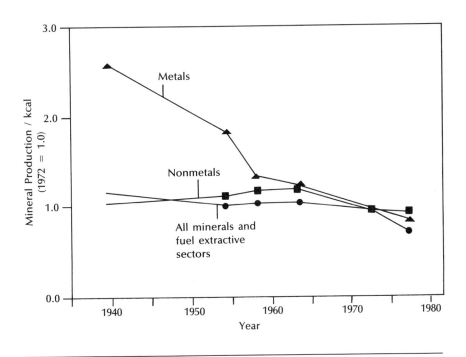

Source: C.J. Cleveland, R. Costanza, C. Hall, and R. Kaufmann, "Energy and the U.S. Economy: A Biophysical Perspective," *Science* 225 (1984): 890–97. © 1984 AAAS

taconite (a plentiful but low-iron-content ore found near Lake Superior).[7]

Cumulative demand, the total quantity of a resource extracted over time, produced these decreases in *nonrenewable* resource quality. However, it is instantaneous demand, the demand over a relatively short interval (practically speaking, a year or less) that affects the quality of *renewable* resources. If demand exceeds the rate of replenishment, stocks of renewable resources decline, and more energy is required to take them from a shrinking pool. As renewable resources are "mined," then, energy costs rise and the quality declines. This response of energy costs to changing instantaneous demand is important

Figure 2–7. Fish Catch (in energy value of edible protein) per Unit of Energy Used by Fishermen versus the Fuel Used by Fishermen

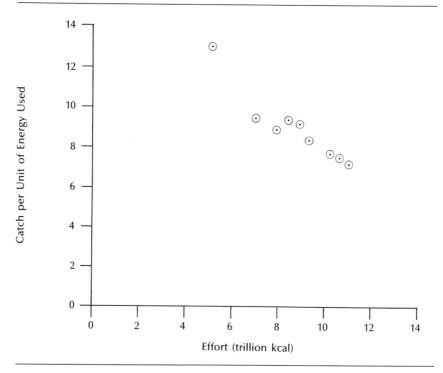

Source: C. Hall, C.J. Cleveland, and R. Kaufmann, *Energy and Resource Quality: The Ecology of the Industrial Process* (New York: John Wiley & Sons, 1986).

because the reverse effect is also possible: if demand is reduced and stocks of the resource are allowed to build up again, its quality may increase.

Rises in energy costs due to "mining" of renewable resources have in fact occurred. In the U.S. fishing industry, the amount of edible energy caught per unit of fossil fuel used in the process has declined by 62 percent in the last twenty years (Figure 2–7). Fishermen are removing more fish each year than reach maturity, thereby mining the stock of reproducing fish. Because the easier-to-find fish have been exhausted, fishermen then must travel farther and trawl longer to achieve the same catch.

The quality of some renewable resources has declined for other reasons. Yields of some resources, like croplands, are actively managed to increase production. Managing natural resources requires people to subsidize natural energies (natural processes that supply nutrients and carry off wastes) with additional energy to increase production. Augmenting or replacing natural energies with supplemental energies (like fossil fuels) does not always increase yields proportionately; this is because biological processes require several inputs in more or less fixed proportions, but the inputs are almost never available in precisely those proportions. For instance, crop growth requires, among other things, seed, water, nutrients, sunlight, and space. Since the odds are remote that all of these will be present in exactly the right proportions, one of them will be in least supply relative to the plants' needs. Adding more of the others may increase productivity somewhat, but not for long. This is Liebig's law of the minimum, mentioned in Chapter 1. Continuing to pour in fertilizer, when the plants really need more water or sunlight, will have waning, and perhaps negative, effects on productivity. (In fact, there is a maximum rate at which biological processes can occur, and at some point this will become limiting.) Figures 2–8a and 2–8b show how progressive additions of fertilizer affect wheat yields. At first, the fertilizer is highly effective, but eventually the supply of this nutrient becomes less important than the limitations imposed by other inputs, and productivity levels off despite additional fertilizer. Eventually yields decline as more fertilizer actually begins to poison the land.

Throughout this century, U.S. farmers have increased crop yields per acre by subsidizing natural energies with fuel, thus raising the energy costs of food. Modern crop strains, which are usually given credit for these greatly increased yields, are actually little more than passive conduits for mounting fuel subsidies. Energy that earlier crop varieties used to collect nutrients has been channeled, in the improved strains, to allow them to be planted more densely and to fatten their edible portions. (Without the requisite heavy doses of fertilizers and pesticides, some modern crops actually fare worse than their unimproved ancestors.[8]) Between 1945 and 1970 per-acre corn yield rose from 34 to 81 bushels (Figure 2–9a) and total corn production

Figure 2–8a. Yield of Two Wheat Strains, Sonora-64 and C-306, as a Function of Nitrogen Fertilizer Applied

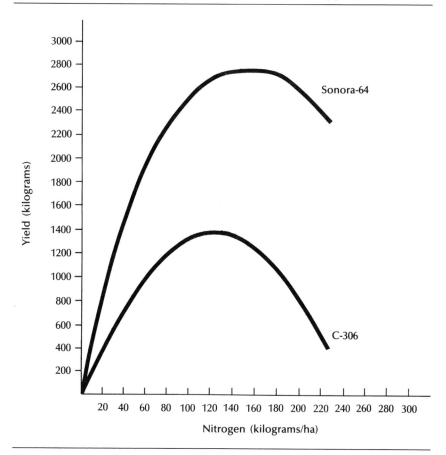

grew 240 percent, but to achieve these gains, energy costs *per bushel* rose 51 percent (Figure 2–9b). The agriculture industry as a whole shows the same trend (Figure 2–10, pg. 52). The historical rise in energy costs may not have been bad, especially since the primary objective was to increase production per worker-hour and per acre. Nevertheless, it's important to recognize that past gains in traditional measures of productivity weren't free but were achieved at a cost, a cost we may not be willing or able to pay in the future.

Figure 2–8b. Additional Wheat Yield Produced by Additional Units of Fertilizer

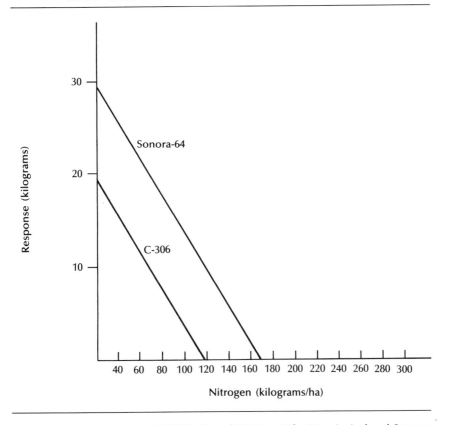

Source: R.W. Cummings, R.W. Herdt, and S.K. Ray, "The New Agricultural Strategy Revised," *Economic and Political Weekly,* October 1968.

Fuel Quality

Most of the U.S. energy budget comes from fossil fuels like oil, gas, and coal (Figures 2–1a and 2–1b). Natural processes replace these fuels only very slowly and, unlike metals, they're gone forever when they're used. The quality of fuels varies considerably, just as with other resources, depending on the ease with which they can be extracted and processed. For instance,

Figure 2–9a.   U.S. Average Corn Yield, 1945 to 1975.

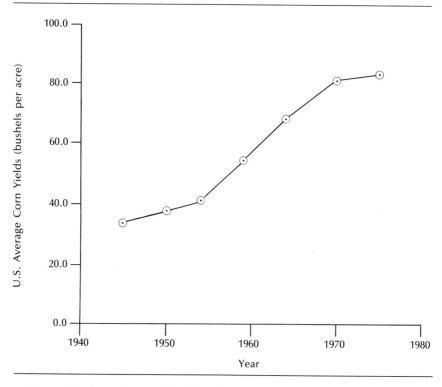

Source: D. Pimentel et al., "Food Production and the Energy Crisis," *Science* 182 (1973): 443.; V. Smil, P. Nachman, and T.V. Long III, *Energy Analysis and Agriculture* (Boulder: Westview Press, 1983).
Note: Circles represent data points.

the oil content of oil shale can vary from less than 5 gallons per ton to 100 gallons per ton, and the energy cost of a gallon varies with the amount of shale that must be processed to get it, with the amount of overburden that must be removed to get to the shale, with the difficulty of obtaining water to process it, and so on. For renewable fuels, energy costs generally increase with rising demand, though the amount of increase depends on the type of fuel in question.

We can measure the cost of fuels the same as we do other resources: in terms of the energy it takes to get a unit of fuel. However, since the product itself can be measured in energy units, this cost can be expressed elegantly by what we call the *energy profit ratio*.[9] This energy profit ratio is the energy in the

Figure 2–9b. Total Energy Cost of a Bushel of Corn, Including Energy Used to Make Chemicals and Machinery

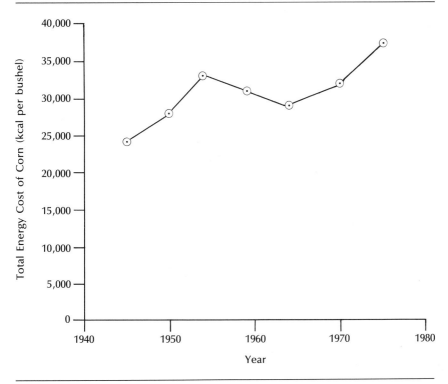

Note: Circles represent data points.

fuel produced divided by the energy used to produce it. The numerator of this ratio is the total energy content of the fuel, while the denominator includes the energy used to find, extract, refine, and transport the fuel. High-quality fuels have a large energy profit ratio, reflecting the small amount of energy they take to produce. Conversely, the lowest-quality fuels may take more energy to produce than they yield, meaning they have an energy profit ratio of less than 1. The energy profit ratio is a tremendously useful yardstick for comparing different fuels or different sources of the same fuel, since it is a direct measure of a fuel's cost, as opposed to its value.

Moreover, we can also calculate the *net energy* obtainable from a particular deposit—that is, the amount of energy made

Figure 2–10.   Index of U.S. Agricultural Output (1957–59 = 100) versus Energy Input, 1920 to 1980

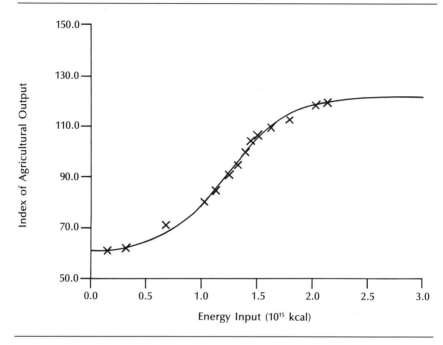

Source: J.S. Steinhart and C.E. Steinhart, "Energy Use in the U.S. Food System," *Science* 184 (1974): 307–16. © 1974 AAAS

Note: Solid line is best computerized fit to data points (crosses). Time also increases from left to right along the curve.

available to society after the energy costs of extraction have been subtracted. For example, if it takes 50,000 barrels of oil (or the heat equivalent in other fuels) to do everything necessary to tap into a particular oil field, and if the field ultimately yields a million barrels of oil, that oil has an energy profit ratio of 20, and society will receive 950,000 barrels of oil in net energy. These 950,000 barrels, not the original million, are the energy we use to fill up our cars' gas tanks, heat our homes, and power the rest of our economy.

It should be emphasized that the energy profit ratio can be used to assess the feasibility of renewable solar-based fuels as well as fossil fuels. We may not have to dig wind or sunlight out of the ground, but we do need labor and capital structures to convert these energies into forms we can use in our homes, cars, offices, and factories. This labor and capital (including windmills, photovoltaic cells, solar water heaters, window glass, and ethanol distillation plants) requires energy to create, maintain, and replace. The energy cost of the needed labor and capital can be divided into the energy produced during the equipment's useful life to calculate the energy profit ratio.

Many people believe that fuel deposits that once were too expensive to exploit can be mined at a profit when the price of energy increases.[10] In other words, recalling the distinction between resources and reserves, more of the resources would become economically exploitable and hence become part of the reserves. Under this view no shortage is ever possible, as rising prices "create" additional reserves.

Unfortunately, that is true only up to a point. As the price of fuel rises, it is true that some resources may be reclassified as reserves (leaving aside the problem that rising fuel prices also raise the cost of exploiting resources)—but in a sensible world that reclassification would stop once the energy profit ratio of resources drops to 1. Society loses energy when it taps fuel sources with an energy profit ratio below 1. And the energy profit ratio of a fuel cannot be improved by increasing the price paid for it. Only technological breakthroughs that reduce a fuel's energy cost can increase the energy profit ratio of known deposits, and these breakthroughs have regrettably been rare.

The energy profit ratio shows why our reserves are always smaller than the total quantity of resources. Although a simple inventory of fuel reserves gives a rough estimate of energy supplies, to stop at that point would be misleading. A nonfuel resource may well be worth escalating energy costs. But the energy profit ratio defines a cutoff point for the sensible exploitation of a fuel resource. In most cases it would be foolish, from society's standpoint, to spend more fuel than is retrieved. Thus, a great deal of fuel may have to stay in the ground because it is simply too energy-expensive to take it out: there would be no net gain of energy.

In some cases, society may be willing to trade a relatively undesirable fuel like coal for lesser amounts of a relatively clean and convenient fuel like oil. This is all right from an energy profit standpoint if the energy profit ratio of the coal used to pump oil is big enough to cover the loss incurred in the oil pumping process. In other words, if the energy used to dig out and transport the coal, plus the energy needed to pump and refine the oil, is less than the energy contained in the oil ultimately obtained, then the aggregate energy profit ratio of the coal plus the oil is still greater than 1. The important question is whether the energy made available to society is greater than the energy used to obtain it from the environment, no matter how roundabout the method.

Energy profit ratios are especially important because dollar prices don't always parallel the energy costs of obtaining fuels. Situations have arisen, and may arise again, in which fuels with energy profit ratios less than 1 have been exploited because it was "profitable" in dollar terms to do so. In Oklahoma, more energy has been used to pump natural gas from stripper wells (wells producing less than the energy equivalent of ten barrels of oil a day) than was contained in the gas.[11] This unfortunate situation arose because the price for "old gas" was set at $1.40 per thousand cubic feet (tcf) whereas "new gas" could be sold for as much as $3.00 per tcf. Thus, it was profitable in dollar terms to use cheap old gas to extract a smaller quantity of expensive new gas, despite the net energy loss to society. It is possible that preferential tax treatment of alternative fuels will create a similar situation.

THE ENERGY FUTURE

By examining past trends of total (gross) fuel reserves and their energy costs of acquisition, and by combining these patterns, we can make reasonably confident projections of future supplies of net energy.

Oil and Gas

A tested method for projecting oil and gas supplies is the so-called Hubbert analysis. In the 1950s M.K. Hubbert, a geologist at Shell Oil, derived a method to estimate U.S. oil reserves and the rate at which they would be exploited in the future.[12] Hubbert believed that oil exploration would be slow and ineffective at first, due to inexperience and lack of demand; that it would quickly become very rewarding; and that ultimately it would again become ineffective as most of the oil would already have been found. Based on this view, the per-year discovery and production of oil, graphed over time, would form a bell-shaped curve (Figure 2–11a). At the beginning of serious industrial exploitation the rate of exploitation would grow exponentially. As the high-quality deposits ran out, though, production would peak and then decline. Lower- and lower-quality deposits would then be exploited and production would tail off.

This Hubbert curve subsequently proved to be very accurate (Figure 2–11b), predicting successfully in 1956 both the date and size of peak oil production in the lower forty-eight states.[13] This analysis was repeated by Hubbert in 1974[14] and again in 1981 by ourselves,[15] adjusting the curve with more recent data, and the results were substantially identical. Both total and peak yield have risen slightly compared to Hubbert's original estimate, but the timing of the peak and general downward trend in production remain. All three analyses indicate that *by the year 2020 domestic oil supplies will be effectively depleted— by then the supply and quality of remaining oil will have become so low that other fuels will be used for most purposes.* Even with the vagaries of wars, business cycles, and political manipulation of prices, the fit between prediction and observations is astonishingly close. Hubbert's accuracy is all the more astounding when we remember that his predictions included production from fields yet to be discovered as well as from known reserves. Government and industry experts laughed off Hubbert's projection as "absurd" when he first announced it, but history has vindicated his position and many knowledgeable people now accept the Hubbert method as valid. (Julian Simon and Barry Commoner, however, are two notable exceptions.)

Even the vaunted Prudhoe Bay field in Alaska, unforeseen in 1956, will have little effect on total domestic production in the long run (Figure 2–12, pg. 58). A Hubbert analysis of the Alaskan oil field by itself does not trace the production curve well because, anomalously, the oil lies in a single field and production had to wait several years for a pipeline to be built.[16] The inaccuracy is

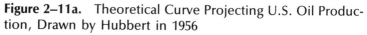

Figure 2–11a.   Theoretical Curve Projecting U.S. Oil Production, Drawn by Hubbert in 1956

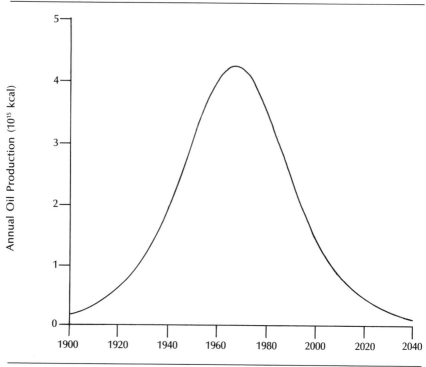

unimportant for total U.S. production totals, however, since Alaska contains less than 5 percent of U.S. reserves.[17]

Subjecting domestic natural gas production to a Hubbert analysis yields similar results (Figure 2–13). Actual production undershot the predicted values during the 1940s and 1950s because an adequate pipeline network hadn't been built yet and a great deal of gas was simply flared. Again, Alaskan gas production differs from predictions based on the Hubbert curve, but the Alaskan find affects total gas production even less than oil. This analysis indicates that *domestic gas will also be effectively depleted by 2020.*

We recognize that Hubbert wasn't the first to warn that fuel supplies will soon dry up. Many earlier warnings were premature.[18] W. Stanley Jevons, a great nineteenth-century British economist, wrote in 1864 that England's industrial economy

Figure 2–11b. Comparison of Hubbert Curve to Actual Production

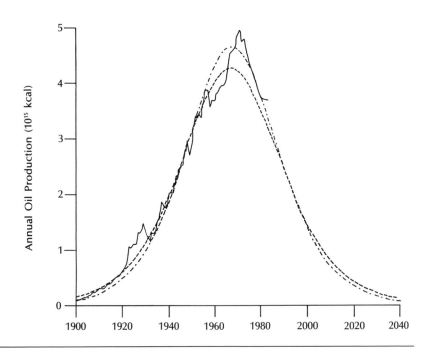

Solid line is actual production; dotted line is Hubbert's 1956 curve; dashed-dotted line is our updated curve based on 1981 data.

Sources: U.S. Department of Commerce, Bureau of the Census, *Historical Statistics of the United States, Colonial Times to 1970* (Washington, D.C.: USGPO, 1975); U.S. Department of Energy, *Monthly Energy Review* (Washington, D.C.: DOE, various years).

would soon collapse due to the impending exhaustion of its coal supply. And in 1920 the director of the U.S. Geological Service predicted that domestic oil production was about to peak and that the United States had better start importing oil and inventing synthetics. He and others failed to anticipate giant new finds. Indeed, largely because such predictions proved to be exaggerated and because oil reserves have grown in the past, Julian Simon and other cornucopians believe that supplies of oil will grow indefinitely. Couldn't they be right? Couldn't we be

Figure 2–12. Hubbert Curve for Oil Production in the Lower Forty-eight States, in Alaska, and the Sum

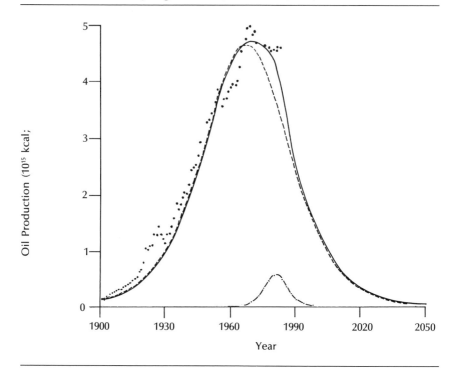

Sources: U.S. Department of Commerce, Bureau of the Census, *Historical Statistics of the United States, Colonial Times to 1970* (Washington D.C.: USGPO, 1975); U.S. Department of Energy, *Monthly Energy Review* (Washington D.C.: DOE, various years).

Note: Dotted line is lower forty-eight states; dashed dotted line is Alaska; and solid line is sum. Dots represent actual production.

guilty of the same shortsightedness as Jevons and the Geological Service?

In brief, no. More large oil discoveries in the lower forty-eight states are highly unlikely because there is not enough room between existing drill holes to contain them. As of 1975 there was one production or exploratory well for every 1.6 square kilometers of sedimentary rock, the only kind known to contain oil, in the continental United States.[19] Since giant oil fields stretch for hundreds of kilometers, the likelihood of new bonanzas would appear remote. Major discoveries in offshore areas also are unlikely. Many of the shallow, placid sites, such as

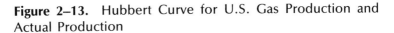

Figure 2–13. Hubbert Curve for U.S. Gas Production and Actual Production

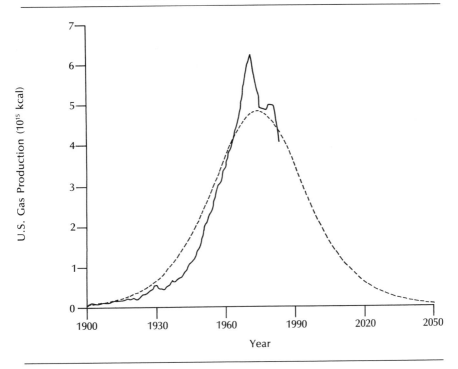

Sources: U.S. Department of Commerce, Bureau of the Census, *Historical Statistics of the United States, Colonial Times to 1970* (Washington D.C.: USGPO, 1975); U.S. Department of Energy, *Monthly Energy Review* (Washington D.C.: DOE, various years). Note: Dotted line is projection; solid line is actual production.

those off coastal Louisiana and Texas, have been thoroughly explored.

The most promising regions for future exploration are in relatively remote regions such as Alaska and the outer continental shelf. However, deep offshore drilling has so far met with relatively few strikes. For instance, oil drillers considered the Mukluk area of the Beaufort Sea, north of Alaska, to be the best hope for finding oil in Alaskan waters. They thought it could contain as much as 5 billion barrels of oil, half as much as the nearby Prudhoe Bay field—but an initial test well came up empty, leading some of the oil companies involved to predict that the whole area would be unproductive.[20] In addition, the deep water and hostile environments of these sites increase the energy (and dollar) costs, thereby diminishing the net yield of oil and gas from them.[21] The average exploratory well in the Beaufort Sea costs $40 million to $50 million, compared to $1.5 million to $3 million for a well in the Gulf of Mexico.[22] Drilling in the Mukluk field has already cost $1.6 billion in lease acquisitions and $140 million for drilling a single well; if the field should really prove to be a bust, it would probably discourage any further attempts to explore this region. Partly in recognition of these realities, in May 1985 the Interior Department cut its estimate of the amount of offshore oil remaining to be discovered by more than half.[23]

Perhaps the most eloquent testimony to the poor prospects of continued oil exploration in the United States is the merger frenzy that has recently gripped the oil industry. The major oil companies now find it more profitable to spend their billions on buying known deposits than on finding new ones. One can hardly blame them: according to one valuation service, Standard Oil of California spent an average of $9.61 per barrel of oil in development costs between 1978 and 1982, while the $80 per share it paid for Gulf Corporation when Socal bought it out in 1984 translates to about $4.40 a barrel for Gulf's reserves.[24]

This is not to say that no new discoveries will be made; the Hubbert analysis indicates that about 50 billion barrels of recoverable oil remain to be discovered in the United States. But discoveries will not keep up with the exhaustion of existing reserves. As older, highly productive wells dry up, they must be replaced by a great many smaller wells to keep production up. That can't happen indefinitely, so production must drop. In late 1982 a giant field, containing between 100 million and a billion barrels, was discovered off the California coast. This find was big enough to excite the whole oil industry.[25] Nevertheless, the United States would need to find at least 50 and perhaps as many as 500 more fields of this size to replace the Class A giant fields that now account for most of current domestic production.[26] As Charles DiBona, president of the American Petroleum Institute, told the *New York Times* in June 1984, "Between now and the year 2000, we're going to have to replace all of our domestic supplies more than once. About three-quarters of the oil that we will be producing if we continue to produce at the present level in the year 2000 must be from fields that we discover after today."

A 1981 analysis published in *Science* by energy analysts Charles Hall and Cutler Cleveland confirmed that the declining quality of shrinking oil supplies is noticeable and important.[27] As Hubbert predicted, they found that, as exploration proceeded from 1946 to 1978, the new wells yielded progressively smaller amounts per foot of well drilled. This decline accounts for about half of the total decline between 1946 and 1978 in the rate, per unit effort, at which the United States finds new oil.

Moreover, Hall and Cleveland found that 40 percent of the year-to-year variation in discovery rates is a consequence of the rate at which new wells are drilled. When exploration goes slowly, only those regions most likely to contain oil are drilled. As exploration gets more feverish, however, drillers become less discriminating, so less oil is found per foot of exploratory well drilled. In other words, haste makes waste: the extra effort yields little but more dry holes. Together, cumulative demand and yearly drilling effort account for 92 percent of the variation in the rate at which the United States discovers oil and gas.

Hall's and Cleveland's most surprising and important finding is this: continued exploration for new oil fields in the United States probably will become pointless (except as a source of petrochemicals) by 2005, although pumping from known fields can still continue for many more years. By extrapolating the historical increases in drilling costs and decreases in oil found per foot of well drilled, Hall and Cleveland forecast that the energy break-even point—at which as much energy is used to conduct exploration as is found—would be reached sometime between 1995 and 2005 (Figure 2–14). Additionally, they concluded that the United States would reap 25 percent more net energy between 1982 and the energy break-even point if exploration proceeded relatively slowly.

Declining quality of the remaining oil reserves causes net energy stores to fall faster than gross supplies. The energy profit ratio for domestic petroleum at the wellhead (which includes energy for location and pumping) since 1919 shows three distinct trends (Figure 2–15): it fell slowly from 1919 until 1955; from 1955 to 1967 it jumped nearly 20 percent; and

Figure 2–14. Historical Relation between Oil and Gas Found per Foot of Well Drilled in High- and Low-Effort Conditions and the Energy Costs of Drilling a Foot of Well

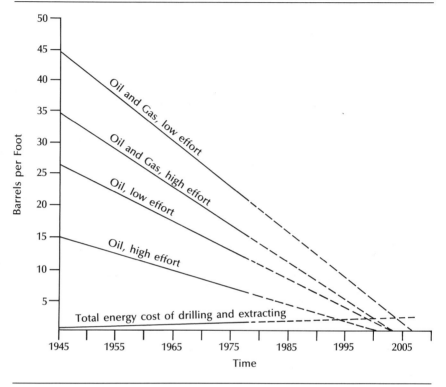

Source: C. Hall and C.J. Cleveland, "Petroleum Drilling and Production in the United States: Yield per Effort and Net Energy Analysis," *Science* 211 (1981):576. © 1981 AAAS.

Note: Solid lines are historic relation; dotted lines are future extrapolations. The energy break-even point occurs when the energy cost line intersects the lines for energy found, between about 1995 and 2005.

since 1967 it has fallen, first slowly, then rapidly. The energy profit ratio for refined petroleum has behaved similarly.

Why, political considerations aside, couldn't imported oil make up for declining domestic reserves? After all, Japan runs its economy almost entirely on imported energy. Moreover, there is no apparent energy cost involved in obtaining oil overseas: we exchange money for energy. But even though the United States doesn't use energy directly to extract imported

Figure 2–15.   Energy Profit Ratio for Domestic Petroleum

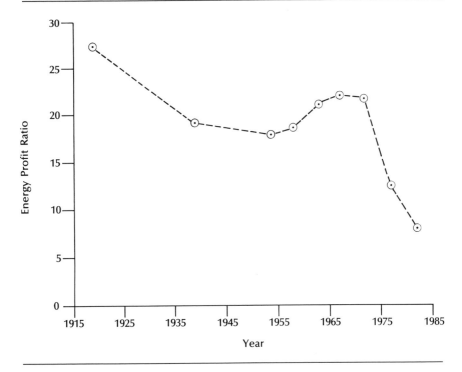

Sources: U.S. Department of Commerce, Bureau of the Census, *Historical Statistics of the United States, Colonial Times to 1970* (Washington D.C.: USGPO, 1975); U.S. Department of Energy, *Monthly Energy Review* (Washington D.C.: DOE, various years); U.S. Department of Commerce, Bureau of the Census, *Census of Mineral Industries* (Washington D.C.: USGPO, various years).
Note: Includes only energy used to extract oil and gas, not energy used in transportation or refining.

oil, the United States must use energy to produce the goods exported in exchange for imported oil. This energy-based exchange allows the calculation of an energy profit ratio for imported oil.[28] These goods may not be bartered directly for oil, but oil sellers would not accept dollars as payment if they could not ultimately be used to buy U.S. products, which take energy to make. Thus, the energy profit ratio for imported petroleum is the ratio of energy contained in a dollar's worth of imported fuel divided by the energy used to make a dollar's worth of exports. For example, in 1979 a dollar bought the United States about

Figure 2–16.   Energy Profit Ratio for Imported Oil

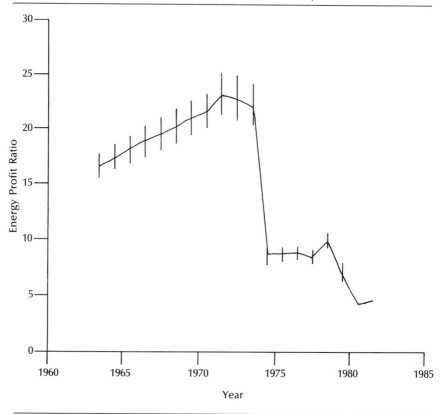

Source: R. Kaufmann and C.A.S. Hall, "The Energy Return on Investment for Imported Petroleum," in W.J. Mitsch, R.W. Bosserman, and J.M. Klopatek, eds., *Energy and Ecological Modelling* (New York: Elsevier, 1981).

Note: Vertical bars represent the variation among the different methods for calculating the energy cost of exports.

47,000 kcal of oil, while it took about 7,000 kcal to produce a dollar's worth of exported goods. This exchange gave the United States an energy profit ratio of 6.7 for its imported oil. (This calculation assumes that the mix of products exchanged for fuel, or for the foreign exchange used to purchase fuel, is similar to that of exports in general. Also, because the calculation of the full energy cost of services is quite difficult, the trade of services for fuel is not considered.)

Based on this formulation of the energy profit ratio, Figure 2–16 shows that the ratio for petroleum imports peaked at about 23 in 1973 and dropped to around 4.6 in 1981. Since 1981 the energy profit ratio for imported oil has risen, as world oil prices have fallen. These figures indicate that the energy bought per dollar has declined more rapidly than the energy needed to produce a dollar's worth of exported goods. The declining energy profit ratio thus defines a "price ceiling" for the cost of oil imports. Logically the real energy cost of imported oil can't quintuple again, as it did in the 1970s, because the energy profit ratio would then be less than one, and the United States would lose energy in the trade. Clearly, there's no point in importing oil if all of its energy is used to make goods to trade for that oil: there would be none left over to fill the nation's gas tanks, heat its homes, or put food on its tables.

In any event, world supplies are finite, though large (Figure 2–17). Although demand is now much less than the maximum possible production rate, this gap could close if less developed nations build an industrial base that depends on fossil energy. If developing nations regain the economic momentum of the 1960s and early 1970s, world oil production will probably peak around the year 2000, and demand may catch up to the maximum possible production rate by then.

Coal

The United States is in a somewhat better position with regard to coal supply. Because the United States has used only a small fraction of its total coal supply, a Hubbert analysis is only speculative: so little of the left side of the Hubbert curve is known that the rest of it cannot yet be projected confidently.[29] Nevertheless, it appears that coal production will not peak until the twenty-second or twenty-third century. Could coal be the answer to "the energy problem"? Certainly the aggressive ad campaign sponsored by the coal industry would have us think so.

We disagree. Besides glossing over the environmental damage resulting from heavy coal use (acid rain, particulate pollution, carbon dioxide buildup in the atmosphere), optimistic

Figure 2–17.   Hubbert Curve for World Oil Production and Actual Oil Production

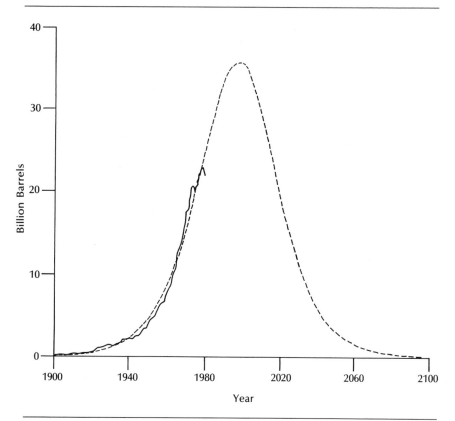

Source: C. Hall, C.J. Cleveland, and R. Kaufmann, *Energy and Resource Quality: The Ecology of the Industrial Process* (John Wiley and Sons, 1986).

Note: Dotted line is Hubbert projection; solid line is actual production.

projections have been based on total coal resources and have ignored the fact that substantially less net energy may ultimately be obtained from these supplies. The quality of mined coal is falling, from an energy profit ratio of 177 in 1954 to 98 in 1977 (Figure 2–18). These estimates include only fuel used at the mine, however, and do not include the considerable amounts of energy used to build the machines used in the mines, to move the coal away from the mines, and to process it. When these costs are included, the shape of the energy profit ratio curve changes and starts to drop in 1967. More important, with this formulation the energy profit ratio for coal slips to 20 in 1977, comparable to that of domestic petroleum. While an energy profit ratio of 20 means that only 5 percent of coal's gross energy is needed to obtain it, the sharp decline since 1967 is alarming. If it continues to drop at this rate, the energy profit ratio of coal will slide to 0.5 by 2040.

There are several good reasons to expect coal's energy profit ratio to continue its decline, albeit at a slower rate. Strip mining is becoming increasingly popular, accounting for over 60 percent of total production in 1977, compared to 38 percent in

Figure 2–18. Energy Profit Ratio for Coal

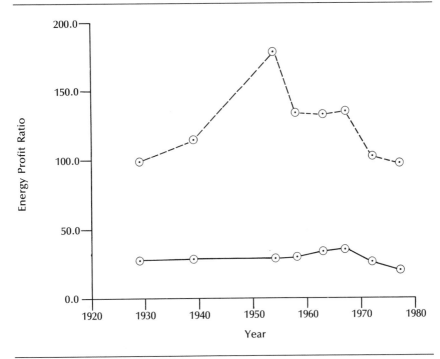

Source: C. Hall, C.J. Cleveland, and M. Berger, "Yield per Effort as a Function of Time and Effort for United States Petroleum, Uranium, and Coal," in W.J. Mitsch, R.W. Bosserman, and J.M. Klopatek, eds., *Energy and Ecological Modelling* (New York: Elsevier, 1981).

Note: Dotted line considers only fuel use at the mine; solid line includes energy used to make mining tools and capital and the energy used to transport coal. Circles represent data points.

1969.[30] Because it involves building and operating complex machinery to physically strip away vast amounts of overlying dirt and rock (and to put it back), it is more energy intensive than underground mining.[31] Increased strip mining will therefore lower the energy profit ratio. The average thickness of veins uncovered can be expected to continue its downward trend, and the depths at which they're found will increase. Most important, the average heat content of a pound of coal has dropped, about 14 percent between 1955 and 1982,[32] and will probably continue to fall.

Thus, just as the total content of manganese in the crust lying under the United States does not give a true measure of U.S. manganese reserves, simple inventories of total fossil fuel deposits are deceptive. It will be profitable in terms of net energy to tap only a fraction of them—perhaps only a small fraction.

Some argue that, as conventional oil and gas are depleted, large amounts of hard-to-get, "deep and tight" gas in the United States could replace them. Some authors, for example, have estimated that more than 1,000 trillion cubic feet of gas could be extracted from unconventional deposits in the United States, about seven to ten times what is contained in existing reserves.[33] But again there is bad news: according to Cutler Cleveland and Robert Costanza, the energy profit ratio of deep and tight gas will be between 3 and 4, which is a good deal lower than that of many other fuels, including several renewable fuels.[34] Indeed, although figures are not available, there is no reason to believe that the same considerations won't apply to the apparently large amount of oil inaccessible to conventional techniques, or to Cornell astronomer Thomas Gold's hypothesized but not-yet-discovered (and perhaps mythical) deposits of so-called abiogenic gas left over from the earth's creation.

Thus, Julian Simon's confidence is misplaced because he doesn't recognize the constraints imposed by the energy profit ratios of our fuel supplies: as the quality of our remaining fossil fuel reserves declines, we must eventually reach a point where it takes more energy to obtain the fuel than the fuel contains. Indeed, Simon offers no concrete suggestions for reversing the decline in the energy profit ratios of fossil fuels or for alleviating its negative effects, beyond expressing a vague faith that "human ingenuity. . . .is boundless" and that "knowledge, imagination, and enterprise" will provide us with all the resources we will ever need.[35]

"Alternative" Fuels

The public has been told repeatedly not to worry about the declining supply of oil and gas. As those sources of energy begin to fail, new alternatives can fill the breach. Barry Commoner, for instance, writes that "methane alone among present fuels can facilitate the transition from our nearly complete dependence on nonrenewable fossil fuels to a solar-energy system".[36] Commoner also touts alcohol as the basis of such a system.[37] Even if rising oil and gas prices don't create new reserves of fossil fuels, surely high prices will make these other energy sources more attractive to the entrepreneurial spirit.

These alternatives will indeed supplement or replace fossil fuels eventually. But as Table 2–2 shows, none currently has an energy profit ratio comparable to those of domestic oil and gas or imported oil during the 1950s and 1960s, when, not by accident, the U.S. economy grew at its fastest rate ever. Some of these alternatives do not even produce an energy profit, and therefore can't be considered net fuel sources. As long as alternatives have lower energy profit ratios than our remaining supplies of oil and gas, the alternatives will probably be more expensive to produce. It will not generally be profitable to invest in alternatives until the energy profit ratio of oil and gas drops to similar levels. As a result, alternatives will just begin to be available in quantity when the supply of oil and gas will have been declining for years: in other words, the development of alternatives is likely to lag the depletion of oil and gas.

All alternatives are not considered equivalent, and a comparison of energy profit ratios illuminates a contemporary debate about which alternatives are best. On one side, advocates of the so-called hard path promote inventive but nonrenewable fuels like oil shale, coal liquefaction, and synthetic gas—as well as solid coal and various nuclear technologies—as the best ingredients for the nation's future energy mix. On the other side, proponents of the renewable "soft path" argue that with solar,

Table 2–2. Estimated Energy Profit Ratios for Existing Fuels and Future Technologies

Process	Energy Profit Ratios
Nonrenewable	
Oil and gas (domestic wellhead)	
1940s	Discoveries ⟩ 100.0
1970s	Production 23.0, discoveries 8.0
Coal (mine mouth)	
1950s	80.0
1970s	30.0
Oil shale	0.7 to 13.3
Coal liquefaction	0.5 to 8.2
Geopressured gas	1.0 to 5.0
Renewable	
Ethanol (sugarcane)	0.8 to 1.7
Ethanol (corn)	1.3
Ethanol (corn residues)	0.7 to 1.8
Methanol (wood)	2.6
Solar space heat (fossil backup)	
Flat-plate collector	1.9
Concentrating collector	1.6
Electricity production	
Coal	
U.S. average	9.0
Western surface coal	
No scrubbers	6.0
Scrubbers	2.5
Hydropower	11.2
Nuclear (light-water reactor)	4.0
Solar	
Power satellite	2.0
Power tower	4.2
Photovoltaics	1.7 to 10.0
Geothermal	
Liquid dominated	4.0
Hot dry rock	1.9 to 13.0

Source: C.J. Cleveland, R. Costanza, C.A.S. Hall, and R. Kaufmann, "Energy and the U.S. Economy: A Biophysical Perspective," *Science* 225 (1984): 890–97. © 1984 AAAS

wind, and water power—as well as conservation—the United States can maintain a robust and sustainable economy.

But neither path leads to a golden future. The hard path's proponents claim that only the apparently huge supply of fossil fuels and uranium can satisfy the huge demand for energy. But these fuels have several daunting drawbacks. All hard-path fuels, except solid coal, have low energy profit ratios, currently ranging from less than 1 to perhaps 10. These energy profit ratios must later drop to even lower levels, since these fuels are nonrenewable and we will have to exploit coal, oil shale, and uranium reserves of ever-worsening quality. As a result, hard-path fuels besides solid coal will probably have an average energy profit ratio over their lifetimes of no more than 5, which is low by current standards. Moreover, the estimates of the energy profit ratios for technologies that are not yet commercially available are probably exaggerated, since experience shows that initial projections of startup costs usually underestimate the actual costs by as much as half.[38] Thus, the amount of net energy obtainable via the hard path could be as much as 50 percent less than what the gross estimates initially suggest: an energy profit ratio of perhaps 2.5.

Even this estimate of the hard path's average energy profit ratio is probably too high because it does not include the energy needed to clean up or prevent the damage to public health and to the environment that hard-path fuels would cause. The combustion of liquefied or gasified coal or of oil from oil shale would result in widespread pollution and a worsening of the greenhouse effect (in which buildup of atmospheric carbon dioxide causes global warming, which in turn would disrupt climate patterns, particularly in agriculturally vital areas), unless very expensive countermeasures were to be taken. Synthetic fuels made from coal would be the worst offenders in this regard.[39] Nor do the costs of exploiting these fossil fuels include the energy needed to reclaim the landscape destroyed by strip mining. The objections to nuclear fission power are too familiar to need recitation here; but the substantial costs associated with, for example, decommissioning obsolete plants or storing radioactive waste were not included in the calculation of this fuel's energy profit ratio—nor, for that matter, were the costs of *not* decommissioning old plants or storing waste.

The hard path also includes two so-called "inexhaustible" fuel technologies: breeder reactors, which generate power and simultaneously turn uranium into plutonium, itself a usable reactor fuel; and controlled nuclear fusion, which releases energy by fusing several light atoms to create a single larger atom (the process behind hydrogen bombs and the sun's energy). These technologies are not advanced sufficiently to allow calculation of energy profit ratios for commercial reactors, but we do know enough to conclude that neither technology will be useful in the time frame of this analysis. The sole commercial-scale breeder reactor in the United States, the federally sponsored Clinch River project, was long regarded as a boondoggle before it was apparently killed in 1983. Besides the staggering dollar cost of such reactors—the relatively small Clinch River reactor was projected to cost $4.5 billion, one-third of which had already been spent[40]—many people were concerned about how to manage the large quantity of highly toxic, weapons-grade plutonium that breeders produce. Fusion technology is still decades away from commercial application. Moreover, at least one leading fusion researcher, Lawrence Lidsky of MIT, believes that the particular fusion technology that is being developed most intensively, the deuterium-tritium reaction, will *never* be commercially feasible.[41] According to Lidsky, it produces large quantities of dangerous radiation that would force plants to be even more sophisticated and expensive, per unit of energy produced, than today's fission reactors. Although this problem might eventually be overcome, fusion energy will almost certainly not be available until long after we have been forced to abandon oil and gas.

The soft path, on the other hand, is indeed renewable indefinitely if demand is kept within sustainable limits. But capturing these solar-powered energies is itself usually an energy-intensive enterprise. Some alternatives, in fact, generate only enough energy to perpetuate themselves and can't produce any surplus for the rest of the economy. For example, the energy profit ratio of alcohol fermented from sugarcane ranges from 0.9 to 1.8.[42] Other solar-based alternatives are better and should improve further with more research.

Because the energy costs of capturing and converting energy to useful forms swallow so much of the energy produced, and because the pressure to maintain material living standards will limit the energy available for the conversion to alternative fuels, we don't believe that substitutes, whether from the hard or soft paths, can fully offset the decline in petroleum before 2025. In essence, existing market forces are tempting the United States to wait too long to wean itself away painlessly from oil and gas and to turn to other fuels.

THE ECONOMIC IMPACT OF DECLINING FUEL QUALITY

The impact of declining fuel quality on economic performance can be understood with a simple model that simulates the relationship between gross energy, net energy, and economic production. For purposes of illustration, the model assumes that society seeks to maintain a constant level of net energy supply. It also assumes that the efficiency with which energy is turned into goods and services also stays constant, so that constant levels of net energy lead to constant GNP. Figure 2–19 shows what happens if the aggregate energy profit ratio of its fuel sources should fall from 15 in year five to 4 in year twenty (the time units are arbitrary—they could be decades instead of years). As the energy profit ratio drops, the amount of gross energy needed to maintain a constant level of net energy rises rapidly. However, as society extracts more gross fuel, all of the increase, and then some, must be used to build fuel-extractive capital equipment, leaving a decreasing amount of net energy. It is *fundamentally impossible* to maintain a constant level of net energy while the aggregate energy profit ratio drops. Only after the energy profit ratio and the need for new fuel-related capital level off can net energy supplies return to the desired level.

Many commentators implicitly believe that we can maintain our vast industrial machine and comfortable lifestyles more or less intact by exploiting large numbers of relatively poor-quality fuel sources. The analysis above, however, indicates that over the next forty years fuel sources with low energy profit ratios cannot completely replace a smaller number of high-quality sources. To keep production of nonenergy goods and services at current levels while the aggregate energy profit ratio drops

Figure 2–19.   The Effect on the Production of Net Energy of a Decline in the Economy's Aggregate Energy Profit Ratio from 15 to 4 over a Fifteen-Year Period

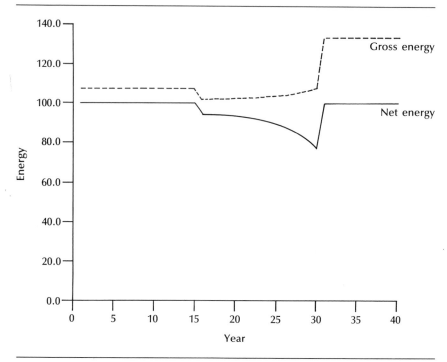

will require more net energy than we can now produce; and to have more net energy in the future means that energy must be diverted now from nonenergy sectors of the economy into energy production. We can't burn our fuel and have it, too. Furthermore, this drain on net energy will be exacerbated by the declining quality of nonfuel resources. That leaves us with two options for averting at least a temporary decline in production of nonenergy goods and services: increasing the energy profit ratio of fuels, thereby increasing the amount of net energy at no additional energy cost; or raising the economy's energy efficiency, that is, increasing the quantity of goods and services we can produce with a given amount of net energy. As this chapter showed, the first option is highly unlikely. A significant rise in fuel quality would be a *deus ex machina*. We turn to the question of efficiency in Chapter 3.

3 ENERGY EFFICIENCY IN THE U.S. ECONOMY

Fire is the best of servants; but what a master!
—Thomas Carlyle

Energy is the driving force, the universal factor, that enables people to convert natural resources to useful goods and services. Neoclassical economists consider our statement of the relation between energy and the economy to be wrong-headed, or at least exaggerated, because they believe that energy can be replaced in economic processes with capital and labor.[1] (In this context, *labor* refers not solely to the energy humans can generate but, more important, to the special qualities of human beings that allow them to focus energy on useful tasks.) But, in fact, such substitutions have been much less effective than economists have claimed. Energy supply is the limiting factor to, and the driving force behind, economic production. As the rest of this chapter shows, energy-based analysis passes the sternest real-world test: it works.

THE NEED FOR ENERGY

The economy can be defined broadly as the sum of all human activities, especially the production, distribution, and consumption of goods and services. It is difficult to imagine an activity that doesn't involve one of these actions—even when asleep we

75

digest food and wear out the sheets a little bit—but there may be such an activity, and since the definition should be as airtight as possible, we will simply say "all human activities."

All human activities entail work in the sense used in classical physics. Work is a force acting over a distance, such as pushing a weight up a hill. Every step in an economic process takes work. It takes work to dig bauxite out of the ground, to grind it up and remove the alumina from it, to smelt it into raw aluminum, to press aluminum bars into cans, to fill a can with beer, to ship the can to a store, to open the can, to drink and digest the beer, and to dispose of the wastes generated at each step in this process. Additionally, the products of work decay unless more work is done to protect them. Roads must be repaired, houses painted, and legal records carefully updated to preserve their value. Thus, humans must continually work both to satisfy current needs and safeguard the products of past labors.

The laws of physics state, somewhat circularly, that doing work requires the capacity to do work. This capacity is called *energy*. In practical terms, work is equivalent to energy and they are measured in the same units; doing ten joules of work requires ten joules of energy. (Physicists are content with this definition, though it might seem a bit insubstantial to nonscientists. It may provide some consolation to note that physicists also define matter in this airy way. Anyway, the one-to-one correspondence between work and energy is the crucial idea.)

Perhaps the most basic law of classical physics says that energy is conserved: that is, it can't be created or destroyed, only transformed. This law was first expressed in this way in the late 1800s. Einstein subsequently found that matter could be considered a form of energy, interconvertible according to the now-famous equation $E = mc^2$. We use this relation in commercial fission reactors, as well as in hydrogen bombs. But nuclear fission, even if developed at an unprecedentedly rapid rate, can supply only a small fraction of our energy demands during the next forty years (see Chapter 4). Controlled nuclear fusion or other applications of the Einstein equation can't be ruled out, but neither is there any evidence that controlled fusion will ever yield an energy or dollar profit. Therefore, we regard fusion energy as we do a lottery ticket: it might win us the jackpot, but in planning for the future, the prudent course is to assume that it won't. Since humans can't create energy, or at least not enough to matter much, it follows that they must find it preformed elsewhere—that is, outside the economy. This "elsewhere" is what we call the environment.

Although energy can't be destroyed, it can be dispersed, and in the process of doing work its form is changed so that it can do less work. The electrical energy used by light bulbs is not destroyed but rather is changed to a little bit of light and a lot of dispersed heat. One could recapture the heat, but according to the laws of thermodynamics, doing so requires more work than the retrieved heat could do. Once changed to heat in this way, energy is as good as lost (unless it's used for space heat, as in cogeneration systems). Similarly, industrial processes "use up" their old supplies and always need new fuel from the environment. Thus, unlike metals and other so-called nonrenewable resources, energy cannot be recycled.

This fundamental dependence on energy is the justification for examining the U.S. economy—and, by extension, its carrying capacity—in terms of energy. In view of our current near-dependence on oil and gas, and the ongoing decline in their supply and quality, it is imperative to understand how the economy uses energy. Only then can we speculate knowledgeably on how the economy will react to a prolonged period of deteriorating energy resources.

ENERGY USE AND THE OUTPUT OF THE U.S. ECONOMY

The amount of energy it takes to produce a given amount of output—defined broadly as the result of any economic activity: producing, distributing, or consuming some amount of goods or services—whether it be moving a case of beer from storeroom to shelf or building 7 million automobiles, is not fixed. But there are theoretical minimum energy requirements for producing a given quantity of output. For example, lifting a ton of bauxite 100 meters out of the ground requires 235 kilocalories (kcal) of energy simply to overcome gravity.[2] It requires another minimum amount of energy to break the molecular bonds holding the rock particles together and grind up the bauxite for smelting, and so on.

In practice, however, even the most efficient processes require much more energy than the theoretical minimum. Energy is always "wasted"; that is, it goes elsewhere than into the actual production of output. Not all the energy contained in a car's gas tank goes into moving the car: a great deal is lost as heat, and more is spent running systems to carry that heat away from the cylinders so that it won't ruin the engine.[3] In general we can't even approach the theoretical minimum. We compare the degree of waste in different processes by calculating the *energy efficiency*.

For any given process, output is related to physical energy consumption and energy efficiency by the following equation:

$$\text{Output} = \text{Energy used} \times \text{Efficiency}$$

This equation applies to any economic activity, from the whole U.S. economy to operating a car. For the entire economy, output has traditionally been measured by the real gross national product (GNP), reckoned in constant dollars; energy has been estimated roughly by total fuel consumption, measured in kilocalories (or some other unit of physical energy like BTUs or joules). The national energy efficiency, then, is the ratio of GNP in dollars to the fuel used in kcal:

$$\text{Efficiency (\$/kcal)} = \frac{\text{Output}}{\text{E Used}} \cong \frac{\text{GNP (\$)}}{\text{Fuel Used (kcal)}}$$

For smaller tasks, if the output is homogeneous, physical measures like numbers of finished cars or tons of steel can be substituted for dollars, but otherwise the equations are the same.

When a population is growing, even to keep material consumption per capita at constant levels requires growing output. The equations show that we can boost output by raising energy consumption, efficiency, or both.

Increasing energy inputs is a time-honored strategy for increasing output. Human numbers and physiology limit severely the amount of work obtainable from simple muscle power. People use machines and nonfood energy to subsidize workers' muscle power in order to increase the amount of work

Figure 3–1. Stacked Representation of Work Done over Time in the United States by Humans, Domesticated Animals, and Machines, as a Percentage of the Total Horsepower in the Economy

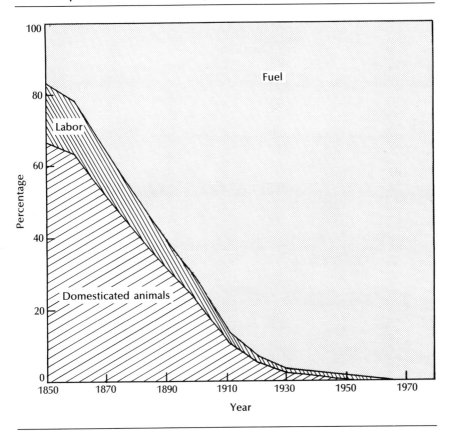

Source: C.A.S. Hall, C.J. Cleveland, and R. Kaufmann, *Energy and Resource Quality: The Ecology of the Industrial Process* (New York: John Wiley & Sons, 1986).

they can do and therefore the amount of output they produce. Thus, an important aspect of our technological capability has been the knowledge that allows us to amplify our own energies with nonhuman fuels.[4]

In 1850 food energy channeled through human bodies did much of the work of the U.S. economy (Figure 3–1).[5] Domestic animals also contributed heavily. Wood was the dominant supplemental energy form, but its bulk and its low energy content limited the work that could be obtained from it. By 1980, however, transitions from wood to coal and from coal to petroleum led to much greater supplies of energy from nonliving sources (Figure 2–1), so that in 1980 human labor accounted for only 0.17 percent of the work done by the economy.

Today, fuel and fuel-derived capital do most of the work necessary to produce output. The output produced per worker-hour, called *productivity*, is thereby expanded tremendously. It might appear that laborers are working harder to produce more goods and services, but in reality those workers, including farmers, are controlling more energy to produce output: they are subsidized by fuels drawn from the environment. When we compare the manufacturing output produced per worker-hour to the amount of fuel used directly to subsidize each worker (ignoring for the moment indirect subsidies like automotive gasoline, home heat, and so forth), it is clear that productivity is closely related to the level of fuel subsidies over the last seventy years (Figure 3–2).[6] From 1909 to 1972 fuel used per worker-hour rose and so did productivity; since 1972 fuel used per worker-hour has remained relatively constant, and productivity has leveled off. The pre-1972 period saw two sustained trends that made rising productivity through increasing fuel subsidies economically feasible: rising fuel supplies, and falling fuel prices relative to the cost of labor. Thus, we should not expect further sustained increases in worker productivity unless both trends are reestablished, which is unlikely, or unless an entirely different strategy is tried. Such strategies may exist: for example, there is evidence that worker productivity is higher in worker-owned factories than in similar factories operating under the traditional labor/management relationship.

Since productivity is related to energy consumption, total per capita production (per capita real GNP) should then correlate with per capita fuel consumption. In fact, from 1850 to 1982 the two follow each other very closely (Figure 3–3). When per capita GNP slumped, so did energy consumption (as in the 1930s), and when per capita GNP rose (as in the 1950s and 1960s), energy consumption did likewise. We make no claims for causality between the two quantities, since such a chicken-and-egg prob-

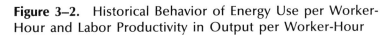

Figure 3–2. Historical Behavior of Energy Use per Worker-Hour and Labor Productivity in Output per Worker-Hour

Source: C.J. Cleveland, R. Costanza, C.A.S. Hall, R. Kaufmann, "Energy and the U.S. Economy: A Biophysical Perspective," *Science* (1984) 225:890-897. © 1984 AAAS

Note: Solid line is energy use; dotted line is labor productivity. Both measures are indexes, 1967 = 1.0.

lem can't be settled with a simple statistical correlation: we simply assert that the two traditionally go together.[7]

The U.S. economy is not alone in its need for energy to generate output.[8] Nations that produce lots of goods and services per person, such as Japan, West Germany, and Canada, consume large quantities of energy per person. On the other hand, poorer nations, such as Egypt, India and Kenya, use lesser per capita quantities of energy. Across the spectrum, there is a strong (but

Figure 3–3. Total Energy Use per Person in the United States and Real per Capita GNP, 1870 to 1980

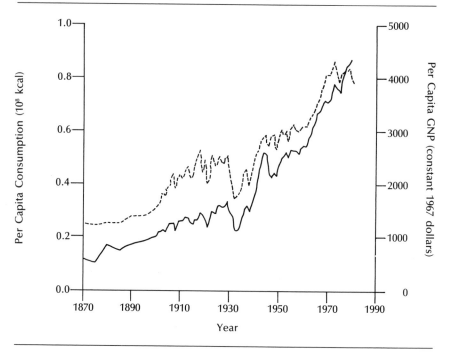

Sources: U.S. Department of Commerce, Bureau of the Census, *Historical Statistics of the United States, Colonial Times to 1970* (Washington, D.C.: USGPO, 1975); U.S. Department of Energy, *Monthly Energy Review* (Washington, D.C.: DOE, various years); U.S. Department of Energy, Energy Information Administration, *Estimates of U.S. Wood Energy Consumption from 1949 to 1981,* (Washington, D.C.: USGPO, 1982).
Note: Dotted line is per capita energy use; solid line is real per capita GNP.

not perfect) correlation between output and fuel consumption (Figure 3–4).

In the last few years, however, per capita GNP in the United States has risen, while energy consumption has remained stable (Figure 3–3). Furthermore, some nations have much higher ratios of GNP to fuel use than the United States (Table 3–1). These observations have led many analysts to contend that the relationship between energy use and GNP is more casual than causal.[9] However, most of these analysts have not looked at the factors that affect this measure of the nation's energy efficiency.

Figure 3–4. International Comparison of Total Energy Use per Person and Real per Capita GNP.

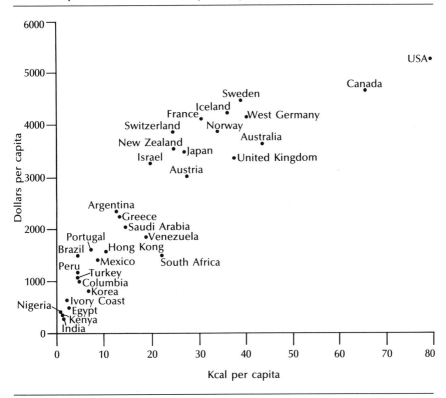

Source: C.A.S. Hall, C.J. Cleveland, and R. Kaufmann, *Energy and Resource Quality: The Ecology of the Industrial Process* (New York: John Wiley & Sons, 1986).

Table 3–1. International Comparison of the Energy/Real GNP Ratio

Nation	$GDP/10^6 kcal
Canada	104.48
United States	92.76
Japan	177.62
Austria	191.75
Belgium	159.21
Denmark	212.31

Table 3–1. continued

Nation	$GDP/10^6 kcal
France	232.02
Germany	181.25
Italy	146.28
Sweden	310.17
Switzerland	347.22
United Kingdom	109.63

Source: United Nations, *United Nations Yearbook of World Energy Statistics* (New York: United Nations, 1981); Organization for Economic Cooperation and Development, *Energy Balances of OECD Countries* (Washington, D.C.: OECD, 1981).

THE DYNAMICS OF ENERGY EFFICIENCY

Ingenuity has enabled people to do all sorts of unlikely things. Humans can't fly under their own power, but our technological capability has allowed us to use fuel energy to propel us into flight. In so doing, we don't violate the laws of gravity or other physical principles: we've simply figured out how to circumvent or neutralize them. Nevertheless, our ability to fly is still constrained by the laws of gravity and aerodynamics. The laws of thermodynamics similarly constrain our ability to use fuel energy to perform economic tasks, but the amount of energy needed to do a given task is not fixed. Human ingenuity may be able to boost the amount of output from each unit of energy—that is, to improve energy efficiency—and thereby offset the decline in energy supplies. (Then again, it may not.) To determine how realistic it is to expect technology and ingenuity to rescue the United States from its present straits, it is necessary to isolate those factors that affect energy efficiency most strongly.

Energy efficiency is the amount of output produced by one unit of energy. For this part of our analysis, we will discuss the efficiency of the U.S. economy as a whole, as measured by the ratio of GNP (measured in constant dollars) to total energy use.[10] A rising ratio of real GNP to energy means the economy is becoming more energy efficient.

Many critics have accused the United States, which uses a tremendous amount of energy to feed, house, and entertain itself, of being energy inefficient. U.S. citizens are only about 5 percent of the earth's population but account for 28 percent of world commercial fuel use. These critics maintain that energy use could be cut sharply without affecting living standards.[11] To back up their claims, they compare the present real GNP/energy ratio in the United States to past values and to those of other countries. The U.S. ratio rose 78 percent between 1929 and 1983 (Figure 3–5), climbing most steeply after 1972 when the dollar price of energy began to rise in earnest. This acceleration encourages those who argue that further price hikes will increase U.S. energy efficiency. Furthermore, the United States uses more energy to produce an average dollar's worth of goods and services than do many other industrial nations, like Sweden, Japan, and West Germany (Table 3–1). By emulating these countries, many assert, the United States could reduce energy consumption without affecting living standards.

Obviously, increasing energy efficiency is desirable: it stretches our fuel supplies and allows us to increase output without using more fuel. But we must be careful not to overestimate the degree to which the United States can cut energy consumption while maintaining GNP. Most discussions of GNP/energy ratios have not identified the factor or factors that affect this measure of efficiency. Without that information, we can't know what practices of other nations we should imitate, nor can we know what we're doing differently from before that has apparently improved our energy efficiency.

A detailed statistical analysis of the real GNP/energy ratio's past behavior shows that three factors seem to have largely determined its year-to-year fluctuations.[12] These factors are (a) the percentage of the energy budget comprising oil, gas, and nuclear and hydroelectricity; (b) the amount of fuel consumed by households, as opposed to manufacturing and other sectors that produce things for resale (or for the military); and (c) fuel prices (though to a much smaller extent). The predominance of these factors suggests that, by and large, we have improved this measure of energy efficiency by becoming *more*, not less, dependent on nonrenewable fuels, and by reducing the amount of energy consumed by households. Fuel prices have only

Figure 3–5. Real GNP/Energy Ratio in the United States, 1929 to 1983

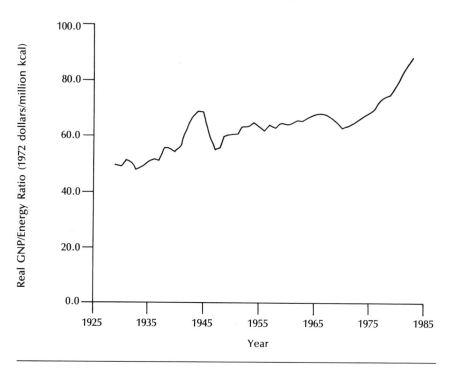

Source: U.S. Department of Commerce, Bureau of the Census, *Historical Statistics of the United States, Colonial Times to 1970* (Washington, D.C.: USGPO, 1975); U.S. Department of Energy, *Monthly Energy Review* (Washington, D.C.: DOE, various years); U.S. Department of Energy, Energy Information Administration, *Estimates of U.S. Wood Energy Consumption from 1949 to 1981,* (Washington, D.C.: USGPO, 1982).

affected efficiency for the last ten years, and even then have been a much smaller influence on the nation's energy efficiency than economists have believed.

The Fuel Mix

Up to this point, we have measured fuel in terms of the heat it produces when burned, typically in kilocalories or BTUs. Heat is a common denominator among fuels, just as dollars are among consumer goods. But heat content reveals nothing about those differences among fuels that affect their usefulness for economic production. These differences influence the real GNP/ energy ratio because 100 kcal of one fuel may be used to create more output than 100 kcal of another. Indeed, we can get a hint of this effect from the varying dollar values of different fuels: we wouldn't pay a premium for a fuel like electricity, which may cost four times as much per kcal as refined petroleum, if we couldn't get more value from it.[13] We sum up these differences with the term *fuel efficiency*, not to be confused with *energy efficiency*.

Fuels vary in efficiency for several reasons. One is differing physical characteristics of fuels. For instance, coal contains more energy per pound than wood does; therefore, coal is easier to store and transport per kilocalorie and is more desirable as a boiler fuel. Oil has a higher energy content per unit weight and burns at a higher temperature than coal. It is also a liquid, which makes it even easier to transport than coal, and it is usable in internal combustion engines. The advantages of internal combustion engines are such that a diesel locomotive uses only one-fifth of the energy (in kcal) that a coal-powered steam engine needs to pull the same train.[14] Moreover, oil-burning systems generally require less attention and are cleaner than solid-fuel systems, as anyone will attest who grew up with a coal furnace in the basement. As a result, oil and gas generate from 1.3 to 2.45 times the amount of economic value per kilocalorie that coal does.[15]

For some uses, especially in manufacturing, electricity is an even more efficient fuel than petroleum. Electricity has supplanted fossil fuels for many applications because it can be converted to mechanical or heat energy at the place where it's needed and can be turned on and off instantly. For example, a factory that was run on coal had its machines connected to a central power plant by an awkward arrangement of drive shafts and pulleys. Running one machine required firing up the whole system. Having an individual electric motor for each machine, however, eliminates this waste of energy and reduces frictional losses of energy.[16] Therefore, energy requirements per unit of output are reduced. Research indicates that a kilocalorie of nuclear and hydroelectricity (as opposed to electricity generated from coal or oil that could themselves serve as fuels)[17] can be used to produce much more output than a kilocalorie of fossil fuel does, as long as the task is suited to electricity's greater fuel efficiency.[18] In short, as more of the nation's fuel budget is provided by these electric fuels, the amount of economic output created with a kcal of energy also increases. Here we see one way in which ingenuity has raised energy efficiency: we have learned how to take advantage of physical and functional differences among fuels. The nation's energy efficiency, as measured by the GNP/fuel consumption ratio, rises; but whether this kind of increase really reflects the ability to do more with less is quite another question.

Changes in the fuel mix over the past few decades explain most—about 72 percent—of the change in the real GNP/energy ratio (Figure 3–6). From 1929 to 1972 the ratio rose steadily as petroleum replaced coal as the major U.S. energy source. Since 1972 nuclear and hydroelectricity's contribution nearly doubled (due mostly to a fivefold jump in nuclear energy production), but the net increase in aggregate fuel efficiency was reduced because the relative importance of petroleum declined.

Household Energy Consumption

But if the decline in petroleum offset the rise in nuclear and hydroelectricity since 1972, then why has the real GNP/energy ratio risen sharply over the same period? The answer lies in rising fuel prices and the differing ways in which GNP reacts to fuel bought by households, rather than by other sectors of the economy.

Because a labor pool consists of human beings, energy is required for its continued existence. Workers need to use energy at home as well as at work in order to be productive. They need fuel to cook their food, heat their houses, and operate their cars. The fuel bought directly by workers and their families can be considered the *energy cost of labor*, the amount of fuel used to keep workers productive. It's clear that the energy cost of labor can vary widely: a worker who lives in Honolulu (with less than 1,000 heating and cooling degree-days each year,[19]) who eats only raw fish and vegetables, and

Figure 3–6. Prediction of the Real GNP/Energy Ratio Based on Changes in the Economy's Fuel Mix versus Actual Values of the Ratio, 1929 to 1983

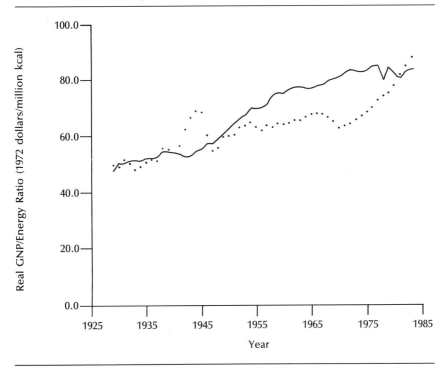

Note: Solid line is prediction based on fuel mix; dots are actual values.

who rides a bicycle or public transportation will make virtually no direct fuel purchases: in other words, such a worker will have a negligible energy cost. Another worker with the same job and the same salary, who lives in Duluth (with nearly 10,000 heating and cooling degree-days a year), who loves to cook two-day spaghetti sauce, and who drives a V-12 Jaguar, a Harley-Davidson motorcycle, and a snowmobile will have an extremely large energy cost. On the other hand, the amount of output (GNP) that the two workers produce are identical, regardless of their fuel-consuming habits away from work. This assumes, of course, that their energy-consuming habits at home don't make them sick or otherwise affect their productivity on the job.

Imagine two companies making identical products with identical methods. However, one firm's labor force consists entirely of workers who ride bicycles and live in unheated flats, while the other firm employs only Jaguar drivers. Each company uses 1,000 kcal of fuel and pays its workers one dollar to produce a hundred dollars' worth of output. A complete accounting of the energy cost of a hundred dollars of output must include the energy equivalent of a dollar's worth of labor—that is, the fuel purchased by workers with a dollar in wages—as well as the 1,000 kcal of direct fuel use. If the bike riders buy an average of 50 kcal of fuel with each dollar of their wages, while the Jaguar drivers buy 500 kcal, the first firm will "use" a total of 1,050 kcal of energy to produce a hundred dollars in output, while the second firm "uses" 1,500 kcal. Clearly, the economy receives more output per kcal of total energy from the first firm than from the second.

The same considerations apply to entire nations. As proportionately less energy is consumed directly in households, the number of dollars in output produced per kcal of energy consumed—the GNP/energy ratio—will rise. Conversely, as household fuel consumption rises, the GNP/energy ratio will drop.[20]

Alterations in household fuel consumption account for about 86 percent of the variation in the real GNP/energy ratio not explained by fuel efficiency, or about 24 percent of the total variation in the ratio. The sharp upswing in the ratio observed during World War II was caused by a large reduction in household fuel consumption, due to gasoline rationing and voluntary cutbacks for the war effort. By contrast, the ratio fell during the 1950s and 1960s when stable fuel prices and rising incomes led people to intensify their household fuel use. The 1973 OPEC price hike caused households to cut fuel use; this largely accounts for the subsequent rise in the nation's apparent energy efficiency. Internationally, household consumption patterns explain 57 percent of the variation in real GNP/energy ratios among nations.[21]

Thus, about 96 percent of the yearly variation in the real GNP/energy ratio between 1929 and 1983 can be accounted for by the efficiencies of fuels consumed and the relative importance of household fuel consumption (Figure 3–7).

Fuel Prices

Many economists believe that fuel prices by themselves have a major influence on the nation's energy efficiency. Rising fuel prices should induce industry and other intermediate sectors, as well as households, to cut back on fuel use and thereby raise the real GNP/energy ratio; falling prices, according to the conventional view, should have the opposite effect. To see whether this hypothesis has any validity, we also considered the history of fuel prices in our statistical analysis.

We found that the fuel mix, household fuel consumption, and fuel prices together account for almost 97 percent of the variation in the real GNP/energy ratio (Figure 3–8).[22] Contrary to

Figure 3–7. Prediction of the Real GNP/Energy Ratio Based on Changes in the Economy's Fuel Mix and Household Fuel Use

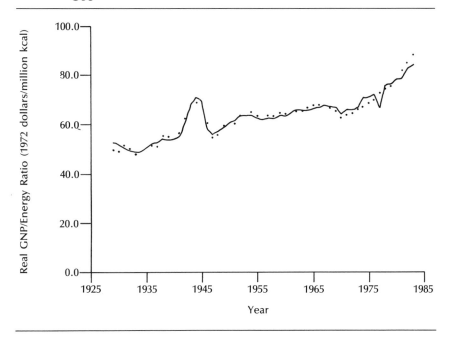

Note: Solid line is prediction based on fuel mix and household fuel use; dots are actual values.

Figure 3–8.   Prediction of the Real GNP/Energy Ratio Based on Changes in the Economy's Fuel Mix, Household Fuel Use, and Fuel Prices

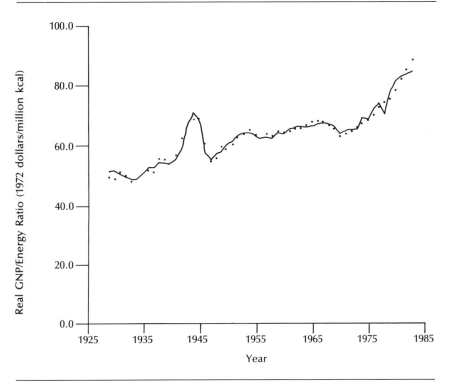

Note: Solid line is prediction based on fuel mix, household fuel use, and fuel prices; dots are actual values.

the conventional wisdom, fuel prices accounted for less than 1 percent of the variation in energy efficiency between 1929 and 1983. In fairness, this average figure understates the recent importance of fuel prices: because fuel prices held remarkably steady between 1929 and 1972, they exerted essentially no effect on energy efficiency until the 1973 oil crisis, after which fuel prices have become considerably more important. We also found that energy's price elasticity of demand (that is, the degree to which energy demand is reduced by a rise in energy prices) has been much smaller than conventional estimates. We discuss these findings in more detail in a later section.

The linkage between the real GNP/energy ratio and the fuel mix, household fuel consumption, and fuel prices has not weakened significantly in the last decade. When we analyze the 1929–1972 period similarly and use the results to "predict" the behavior of the real GNP/energy ratio from 1973 to 1984, based on changes in the aggregate efficiency of the nation's fuel mix, household fuel consumption, and fuel prices, we find that the predictions match actual values of the GNP/energy ratio in the 1973–84 period very closely (Figure 3–9).[23]

Statistical correlations alone do not prove causality. (Indeed, causality can never be proved absolutely, only disproved.) Nevertheless, a very strong correlation (in addition to the theoretical considerations discussed above, which led us to look for the correlation in the first place) indicates a strong likelihood of

Figure 3–9. Prediction of the Real GNP/Energy Ratio Based on 1929 to 1972 Data versus Actual Values of the Ratio, 1973 to 1984

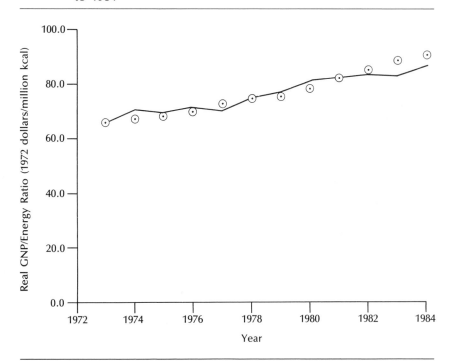

Note: Solid line is prediction; circles are actual values.

causality. Other analysts have advanced other theoretical mechanisms to account for the GNP/energy ratio's behavior, but their studies either looked only at particular sectors of the economy or failed to quantify the mechanisms statistically for the economy as a whole. They can't identify which factors most strongly affect the economy's energy efficiency, or even whether the postulated mechanisms have any effect at all. Consequently, we can claim that we have identified—and measured—the strongest candidates yet for the true determinants of the GNP/energy ratio.

The events of the past dozen years have made increasing the economy's energy efficiency a high national priority. Many people who accept that fuel will never be as plentiful as in the 1950s and 1960s believe that we can continue to increase economic production by increasing our energy efficiency. These results, however, indicate that our ability to keep increasing the amount of GNP we produce with each kcal of fuel is severely constrained. This doesn't mean that it will be impossible to increase efficiency in the future; rather, it means that we will be unable to continue some strategies that were successful in the past and that other conservation efforts will involve significant tradeoffs.

Past strategies for increasing the nation's energy efficiency included using a greater proportion of oil, gas, nuclear power, and hydroelectricity. But petroleum is running out, imported oil is thought to be unreliable, the choicest large hydroelectric sites have already been developed, and nuclear power is widely considered too expensive and too dangerous. We could increase the amount of small-site hydro and photovoltaic electricity or pursue breeder or fusion technologies, but, as will be argued in Chapter 4, these power sources can't completely offset the expected general decline in the real GNP/energy ratio before 2025. In fact, coal, the leading candidate to replace oil and gas, is roughly half as efficient, so that replacing oil and gas with coal will *depress* the GNP/energy ratio. And, as discussed in more detail in a later section, cuts in household fuel use have largely involved sacrifices of one kind or another. Since it is human nature to make the easiest adjustments with the greatest rewards first, we may meet growing resistance to further reductions.

THE U.S. ECONOMY: PAST, PRESENT, AND FUTURE

Our quantitative examination of the relationship between energy supplies and economic production can shed new and intriguing light on some familiar questions. For instance, it can explain why the real dollar prices of many resources have fallen over the last century, a trend that Julian Simon, the late Herman Kahn, and other cornucopians have used to argue that resources are becoming more, not less, abundant. It also shows why, in the late 1970s and early 1980s, it was possible to have high inflation and interest rates and sagging economic growth simultaneously, and why stimulatory fiscal and monetary policies have not worked as well as they once did. The ability to explain these real-world problems is desirable in its own right, but it also demonstrates the power of energy-based economic analysis in general.

The Falling Price of Resources

The rising supply, efficiency, and energy profit ratio of fuels from the mid-1800s to the early 1970s simultaneously helped and hurt the U.S. economy. On one hand, they enabled us to build living standards to unprecedented heights, even as the population grew tenfold. On the other hand, the power they conferred allowed us to paper over many of the warning signs that we were using other resources unsustainably. As cumulative demand for natural resources lowered the quality of nonrenewable resources, the increasing energy costs of their extraction were of little apparent consequence; we simply took more cheap (both in energy and dollar terms) fuel from the environment to pay these costs. The same is true for the increasing instantaneous demand for potentially renewable resources. Increased demand encouraged farmers to grow more food on the same acreage; but energy was so plentiful that the energy costs of more and bigger tractors, fertilizers, pesticides, and irrigation water were relatively unimportant. The nation "solved" its resource problems by throwing energy at them.

We could believe, as Julian Simon still believes, that the rapid pace of resource use was no cause for worry because the real dollar costs for most natural resources (except timber) declined during the period of relative energy abundance.[24] The price of these resources declined in spite of rising energy costs because the supply, energy profit ratio, and efficiency of the nation's fuel mix were still improving. As demand for natural resources and their energy costs rose, we simply wrung more fuel from the environment to pay them. Because the dollar price of fossil fuels was so low compared to that of labor, these fuels were used to do most of the work needed to meet the increased demand, and at far less expense per unit of resource obtained than if the work was done entirely by human labor. The increasing use of fossil fuels in resource extraction let the unit price of most resources fall. Moreover, we didn't have to divert energy from other parts of the economy, and therefore we didn't have to forgo other goods and services. We were able to have more of everything.

In sum, until the early 1970s, the United States luxuriated in net energy. We didn't hesitate to spend more energy to build up crop yields or increase fish hauls or mine low-quality copper ores because we were so energy rich that the higher expenditures were insignificant compared to our total hoard of fuel and our ability to increase it. Thus, to realize the expectation of Simon and his fellow cornucopians that natural resources will continue to become cheaper and more "abundant" in the long run, the net supply of fuel must continue to rise and its dollar price must continue to fall—an expectation contradicted by the Hubbert analysis and by common sense.

The Failure of Traditional Economic Policies

Despite the abundant supply of fuel prior to the 1970s, though, the performance of the U.S. economy was not an unbroken string of triumphs. Several economic downturns, including the Great Depression, occurred when unexpected economic events caused demand to slacken. Starting with the New Deal and World War II, such downturns were cured by increasing the money supply (monetary policy) and/or government spending (fiscal policy). By putting more money in people's pockets or by having the government buy goods and services directly, these policies spurred demand and got the economy growing again. They were successful prior to the 1970s because the energy needed to meet the stimulated demand was easily available.

But since then our fuel budget has undergone several upheavals. Domestic production of oil and gas peaked in the early 1970s. It is now declining, and there is little hope for future improvement. Even as the supply of high-efficiency fuels has fallen, the energy profit ratios for major fossil fuels used by the U.S. economy have plummeted: for coal and domestic oil and gas since 1967 and for imported oil since 1971. Additionally, most new primary electric capacity came not from hydroelectric turbines, which have an energy profit ratio of 11, but from nuclear reactors, with energy profit ratios of about 4. If gross supplies of energy decrease, and if the fraction of those supplies available to produce useful goods and services shrinks, output must fall unless energy efficiency increases.

Of course, the biggest upheaval affecting the U.S. fuel budget was the huge run-up in fuel prices in the 1970s. It is not immediately obvious that declining fuel quality or oil production in the United States had anything to do with those price hikes—but, nevertheless, it did. That the 1973 oil embargo occurred shortly after U.S. domestic oil production peaked was no accident. Rather, that was the earliest date that oil exporting countries had the economic power to dictate oil prices on a sustained basis. Here's why: before the early 1970s the United States could still expand its domestic production to meet increases in demand, and domestic oil was relatively cheap. If the economy needed a little more oil, it could get it from domestic producers. But once domestic production peaked and demand continued to grow, the United States needed a lot more oil and had to look abroad for it. This cast foreign producers in the role of "marginal supplier" and greatly increased their influence on world oil prices. OPEC could then double the price of its oil and make that price stick because the United States could not replace much of its oil imports with domestic supplies. Thus, declining domestic fuel quality set the stage for OPEC's rise to power.

These considerations go a long way toward explaining the unprecedented behavior of the economy since 1973. Most of this period has been characterized by low economic growth and high inflation: conditions that are supposed to be mutually exclusive. They have occurred, however, because this economic slowdown was not an internal crisis of demand, as were the recessions of the 1940s, 1950s, and 1960s, but an external crisis of supply. Quite simply, the flow of net energy and other natural resources into the economy hasn't been increasing as it did in the past because rising fuel prices discouraged the use of this fundamental ingredient of economic activity. Consequently, the flow of goods and services from the economy has slowed down. Some analysts estimated that rising fuel prices in 1976 reduced the economy's potential output by 3 to 7 percent.[25]

Government policymakers treated the slowdown as they did previous ones, with stimulatory monetary and fiscal policies. But these efforts did not have the same "pump priming" effect when energy and natural resources couldn't be drawn as easily from the environment. If the money supply is expanded, all other things being equal, the demand for goods and services rises and the U.S. economy needs a greater supply of energy to satisfy this increased demand. If energy cannot be drawn from the environment as quickly as the money supply expands, demand by dollar holders exceeds the supply of goods and services. When demand is greater than supply, prices rise, a phenomenon known as inflation. Indeed, all inflationary periods of the last ninety years, including the unprecedented inflation of the 1970s and early 1980s, were times when demand (money supply) increased faster than supply (energy use).[26] By correlating changes in the ratio of money supply to energy consumption with the consumer price index, we can account for almost all the variation in prices since 1890 (Figure 3–10). The relatively low inflation seen in the last few years fits this pattern: a tight-money policy coupled with stable energy use kept consumer demand in line with the supply of goods and services. This is not to say that all inflationary periods have been caused by tight fuel supplies: in the past, inadequate industrial capacity or insufficient labor were probably the main factors that kept output (and energy use) from growing as fast as the money supply. Recently, however, we have seen inflation occur during periods

Figure 3–10.   Consumer Price Index since 1890 and as Predicted by Regression Involving Energy Consumption Relative to the Money Supply

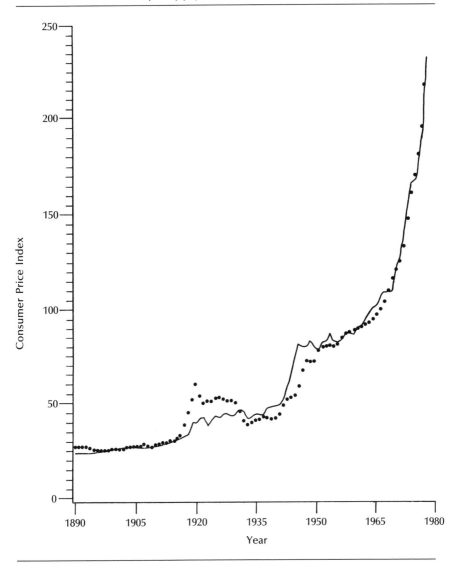

Source: C.J. Cleveland, R. Costanza, C.A.S. Hall, and R. Kaufmann, "Energy and the U.S. Economy: A Biophysical Perspective," *Science* 225 (1984):890–97. © 1984 AAAS
Note: Dots are actual values of the CPI; solid line is prediction; 1967 = 100.

of high unemployment and low capacity utilization, which leads us to conclude that the limits to fuel supplies are now a principal cause of inflation.

Declining supplies of fuel and other natural resources also reduce the effectiveness of fiscal policy. In the past, when government spending rose, fuels and resources needed to produce the goods and services it purchased were forthcoming from the environment. However, increased government buying won't stimulate sustained growth when fuel can no longer be drawn without limit from the environment. Consequently, increased government spending takes fuel and natural resources away from other sectors of the economy: 10 million barrels of oil used to build an aircraft carrier are 10 million barrels of oil that are no longer available to replace aging industrial capital.[27] In an age of limited energy supplies, increased government spending crowds out other sectors without increasing the total output—especially if those purchases are made with borrowed money. Indeed, this crowding-out may be one reason that large federal budget deficits now have such a strong impact on interest rates. We are not attacking all government spending as unwise or burdensome; we simply wish to point out the zero-sum nature of the nation's energy budget. By the same token, increased energy use by the private sector means that less energy is available for educating our children, delivering our mail, running our firefighting equipment, or providing any of the other government services on which we depend.

Thus, Ronald Reagan was at least partly correct in 1980 when he called stagflation a supply-side problem. But the problem wasn't that government regulations were tying the hands of private enterprise or that corporations didn't have enough money or incentive to invest.[28] It was that the natural resources, especially energy, were simply no longer sufficient to permit 4 percent annual growth in real GNP. Inflation occurred because demand was stimulated without similarly increasing the supply of fuel needed to satisfy the higher demand. These problems will not go away unless either (1) the supply of net energy is increased, or (2) fiscal and monetary policies are set consistent with the energy supply. Although the current "oil glut," caused by the recession still dogging the rest of the world, may allow an increase in energy consumption and therefore some real economic growth, no one should be lulled into thinking a glut can last for long. All evidence suggests that if and when the world's economies build up steam again, the "glut" will vanish. Adjusting fiscal and monetary policies to energy realities can't offset declining resource quality, but it can at least eliminate the corrosive effects of inflation.

If present trends continue, and there is every reason to believe they will, the quality of fuels available to the U.S. economy will deteriorate. Total energy consumption will stagnate, and because the fuel mix will be increasingly made up of coal and other low-efficiency fuels, total energy efficiency will fall. In the next chapter, we will use a simple computer-based model to see what these trends portend.

But one trend is certain. In the future, the United States will no longer be able to conceal the effects of unsustainable resource use by using more energy to extract natural resources from a deteriorating base. As high-quality and high-efficiency fuels disappear, the environment and the quality of its resources will reappear in economic calculations, whether neo-classical economists recognize it or not.[29] In the last ten years alone, the fraction of GNP accounted for by natural resource extraction has grown from 4 percent to 10 percent.[30] Because of the prohibitive energy cost of processing low-quality ores, mining dirt to satisfy demand for some elements is not feasible, contrary to what some maintain.[31]

The Role of Technology

The problems of declining resource quality and supply would matter little if society could learn to get more output from the same quantity of resources and other inputs. Technological advances that stretch our resources are the most commonly proposed solution for the problems of declining quality and supply.[32] Unfortunately, though, our analysis indicates that the ability of technical change to increase the goods and services produced from the same amount and mix of fuels is much smaller than most economists claim. Our estimate of energy's price elasticity of demand, for example, is -0.19 (meaning that a 1 percent increase in fuel prices would cut fuel demand by 0.19

percent), significantly less than the range of -0.51 to -1.36 previously estimated.[33]

There are several reasons to believe that previous assessments of technology's ability to save energy were overly optimistic. For one, many analyses ignored important changes in the kinds of fuels used in the economy and in the division of fuel supplies between household and intermediate sectors. As a result, changes in efficiency due to these factors were mistakenly attributed to technological advances and/or fuel prices.

Another mistake made by conventional economists is to extrapolate results obtained from studies of individual sectors to the entire economy. According to economic orthodoxy, fuel, labor, and capital are independent and equally important inputs into the economy. Fuel supposedly can be replaced by capital and labor, thereby maintaining output while reducing the quantity of energy used to produce that output. Such replacement certainly occurs at the level of single companies.[34] As the dollar price of fuel rises relative to that of capital and labor, the smart manager will alter production processes to replace direct fuel use with cheaper capital and/or labor and to reduce the fuel used directly to produce a unit of output—the opposite of what was done earlier in the century when fuel prices fell relative to wages and capital costs.

It is often assumed that, if one company could make such a substitution, all companies could, and the nation's aggregate energy efficiency would rise. A 1983 report from the Congressional Office of Technology Assessment, "Industrial Energy Use," attempted to measure the potential for energy savings in manufacturing sectors. It studied fuel consumption in several industries and concluded that energy needs could be reduced by as much as 50 percent.

This sort of analysis, however, overestimates the degree to which fuel can be displaced within the entire U.S. economy, because it fails to consider the fuel used elsewhere in the economy to produce and support the additional capital and labor. If *all* companies substituted labor and capital for fuel, more fuel would be needed somewhere in the economy to increase the amount of labor and capital, and the nation's net savings in energy are reduced. In agriculture, for example, the amount of fuel used *directly* on a cornfield to grow a kilogram of corn fell 14.6 percent between 1959 and 1970. However, when the calculation includes the fuel used elsewhere in the economy to build the tractors, make the fertilizers and pesticides, and so on, it turns out that the total energy cost of a kilogram of corn actually rose by 3 percent during that period.[35] In the manufacturing sector, the OTA found that the amount of energy used directly to produce a real dollar's worth of output dropped by 18 percent between 1972 and 1982. However, these direct fuel savings don't appear in our analysis of the nation's energy efficiency because part of manufacturers' energy savings were offset by energy used to replace capital made prematurely obsolete by high fuel prices.[36] Direct fuel savings were further offset by the higher overall use of capital per unit of output.[37]

Figures 3–11a and 3–11b highlight the importance of considering the indirect as well as the direct uses of fuel in producing goods and services in the general economy. The first figure includes only direct fuel use, and it shows a nearly random scatter of points. Including the indirect energy costs of capital, labor, and government services compresses the points into the neat line shown in Figure 3–11b. Thus, the total energy cost of a dollar's worth of financial and insurance services, for example, is nearly identical to the energy used to produce a dollar's worth of primary nonferrous metal products.[38]

In other words, one can shift energy use from one sector to another in a kind of shell game, by switching between direct fuel uses and indirect uses in the form of labor and capital. However, it is not so easy to cut fuel use in the economy as a whole. You can hire more workers and thereby get rid of some fuel-guzzling machines; but assuming that most of the new workers were previously out of work, they will then have more money to spend, part of which they'll use to buy fuel. Nationally, the average employed person consumes twice the fuel used by an unemployed person.[39] Some if not all of the apparent energy savings will therefore be erased. Likewise, you can buy a new and sophisticated "fuel-efficient" machine to replace an old machine or some workers, but the new machine could take more energy to build than its predecessor and so eat up most or all of the apparent savings. It might be argued that if the new machine takes more energy to build and run than what it

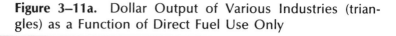

Figure 3–11a. Dollar Output of Various Industries (triangles) as a Function of Direct Fuel Use Only

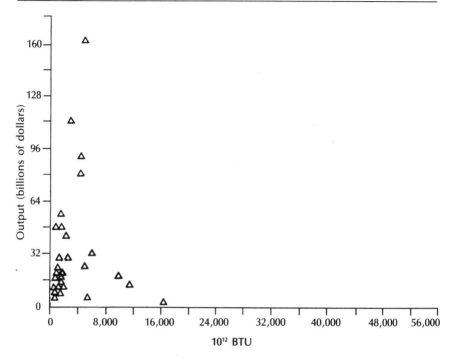

replaced, it will cost more in dollars and hence not be economically attractive; but that argument assumes that energy costs are the primary determinant of dollar costs. Such an assumption is hardly valid in a world of tax incentives, capital write-offs, price controls, and plain stupidity.

Finally, some economists argue that *deindustrialization*, the shift from heavy smokestack industries to light manufacturing and services, has increased the real GNP/energy ratio over the last decade and will continue to do so.[40] This sounds plausible, but these studies haven't supported their hypotheses with hard data. Neither the percentage of GNP produced by services nor the fraction of net national income produced by heavy manufacturing (such as chemicals, oil refining, and primary metal production) have had a statistically significant effect on the real GNP/fuel ratio between 1929 and 1983. Deindustrialization might increase the energy efficiency in the future, but we think it should be regarded as analogous to fusion power: it would be

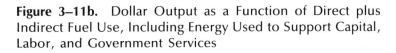

Figure 3–11b. Dollar Output as a Function of Direct plus Indirect Fuel Use, Including Energy Used to Support Capital, Labor, and Government Services

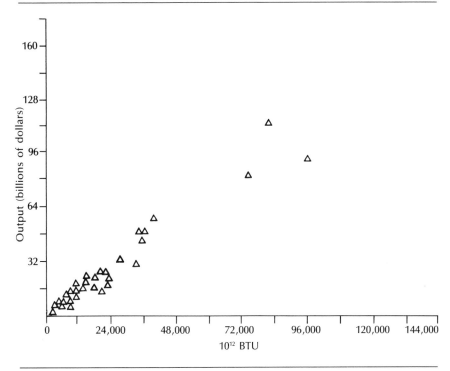

Source: R. Costanza, "Embodied Energy and Economic Valuation," *Science* 210 (1980): 1219–24. © 1980 AAAS
Note: Triangles are industries.

very helpful, but the nation is gambling with its material living standards if it *assumes* that it will be successful.

Energy conservation in industry, through cogeneration, insulation, and preheating, could be substantial. However, it's extremely tempting, when assessing the benefits of a new process or technology, to look only at direct fuel savings. Decisions regarding substitutions among labor, capital, and fuel, in the hope of achieving energy savings via technology, must include *all* the energy costs associated with that technology.

It's not that substitutions *cannot* enhance energy efficiency. Even a price elasticity of -0.19 could increase energy efficiency substantially if the incentives to save energy remain strong. In Chapter 7 we describe how the price incentive to reduce energy use can be reinforced to raise efficiency further. But the potential for increase is limited and, as the next chapter shows, probably insufficient to offset the coming decline in fuel supply and aggregate fuel efficiency.

Conservation

The word *conservation* comes up a great deal in discussions of the nation's energy future and usually is meant to signify all kinds of reductions in fuel use. We showed that shifting fuel use away from the household sector is an effective way to increase the real GNP/energy ratio. Reductions in household fuel use are a proven way to boost U.S. energy efficiency.

Energy conservation is generally understood to be any practice that cuts the use of energy. It may be more useful, however, to think of these practices as divided between conservation *per se* and curtailment. Actual conservation is a rather specialized way to reduce fuel use, and our ability to practice it is constrained in the short run. Through conservation *per se*, the same amount of work is done with less energy. For example, we can reduce the amount of heating oil needed to warm our homes to 67°F by insulating our walls or by installing a more efficient furnace. However, we can also cut fuel use by simply getting along with less: we can just turn the thermostat down to 63°F. This type of reduction is curtailment rather than true conservation. Between 1972 and 1984 the percentage of GNP attributable to personal expenditures on fuel shrank from 4.28 to 3.41 percent. If households conserved energy, our lifestyles were unaffected by this reduction. To the extent that these saving were achieved by curtailing fuel-consuming activities, however, our lifestyles have been changed, perhaps for the worse.[41]

Driving cars and heating homes account for most of the fuel used in the household sector. The Department of Energy estimates that gasoline consumption by private autos in 1980 was 25 percent less than it would have been had our driving habits and gas mileage stayed as they were in 1973.[42] Of this reduction, about half can be attributed to the increased gas mileage of the average car. The other half results from from reductions in auto travel and speed. Both involve some measure of curtailment, of sacrifice: we now drive cars with less passenger room and that offer less protection in collisions, we drive them less often, and we take longer to get where we want to go. Smaller cars also bring benefits—they're easier to maneuver—and some people may not miss what they've given up, but the fact remains that many of these cutbacks involved sacrifice by many people. We find indirect corroboration of this point in people's response to stable or falling gasoline prices: invariably, average highway speeds and sales of larger cars again increase. A dominant role for curtailment is also found in home heating.[43] Both the DOE and the American Gas Association estimate that reduced consumption was caused more by turning thermostats down rather than by true conservation measures. Colder houses reflect sacrifices. To be sure, the severity of the sacrifice is a subjective judgment; nevertheless, the fact that people could have saved money before the 1973 price shocks by buying small cars or by turning their thermostats down, but chose not to do so, indicates that their post-1973 behavior was not entirely willing.

We are not arguing that *all* curtailment has reduced living standards; some of it involved the correction of bad habits such as heating and lighting empty rooms. Nor are we claiming that people's values remain unchanged or that cutbacks hurt forever; year-round climate control is no longer important to many people. We *are* arguing, however, that it is a mistake to believe that reductions in fuel use entail no tradeoffs. Overpromising the benefits and ignoring the costs, as many previous analyses have done, will ultimately lead to a backlash against all conservation efforts. The resurgence of "muscle cars" and the disappointing sales of energy-efficient home appliances indicate that such a backlash may already be occurring.

The past importance of curtailment indicates that much of the recent increase in the GNP/energy ratio was accomplished by reducing many people's living standards. On the other hand, conservation *per se* could play a more important role in the future—but new strategies will have to be found to encourage people to spend the money needed to accomplish it. Chapter 7 describes both the existing obstacles to conservation *per se* and ways to remove or get around them.

The fact that curtailment seems to have reduced material living standards while, ironically, increasing the amount of GNP we produce with a unit of energy illustrates the weakness of GNP as a measure of living standards. Many people have pointed out that many of the goods and services lumped together in GNP do not make our lives any better or happier and that rising GNP is not necessarily a good thing in itself. Perhaps the most eloquent expression of this came from Robert F. Kennedy:

> For the gross national product includes air pollution and advertising for cigarettes, and ambulances to clear our highways of carnage. It counts special locks for our doors, and jails for the people who break them. The gross national product includes the destruction of redwoods and the death of Lake Superior. It grows with the production of napalm and missiles and nuclear warheads, and even includes research on the improved dissemination of bubonic plague. The gross national product swells with the equipment for the police to put down the riots in our cities; and although it is not diminished by the damage these riots do, still it goes up as slums are rebuilt on their ashes. It includes Whitman's rifle and Speck's knife, and the broadcasting of television programs which glorify violence and sell goods to our children.

As energy supplies become tighter and as our society has to choose which goods and services to keep producing at current levels and which to give up, it may be possible to make most of the cutbacks in activities that degrade the quality of life. It will certainly be difficult, but at least the possibility exists.

CONCLUSION

In this chapter we examined one of the two components of economic growth—the knowledge people have gained for creating a more comfortable and secure world for themselves—and compared its state of development to the other component—the supply of energy and other natural resources needed to implement that knowledge. During most of the preceding century, human knowledge has limited the rate of economic growth. Because the supply of high-quality resources was relatively large compared to our knowledge of how to use them, advances in chemistry, physics, biology, and engineering were easily translated into a higher standard of living for a growing U.S. population. The nation prospered by finding new ways to subsidize human effort with expanding quantities of increasingly efficient fuels. This allowed us to produce more output per person while appearing to reduce the extra amounts of energy needed to achieve this increase.

However, the declining supply, energy profit ratio, and efficiency of fuels and other resources have turned the tables on the United States. The principal limitation to economic growth now comes from the supply of resources needed to implement our still-growing knowledge. The shift in the technology's limiting factor forces us to change the way in which we approach the future. It is no longer enough to ask whether human understanding can solve our problems; we must also ask whether we have the natural resources needed to implement the solutions.

The change has important implications for the size of the United States' carrying capacity. As long as human knowledge limited economic growth, growth in carrying capacity was more or less an automatic companion to expanding knowledge. We could and did use our knowledge to increase both the average standard of living and the size of our population. It is a short but enormously mistaken step to assume that it must always be possible to use our increasing knowledge to increase our carrying capacity.

The dynamics of a system limited by its natural resources are very different from one limited by its technical understanding. Thus, we cannot extrapolate past successes into the future. Nevertheless, our present economy and our understanding of its operation were both formed during the period of relative resource abundance and knowledge scarcity. It will take some time, at least a few decades, to adjust to the new order. In the next chapter we will use the quantitative relations developed in Chapters 2 and 3 to examine how the existing economy might react to long-term resource limitations.

4 A MODEL OF ENERGY AND THE U.S. ECONOMY

Watch out w'en youer gittin' all you want. Fattenin' hogs ain't in luck.

—*Joel Chandler Harris*

Imagine that, over the last few decades, you and your family have acquired a comfortable, well-appointed house with all the modern conveniences. You've grown accustomed to enjoying a wide variety of fine foods and clothes, to traveling where you wish in an option-loaded automobile, and to owning a variety of labor-saving gadgets. In sum, your wealth has burgeoned fast enough to support a growing family at an ever-greater material standard of living. Many readers won't need to imagine this scenario: they've lived it.

Now imagine that your income and savings are dwindling, slowly but inexorably. Imagine further that the cost of everything is rising. In the not-too-distant future, many of the goods and services you've taken for granted won't be available, period. And your in-laws are hinting that they want to live with you. What will happen to you and your lifestyle?

This is the position in which the United States now finds itself. We have built an enormous economy that has provided us with unprecedented affluence, but it is founded on a finite and dwindling base of fuels and other resources. The flow of domestic fuel that keeps the economy running becomes smaller with each passing year, at a time when that part of the economy devoted to finding nonfuel resources is making escalating

111

demands for fuel. Increasing reliance on imported fuels could ease this problem for a while, but with significant costs. Thus, unless we increase enormously the efficiency with which the economy converts energy to goods and services, our economic output must drop. If this is the case, what does the future hold for our country, our economy, and our lifestyle?

One way to answer this question is with a computerized numerical model. Such a model allows us to combine projections concerning many different parts of the economy so that we can evaluate their overall effect in ways that would be impossible if the calculation had to be done by hand. Although a model doesn't predict the future, it can define more clearly the risks and the tradeoffs involved in different strategies for coping with the declining resource base.

To build a model, the modeler identifies those parts of the system (in our case, the conversion of energy and other inputs into the goods and services aggregated into GNP) that are most important to its operation. The parts are then linked through equations that represent the modeler's view as to how the parts interact. Since these aspects of model-building are at least partly subjective, the model's results depend on the preconceptions and biases that the modeler builds into it. The computer simply performs the tedious mathematical calculations that follow from the linkages and from the assumptions about those linkages. Such calculations, such projections, are only as reliable as those assumptions.

A vital part of modeling is scenario analysis, in which the model is run several times using different values for the input variables in each run. The first run is often done with middle-of-the-road estimates for the input variables, or with simple extrapolations of current trends, and is often called the *reference scenario*, to which the results of subsequent runs will be compared. Later scenarios might ask, What if federal expenditures grow by an extra 0.5 percent a year? What if oil prices fall instead of rise? What if the money supply expands faster than anticipated? The model responds to these questions by calculating new values for the output variables, things like automobile purchases, oil demand, interest rates, and so forth. Scenario analysis pinpoints those input variables that have the greatest effect on the model output, thereby identifying the variables that most strongly influence the system's behavior. In other words, scenario analysis reveals how different the future would be (according to the model's equations, of course) if people bought 10 percent more cars and 10 percent fewer computers than the "best guess" indicated.

CHANGING MODELS TO REFLECT CHANGING CONDITIONS

A sizable number of national economic models already exist, and it might be asked why we need to build yet another. The answer is that conventional economic models were built by and for neoclassical economists and therefore reflect the strengths and weaknesses of neoclassical economics. One of our main arguments has been that neoclassical economics was developed during a period of resource abundance relative to the ability or need to exploit resources, and hence concentrated on the internal workings of the human economy. Models therefore focused on internal supply and demand conditions while relegating external conditions in the resource base to the background. That is, economic models attempted to predict the supply and demand for various goods and services given certain market expectations, such as how much the government will spend or what kind of monetary policy the Federal Reserve Board will set. The simulated level of economic activity could be adjusted by changing the assumptions about these internal economic conditions. Many models start by presuming that the economy will grow at some predetermined rate, say 2.5 percent per year, and calculate the amount of energy needed to produce this output—without considering whether that amount of energy would even be available. These "internal" models just assume that it will.

The strengths and weaknesses of this approach can be seen in one of the most widely used models, which was put together by Data Resources Inc. (DRI), the well-respected Massachusetts consulting firm.[1] Given assumptions about 225 *input variables*, such as the price of fuel, population growth, and government taxing and spending policy, this model projects 982 *output variables*, such as the dollar value of cars bought, the level of GNP, and so on. This model, which is similar to most others in its basic philosophy, is usually used to make five-year projections. Within this short time scale, the DRI model is as effective as any forecasting tool, since declining resource quality has rarely been noticeable over periods shorter than a decade.

Occasionally, however, the DRI model is used to make twenty- or thirty-year forecasts, and then its shortcomings become too large to ignore. Essentially, DRI assumes that certain recent trends will continue in the future, without making any attempt to see what lies behind those trends. For example, DRI did not try to find out what makes the real GNP/fuel use ratio change from year to year. Since this ratio has been rising during the last decade, the DRI model simply assumes that it will continue to rise. But we made the following calculation: we put DRI's own projections for the consumption of oil, gas, nuclear power, and hydroelectricity, for the fraction of GNP spent by households on fuel, and for fuel prices into our equation (described in Chapter 3) relating these factors to the GNP/energy ratio. The resulting ratio rises faster than DRI's over the next decade, but soon drops below the DRI prediction (Figure 4–1). In other words, DRI implicitly assumes that the ways in which the economy converts energy to goods and services are going to change. Similarly, DRI assumes that rising energy prices will "create" new domestic supplies of oil and gas to run the US economy. As shown in Figure 4–2, domestic oil and gas flows predicted by the highly accurate Hubbert method are far lower than the domestic production DRI predicts: DRI assumes, without support, that the Hubbert method is wrong.

These problems are not confined to the DRI model. For example, in 1977 the Workshop on Alternative Energy Strategies project (WAES), sponsored by the National Academy of Sciences, saw domestic petroleum production growing to 12 million barrels per day by 1985 if crude oil prices surpassed $17.25 a barrel in constant 1975 dollars.[2] In 1982 a barrel of imported oil cost $20 in 1975 dollars, yet domestic production was only 8.7 million barrels per day.

Conventional economic models fall into these traps because they operate under one basic assumption: that the production of

Figure 4–1. The Real GNP/Energy Ratio Predicted by the DRI Model and by Our Model Based on DRI's Data on Fuel Mix, Household Fuel Use, and Fuel Prices

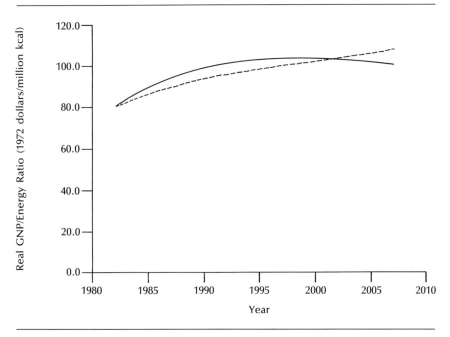

Source: Data Resources, Inc., *US Long-Term Review* (Lexington, Mass.: McGraw-Hill, Spring 1982).
Note: Dotted line is DRI projection; solid line is our model's projection.

fuels and other resources is determined solely by conditions within the economy. As we have stated before, this assumption no longer holds (although we recognize that demand can influence resource extraction). We believe that the reverse is now true: that physical changes in the resource base limit U.S. fuel production, which in turn influences economic conditions, and that this effect will become inexorably stronger as world oil production becomes similarly constrained. This assumption is antithetical to the philosophy behind "internal" economic models, and hence cannot be built into them *post hoc*. If our goal is to see how the physical limits to the availability of energy may influence the economy in the long term, it is necessary to start from scratch.

Figure 4–2. Amount of Domestic Oil and Gas the DRI Model Assumes Will Be Produced versus the Hubbert Projection of Oil and Gas Production

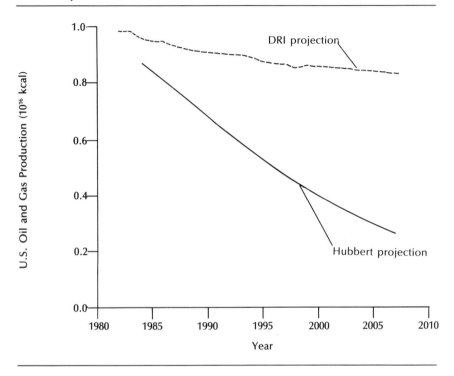

Source: Data Resources, Inc., *US Long-Term Review* (Lexington, Mass.: McGraw-Hill, Spring 1982).

AN ECONOMIC MODEL BASED ON FUEL PRODUCTION

In our model, the quantity of available fuel and the efficiency with which it is used determine the quantity of goods and services producible. This structure explicitly links industrial production to the resource base that increasingly limits it. Specifically, we assume that physical conditions limit the amount of fuel available to the U.S. economy and that the economy will always use all of this potential fuel supply. That is, our model simulates the output that could be achieved if all the fuel physically available from the environment were used. A corollary to this assumption is that nonfuel resources will always be in adequate supply.

Obviously our approach has limits of its own. For the purposes of our model, we have replaced the assumption that resource quality never limits economic production with the assumption that internal conditions never limit production. Of course, future internal conditions will occasionally depress energy consumption below the maximum level. For example, if the federal budget deficit isn't controlled and if foreign dollar-holders slow down their rate of investment in the United States, zooming interest rates may depress the economy and with it the demand for energy. But although internal economic conditions will continue to affect the level of economic activity, we believe that energy availability will soon replace internal conditions as the primary limitation on economic production. Because our model assumes that all the energy physically available will be consumed each year, our model cannot perform one of the main tasks expected of internal models, predicting short-term business cycles. We know that underutilization of production capacity will still occur, because of high interest rates or unemployment or other factors, so policymakers will still need short-term internal forecasts. But such overestimations do not weaken the analysis of long-term trends stemming from expected changes in the natural resource base. (Indeed, many of the internal limits may ultimately be traced to limits on fuel supplies. High interest and inflation rates, hitherto considered internal supply-and-demand conditions, are now greatly affected by the natural resource base.)

The long-term focus of our analysis reduces the complexity needed in our model. Because we let fuel supplies and energy efficiency determine the model's simulated production of output, our model doesn't need the hundreds of input variables that must be fed into the DRI model. Our basic view of the U.S. economy and the resource base to which it is tied is presented in Figure 4–3 (see box). It includes only the most important determinants of its long-term per capita output: fuel supply, energy efficiency, and the number of people among whom GNP is divided. The left side of Figure 4–3 shows fuel entering the economy, including domestic oil and gas, imported oil, coal, hydro and nuclear electricity, and possible alternative fuels. The middle of the figure shows the historical determinants of aggregate energy efficiency: the fractions of the U.S. fuel budget supplied by petroleum and nuclear and hydro electricity, fuel consumption by households, and fuel prices. Multiplying total energy input (measured in kcal) by the economy's energy efficiency (measured in constant 1972 dollars per kcal) yields real GNP. Finally, the right side of the figure shows what this output means to the individual consumer: per capita GNP, measured in constant 1972 dollars.

Our analysis extends to the year 2025. We chose this date because the next forty years will see significant changes in the natural resource base, changes that will be felt by everyone: By 2025 U.S. petroleum fields will have been pumped nearly dry, and 88 percent of the world's original reserve of oil will have been depleted.[3] Since oil and gas now account for about 75 percent of the U.S. energy budget, by 2025 the mix of fuels flowing into the U.S. economy, and the economic structure built around the mix, should be substantially different.

We have relied largely on expert studies for the input variables, such as future fuel supplies, household fuel consumption, fuel prices, and population, which we use for our *reference projection*. These studies include Hubbert analyses of domestic oil and gas and imported oil, reports from the Department of Energy regarding nuclear power, Census Bureau demographic projections, and so on. We will discuss, one by one, the details of these forecasts and the effects of possible errors in them in the scenario analysis section. (A *scenario*, in modeling parlance, is a complete set of values for the input variables. It may also be called a model *run*.)

The equation by which our projections of fuel supplies are turned into GNP is based on the one described in Chapter 3. In this equation, the percentages of the national fuel budget supplied by oil, gas, nuclear power, and hydroelectricity, the percentage of GNP spent on household fuel purchases, and fuel prices together determined 97 percent of the variation in the real GNP/energy ratio between 1929 and 1983. Projections of these quantities, of other fuel supplies, and of population are

Figure 4–3. Simplified Flow Diagram of the U.S. Economy

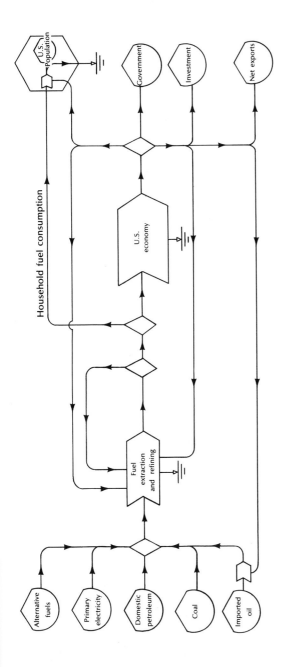

Note: Lines represent direct and/or indirect flows of energy. The storage tanks represent stores of energy. Diamonds represent decision points at which energy flows are aggregated or sent to different uses. The arrow-shaped boxes represent processes in which energy is used to do work. The ground symbol represents waste heat generated by these work processes. The hexagon represents a self-propagating, self-controlling unit, such as the U.S. population.

Our simplified view of the U.S. economy, the fuel sources it draws on, and where its output is allocated. Fuels are extracted from five environmental resource pools: (1) domestic oil and gas fields; (2) non-U.S. oil fields; (3) domestic coal beds; (4) primary electricity generated from falling water and uranium; and (5) alternative fuels ("hard path" and "soft path"). Once extracted and refined, the fuels are either used to extract and refine more fuels, consumed in households, or fed into intermediate economic sectors where they are turned into goods and services. Typical economic accounting schemes, such as GNP, count the value of all goods and services, but many of these do not really support the quality of life. Some of the fuels extracted and refined, as well as some of the goods, services, and investment produced by the economy, must be used to extract and refine more fuels. In addition, some of the net exports cannot be traded for "useful" goods such as cameras and TVs but must be exchanged for fuel. Thus, as the quality of fuels available to the U.S. economy declines, so too does the proportion of direct and indirect energy flows used to support standards of living.

used to calculate year-to-year values of the GNP/energy ratio. These yearly values are multiplied by the projected level of total fuel consumption to yield GNP; dividing GNP by the population size gives per capita GNP. We showed in Chapter 3 that an equation for the GNP/energy ratio based on data from 1929 to 1972 "predicts" the 1973 through 1984 period very well, strong evidence that our methodology is sound.

The most important result of our model is its demonstration of how the current economy—in which per capita GNP is determined by the factors described above—might behave when the quantity, quality, and efficiency of the fuel mix is no longer rising. Thus, if we can project the quantities and types of fuel the economy will use, the amount consumed directly by the household sector, and fuel prices, the model will project the upper limit to economic production.

Of course, the basic structure of the economy could change. If it did, the basic equations by which the model simulates the conversion of fuel into goods and services would no longer be valid. But there is no way to predict how or by how much the economy could change at a fundamental level. Our approach is one of caution and prudence, so it's more important to us to show what could happen if the cavalry doesn't ride over the hill in time.

Briefly, we will present the model's results as follows: first, we show the results of the reference scenario. We use the reference scenario as a middle-of-the-road first pass, a pedagogic tool; we don't present it as our vision of the future. Then, in the scenario analysis section, we describe the assumptions behind each input variable in the reference projection and adjust them one at a time to show the impact different projections might have on per capita economic output. For example, we will see whether it matters if the Hubbert analysis underestimates domestic oil supplies by 25 percent. If varying the oil supply by 25 percent doesn't make an appreciable difference in the model's output, then large underestimations in the Hubbert analysis will not alleviate the overall effects of declining fuel quality.

Figure 4–4 shows the results of our reference scenario. These are the results: from 1982 to 1995 energy supplies can permit economic output to grow rapidly. However, by the mid-1990s,

Figure 4–4. Results of the Reference Scenario: Historical Data from 1929 to 1983 and Projected per Capita GNP from 1984 Onward

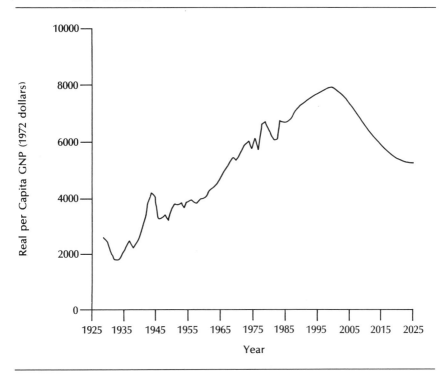

per capita GNP stagnates and then deteriorates briskly until 2025, when it reaches a plateau at a level similar to that of the late 1960s.

We emphasize again that this reference projection is not meant as a bald prediction of What Will Happen. Rather, the reference scenario is a heuristic device in which various middle-of-the-road projections yield one hypothetical scenario to which other scenarios will be compared. For one thing, it assumes that all available fuel will be consumed every year. For another, the reference scenario purposely included no contribution from alternative fuels, even though we fully expect that some hard and/or soft path fuels will play a major role by 2025, because we want to show starkly the need to begin developing appropriate alternative fuel sources soon.

SCENARIO ANALYSES

In the next sections we will state exactly what the reference scenario assumed and then evaluate various alternate assumptions.

Future Fuel Supply

We will first examine the five types of fuel used by the economy shown in Figure 4–3: domestic and imported petroleum, coal, nuclear and hydro electricity, and alternatives (Figure 4–5).

Domestic Oil and Gas. Hubbert curves have estimated rates of petroleum production very accurately, regardless of fluctuations in price or other economic conditions. Even in the last dozen years, in which oil prices have quadrupled and drilling effort has tripled, domestic oil production has continued to follow the pattern of discovery and production that Hubbert predicted in 1956. We have no reason to expect the Hubbert method to be any less accurate in the future. Since the U.S. exports virtually no oil, all domestic production can be assumed to flow into the U.S. economy. Therefore, our reference projection for domestic petroleum inputs to the economy is obtained by adding together the Hubbert curves for petroleum from the lower forty-eight states and from Alaska (Figure 4–6, solid line).

Despite our confidence in the accuracy of the Hubbert method, we ran two alternate scenarios: one in which annual domestic oil and gas production is 25 percent lower than the Hubbert projection across the board, and one in which oil and gas production is much higher than the Hubbert projection to simulate unexpectedly high production from enhanced-recovery procedures, such as pumping carbon dioxide or water into "exhausted" oil fields (Figure 4–6, dotted lines). At no time since 1900 did actual oil production differ from the Hubbert curve by this much.[4] But even with these changes the overall pattern of future output remains the same (Figure 4–7). That is because domestic petroleum will still be nearly exhausted by the year 2025 even with

Figure 4–5. Stacked Representation of the Reference Scenario's Energy Mix (includes no alternative fuels)

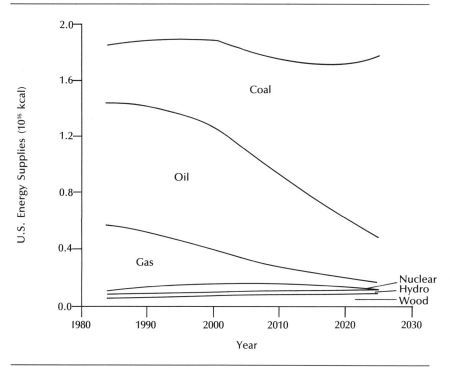

this much of an increase. Even large errors in our estimate of petroleum production wouldn't matter much.

Imported Oil.   Hubbert curves are available for world oil production (Figure 2–17), but the picture here is more complicated than for domestic petroleum. The share of world production imported by the United States depends on several factors. Much of the world's oil lies under politically volatile regions where events could interrupt the flow of oil long before the fields run dry. As the world's smokestack industries increasingly relocate to developing countries, as steelmaking has already begun to do in Brazil, Korea, Taiwan, and elsewhere, these nations will consume a higher proportion of world oil. Heavier competition for oil will mean that the United States will find it increasingly difficult and expensive to obtain its traditionally enormous

Figure 4–6. Reference Assumption of U.S. Petroleum Production Based on Hubbert Curves for Oil and Gas (including Alaska) and Two Alternate Assumptions

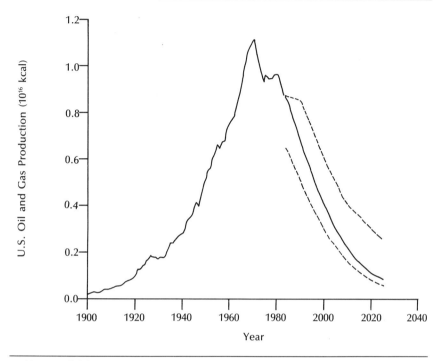

Note: Solid line is historical data and the reference projection; dotted lines are alternate assumptions.

share of non-U.S. oil production. (We ignore foreign gas production because we, along with most experts,[5] believe that cross-ocean transportation of natural gas will be too expensive and dangerous to figure significantly in the U.S. energy budget before 2025.)

The last year in which the United States was not a net importer of oil was 1947; by 1977 the United States was consuming 16 percent of all oil produced outside its borders. Currently the United States imports about 12 percent of non-U.S. oil production. For the reference scenario we allowed the figure to rise to 15 percent in 2010, then to decline to 13 percent by 2025. As we did with domestic oil and gas, we then varied the share of non-U.S. oil production bought by the United States by 25 percent to determine what effects changes in our reference

Figure 4–7. What Happens If Domestic Petroleum Production Varies from the Hubbert Curve?

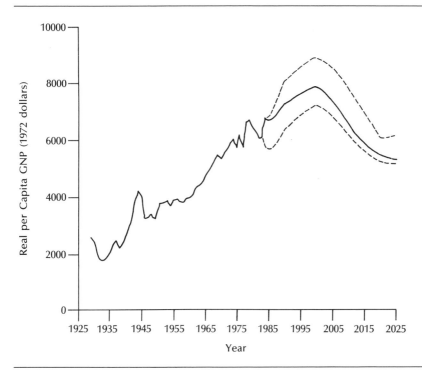

Note: Solid line is historical data and the reference scenario. Dotted lines represent real per capita GNP if Hubbert curves underestimate (upper line) or overestimate (lower line) domestic production.

estimate might have on the model output. The overall results of importing more or less energy differ little from the reference scenario (Figure 4–8). The difference at the end of the model run is small, since total world production by then is low, and a 25-percent greater or lesser share flowing to the United States would be almost insignificant in absolute terms.

It's interesting that the model highlights the need for imported oil to support the level of economic activity shown in these scenarios. In 1998, the year of peak per capita GNP in the reference scenario, imports would supply 61 percent of oil consumption; by 2025 the fraction reaches 80 percent. Currently about 30 percent of U.S. oil consumption is imported. Thus, much of the model's short-term economic growth is due to

Figure 4–8. What Happens If the Flow of Imported Oil Varies by 25 Percent over or under the Reference Assumption?

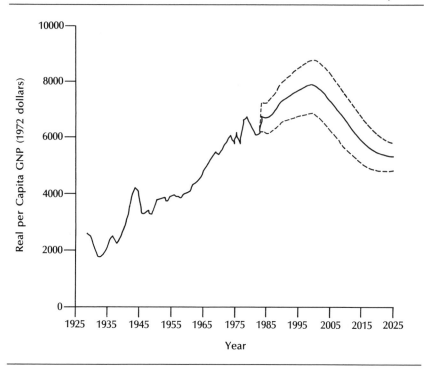

Note: Solid line represents historical data and the reference scenario. Dotted lines represent results of alternate assumptions.

imported oil. Since it's now impossible to replace foreign oil with alternative fuels before the end of the century (we would have to begin building all the required synthetic fuel or nuclear fission plants this year to have them on line by 2000), proposals to make the United States energy independent are plainly ridiculous.

Coal. The rate of coal consumption is much more complicated to predict than that of oil. As we noted in Chapter 2, it is too early to draw a Hubbert curve for coal. Moreover, the degree to which coal can replace other fossil fuels is limited by the serious damage it inflicts on the environment and on human health, government regulations, difficulties involved in transporting coal, and the fact that the existing economy requires liquid fuels for many activities.

Nevertheless, its relative abundance and petroleum's impending exhaustion assure coal's attractiveness to many. In our reference scenario we therefore assumed that coal use grows at a 2 percent annual rate until the year 2000, after which it swells by 3 percent each year. This estimate is similar to projections by the Committee on Nuclear and Alternative Energy Systems of the National Academy of Sciences/National Research Council (CONAES), the Department of Energy (DOE), and others. We didn't directly evaluate the large uncertainties associated with our forecast of coal consumption. If coal consumption were to rise significantly faster than this reference projection, it would almost certainly be through conversion to liquids or gases. Liquefied and gasified coal are considered synthetic fuels and are therefore part of the hard path, which we will analyze in a later section dealing with alternative fuels.

Conventional Nuclear Fission and Hydroelectricity. Two sources of electricity, hydroelectric and nuclear fission plants, make a small but important contribution to the U.S. economy. Unfortunately, most suitable sites for large hydroelectric stations have already been developed. There are many sites for small-scale, low-head hydro dams that could be helpful locally, but there are not enough for total U.S. hydro generation to increase its percentage of total energy output more than marginally. For instance, it has been estimated that full exploitation of small hydro sites in water-rich New England could increase its total electric generating capacity (including nuclear and fossil fuel plants) by perhaps 7 percent.[6] The CONAES study projected that hydroelectric capacity will grow by 27 percent between now and 2025, which we used for our reference assumption. Since these supply restraints seem practically unbreakable, and since hydroelectricity accounts for only a very small fraction of the nation's energy use, we didn't run alternate hydroelectric scenarios.[7]

The future of conventional nuclear fission power, on the other hand, is extremely clouded. Although the quality of domestic uranium supplies is dropping,[8] there is still enough to support as much as 320 million kilowatts of capacity—five to six times the present installed capacity—for the period up to 2025.[9] On the other hand, public fear, dislike, and distrust of nuclear power—which involves issues as diverse as meltdown, waste disposal, rate shock, utility bankruptcy, terrorist activities, and potential contribution to the arms race—has never been put to rest, and it seems reasonable to believe that it never will.

A very tangible limitation on the nuclear industry is that support for new reactor construction from bankers and investors has disintegrated. While a great deal of controversy surrounds the "real" dollar cost of nuclear power, government subsidies to the civilian nuclear program can't hide its energy cost: the energy profit ratio for nuclear power is about 4, compared to 11 for large-site hydroelectric power. Despite mushrooming subsidies, no new plants have been ordered in this country since 1979. Furthermore, reactors have been postponed or cancelled outright while under construction: for example, the Washington Public Power Supply System's Project 1 was mothballed when it was 62.5 percent complete.[10] Because investors have lost faith in the power once promised to be "too cheap to meter," the total nuclear power capacity of the United States (operational, under construction, and planned) slipped from 236 million kilowatts in 1976 to 123 million in late 1984.[11]

In our reference scenario, we used DOE's baseline projection, which assumes that no operating reactors will be shut down and that all reactors more than 20 percent complete will be finished and commissioned (a rather generous assumption, given the recent spate of cancellations of nearly finished reactors). This scenario also assumes that no new plants would be ordered, and that existing plants, as their thirty-year lifespans are reached, will be retired and not replaced.[12] Nevertheless, because the upper limit to nuclear generating capacity is well above current operating levels, there is a lot of room for error in our reference projection. Two possibilities are that all reactors under construction will be cancelled or that the nuclear industry will undergo a rebirth beginning in the late 1980s so that older reactors scheduled for shutdown after the year 2000 will be replaced without too much slippage.

The effects of these scenarios are shown in Figure 4–9. Note that, if reactor construction were halted, most of the short-term

Figure 4–9. How Important Will Nuclear Power Be?

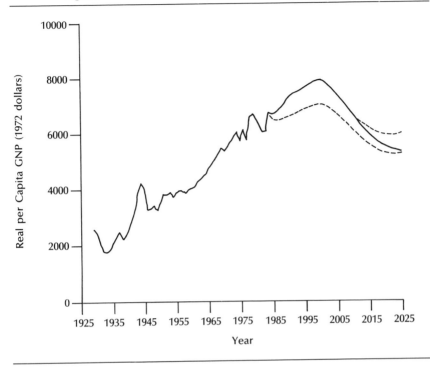

Note: Solid line represents historical data and the reference scenario. Dotted lines represent real per capita GNP if reactors scheduled to go off-line after 2000 are replaced (upper) or if all reactors incomplete in 1982 are cancelled and no new plants are built (lower).

growth phase in the reference scenario would be lost. If, on the other hand, more nuclear power plants are ordered soon, the drop in per capita GNP would be cushioned a little—and this scenario contains a variety of hidden and perhaps unmeasurable costs that would make its actual practice even less promising. Most important, the low energy profit ratio for fission implies that one-quarter of the increased GNP attributable to nuclear power would simply reflect the cost of building reactors rather than consumer products made with the electricity. In addition, there are currently unknown but inevitable costs, including the costs of keeping nuclear fuels and wastes out of the environment and out of the wrong hands, and the costs of decommissioning obsolete reactors. They will be paid, not only in dollars and energy, but also in sacrifices in the quality of life. It is unlikely that such sacrifices will be considered worth the gains in goods and services.

Alternative Fuels. Most thoughtful people have been brought, if reluctantly, to understand that domestic petroleum will be exhausted in the not-too-distant future, foreign oil production will soon peak, and nuclear power will never provide the surfeit of cheap energy envisioned by every president from Truman to Nixon. Consequently, the United States is casting about for—though not aggressively pursuing—alternatives. In Chapter 2 we mentioned the two major options that have been proposed: the hard path, in which oil shale, liquefied and gasified coal, and nuclear fusion and breeder technologies serve the nation's energy needs, and the soft path, in which a smorgasbord of renewable energy sources are utilized. For pedagogic reasons stated earlier, the reference scenario did not include either hard-path or soft-path fuels. In this section, we evaluate the contributions these alternative fuels might make by the year 2025.

Estimates for the production of oil shale and coal liquefaction and gasification have been given in a number of studies, including those by the Committee on Nuclear and Alternative Energy Systems (CONAES), WAES, and the U.S. Bureau of Mines.[13] We chose a few of the moderate scenarios to assess the feasibility of these options (Figure 4–10). We dismissed the rosier estimates because we believe that unfavorable economic conditions and the long lead times associated with synthetic fuel plants will inhibit their development. Recently, for example, several synthetic fuel projects have been cancelled. Such delays in bringing synthetic fuels onstream will further postpone any significant contribution from these fuels: in fact, it's now impossible for synthetic fuels to be available in quantity before the turn of the century. Moreover, oil shale and coal conversion technologies require massive amounts of water; since most of our oil shale and coal is found in arid western states, where limited water supplies must also satisfy irrigation and municipal needs, synthetic fuels face yet another hurdle. And, as was pointed out in Chapter 2, obstacles to the commercial feasibility of nuclear breeder and fusion technologies will almost certainly not be cleared away before 2025.

Figure 4–11 shows the effects of what we consider a realistically vigorous effort to follow the hard path. The hard path is unable to forestall the decline in per capita GNP after the year 2000, but it's clearly better than nothing at all: in 2025 the projected level of per capita GNP is just about equal to the 1984 level.

To evaluate the soft path, we took estimates from the Solar/ Conservation Study performed by DOE's Solar Energy Research Institute (SERI).[14] This study projected the potential contributions of biomass, passive solar, photovoltaics, windmills, and other soft-path fuels to the nation's energy budget. In our soft-path scenario, based on SERI's projections, the contribution of solar-based alternatives (including wood) rises to 19 percent of U.S. energy supply by 2025 (Figure 4–12). This rate

Figure 4–10.   Stacked Representation of the Fuel Mix of a Hard Path Economy

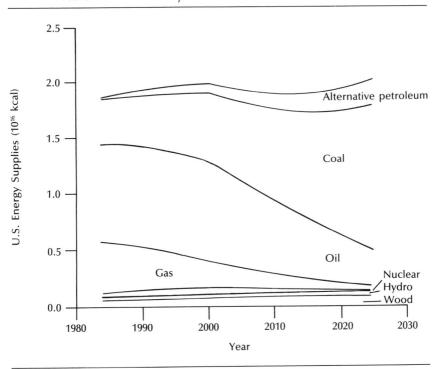

Note: "Alternative petroleum" includes liquefied coal and oil from oil shale.

Figure 4–11.   Where Does the Hard Path Lead?

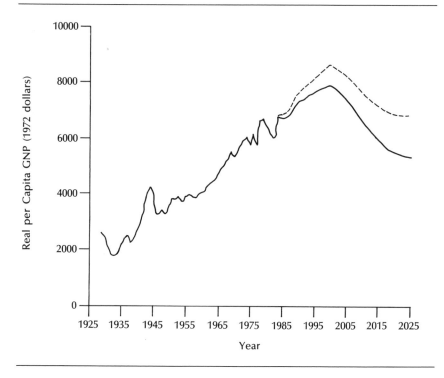

Note: Solid line is historical data and the reference scenario. Dotted line projects real per capita GNP if the economy receives the fuel supplies shown in Figure 4–10.

of growth of soft-path fuels is only slightly more effective than the hard path in offsetting the effects of petroleum's decline (Figure 4–13). Thus, by the year 2025 neither the hard-path nor the soft-path alternative can be developed fast enough to replace petroleum completely, although the soft path is increasingly favored as one looks further into the future.

Future Energy Efficiency

It should be clear that continued growth in the energy available to the United States on a per capita basis, in the forty-year timespan of this analysis, is virtually out of the question. But fuel inputs to the economy don't entirely determine output: the

Figure 4–12.   Stacked Representation of the Energy Mix of a Soft Path Economy

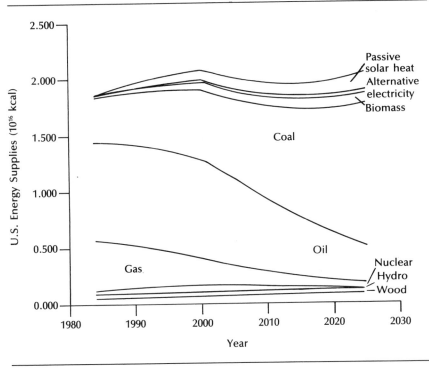

Note: "Alternative electricity" includes photovoltaic and windmill energy.

economy's energy efficiency must still be considered. Although many people believe that substitutions and shortcuts in industrial techniques have been the primary causes of increased national energy efficiency, we have demonstrated that three factors have almost completely determined the nation's aggregate energy efficiency during the last half-century: the percentage of demand supplied by petroleum, nuclear power, and hydroelectricity; household fuel purchases; and fuel prices. Our projections of future energy efficiency therefore depend on anticipated changes in these factors. The effects of the fuel mix on national energy efficiency can be derived from the various projections of fuel supplies and were implicitly included in the scenarios already described. The fraction of fuel usage in house-

Figure 4–13.   Where Does the Soft Path Lead?

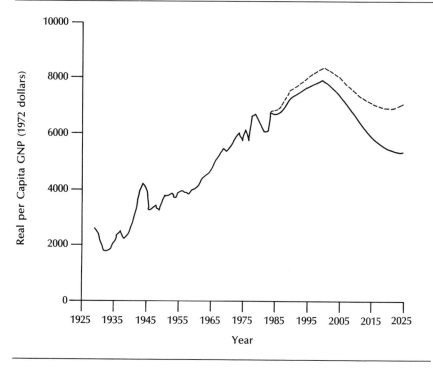

Note: Solid line is historical data and the reference scenario. Dotted line projects real per capita GNP if the economy receives the fuel supplies shown in Figure 4–12.

holds and fuel prices, however, must be estimated independently.

Household Fuel Consumption.   We used a somewhat intricate method to project household fuel purchases. Since the level of household fuel consumption is essentially determined by an internal economic process, we adapted a model developed by Thomas Lareau and Joel Darmstadter to help us simulate it.[15] The average amount of fuel purchased by individuals depends on the price of fuel and consumer income and on how consumers respond to changes in these parameters. Lareau and Darmstadter examined how consumer purchases of various fuels respond to changes in income and fuel prices. The patterns of response, in conjunction with projections of fuel prices and consumer income, allow us to project fuel purchases.[16]

When all of these estimates were put together, the reference projection was that total household fuel consumption, measured in constant 1972 dollars, would decline gradually for the next fifteen years and then fall quickly after the turn of the century to a level that, by 2025, is less than half of its 1983 value. This scenario, based on a steady, slow rise in fuel prices, clearly represents substantial household conservation and/or curtailment.

We also ran an alternate scenario in which, for whatever reason, the price of fuel merely keeps pace with the prices of other goods and services. Making this single change in the reference projection, so that the real price of fuel stays constant, leads to a rise in household fuel use and slowing in conservation in other sectors as the incentive to conserve or curtail is eliminated. Figure 4–14 shows the effects on the nation's energy efficiency of this assumption versus the reference scenario: the real GNP/ energy ratio starts falling immediately if fuel prices stay constant, ending up by 2025 at less than half the efficiency projected in the reference scenario. Without the incentive to conserve provided by rising energy prices, all short-term economic growth is choked off and per capita GNP in 2025 is much lower than in the reference scenario (Figure 4–15).

This finding that rising fuel prices increase GNP while constant prices decrease it is astonishing, and not very realistic: it is an artifact of our initial assumption that all available fuel supplies would be used, regardless of other economic conditions. In reality, rising fuel prices encourage curtailment of fuel use as well as conservation. Curtailment means an overall reduction in economic activity that offsets gains in production induced by increased efficiency. Our model, however, included only the conservation effect and assumed that there is never any curtailment. Nevertheless, curtailment does not account for the whole gap between the lines in Figure 4–15: constant fuel prices could easily lull us into a false sense of security during the period of potential growth (1985–2000), which would leave us unprepared for the rapid decline in U.S. energy supplies occurring after world oil production begins to fall. The ongoing resurgence of high-powered cars is powerful evidence that such complacency is already spreading.

Figure 4–14. The Effect of Alternate Assumptions Regarding Fuel Prices on the Real GNP/Energy Ratio

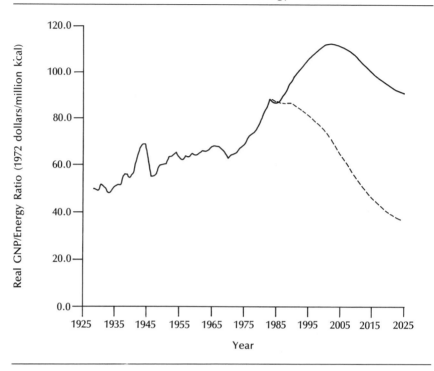

Note: Solid line is historical data and the reference scenario. Dotted line shows the effect on national energy efficiency if fuel prices stay constant at the 1983 level in real terms.

Population Size. The factors we have discussed up to now, fuel supply and energy efficiency, determine total GNP. However, an equally important additional factor determines per capita GNP: population size. Future population depends most heavily on fertility rates and net immigration. The total fertility rate (TFR) is the average number of children each woman bears in her lifetime. In the past, the U.S. TFR has ranged from 7 in 1800 to 1.8 in 1975. It now stands at about 1.8. Most estimates for its future behavior fall between 1.4 and 2.7, assuming no concerted effort is made to encourage or discourage childbearing. Net immigration is simply the number of people moving into the United States minus the number leaving.

Figure 4–15.   Results of Alternate Fuel Price Projection

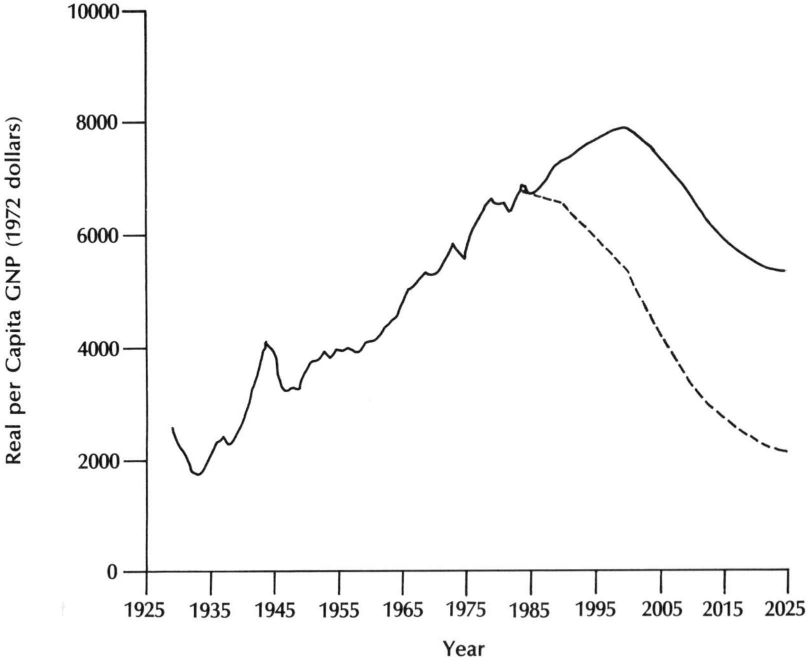

Note: Solid line is historical data and the reference scenario. Dotted line projects real per capita GNP if fuel prices stay constant in real terms.

Our reference population projection came from the U.S. Census Bureau, whose middle-of-the-road estimate assumes a TFR of 1.9, net immigration at 450,000 per year, and an average life expectancy of 81.0 years.[17] We also ran the Census Bureau's high-growth scenario, with immigration at 750,000 a year, TFR at 2.3, and a life expectancy of 77.4 years; and its low-growth scenario, with fertility rate of 1.6, immigration at 250,000 a year, and a life expectancy of 85.9 years. Either scenario is achievable, depending on how national and individual attitudes toward health care, immigration, birth control, and abortion evolve. But Figure 4–16 shows that neither the high nor low population scenario changes the reference results significantly until near the end of the model run. However, it is clear that population growth becomes increasingly important as time goes on.

PER CAPITA GNP, FUEL, AND THE QUALITY OF LIFE

Throughout this chapter, we've used real per capita GNP as a measure of output per person, knowing that this is not a good indicator of the quality of life. We did so for two reasons: there *is* no good indicator of the quality of life, and one of our principal goals was to examine how today's economy may fare under future conditions of fuel supplies. This goal required us to use an output measure that has traditionally been used to judge the

Figure 4–16. How Important Is Population Growth?

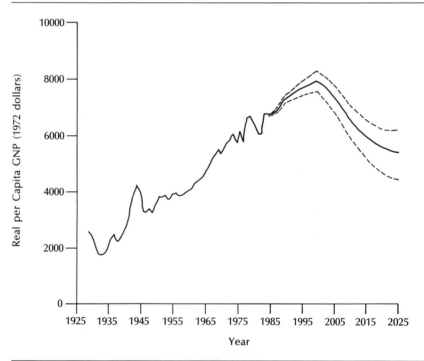

Note: Solid line is historical data and the reference scenario. Lower dotted line projects real per capita GNP if the Census Bureau's high-growth projection is realized; upper dotted line results if population follows the low-growth projection.

economy's health. Per capita GNP fits this description and is familiar and easily grasped as well.

Yet, in addition to the problems with GNP pointed out by Robert Kennedy and others, energy analysis reveals two other distortions that may become increasingly important as the supply and quality of fuel declines.

It should be clear why most of the scenarios described above portray a future in which per capita GNP rises a little, only to falter and decline. The declining supply of fuel per capita—particularly oil and gas—overrides all forces that tend to increase per capita production. However, the declining quality of fuels also will have a negative effect on quality of life that is not reflected by GNP. Ideally, the increased effort needed to obtain lower-quality fuels should not be included in measurements of the useful goods and services that make the United States an affluent nation.

Real GNP includes the fuel, labor, and capital used to extract fuel from the environment and refine it to a usable state.[18] Of course, these activities are vital, but the product of them—fuel—does not *itself* improve living standards. Heating oil is not valued for itself but because it can be used to make a house warm in winter. To state it more generally, the average U.S. living standard is considered high, not because we have large quantities of fuel to burn but because we have the goods and services that the fuel allows us to produce and enjoy. Fuel is valuable only because it can be used to produce the material necessities and comforts of life.

As the energy profit ratios of fuels decline, more and more fuel, capital, and labor will have to be plowed back into getting more fuel. As we showed at the end of Chapter 2, maintaining constant supplies of net energy and nonenergy-related goods and services is impossible in the face of declining energy profit ratios. However, GNP *can* remain constant or even grow: the part attributable to fuels swells, while everything else shrinks. Such a situation reflects a real decline in living standards, though not in per capita GNP. Thus, just as gross energy supplies overestimate the true (net) amount of fuel available, using GNP as an indicator of living standards overestimates the availability of nonfuel goods and services. In the past, when energy profit ratios were large and a relatively tiny effort yielded enough fuel to run the economy, the overestimation was negligible. Fuels with large energy profit ratios are becoming a thing of the past, however, and as we strive to replace oil and gas with alternative fuels, the overestimation will become too great to ignore. Falling energy profit ratios mean that per capita GNP and the amount of nonfuel goods and services produced will increasingly diverge.

To get a sense of the importance of this effect of declining fuel quality, we projected trends for the energy profit ratios of fuels used in our hard-path scenario, and from them calculated the aggregate energy profit ratio for all fuels in the U.S. energy budget. We then reduced GNP by the fraction of the energy budget used to find and extract fuels, leaving what might be called the "nonfuel national product" (Figure 4–17). Soft-path fuels would show a similar pattern, since their energy profit ratios are similar to those of the hard path. The gap between GNP and nonfuel national product grows as petroleum is replaced by lower-quality fuels.[19] Thus, the nonfuel national product produced by these alternatives is significantly worse than GNP leads us to believe. Again, because the hard and soft paths have similar energy profit ratios, the two paths produce about the same nonfuel national product—but the two paths may still have quite different effects on the unmeasurable aspects of the quality of life. For example, the tight security needed to protect the highly centralized facilities and dangerous products and by-products of the hard path could erode many liberties, such as privacy and freedom to travel, that we now take for granted.[20] Also, the production of synthetic fuels entails strip mining to obtain the needed coal and oil shale, and the disposal of huge amounts of slag, both of which would imperil the environment. These potential side effects of the hard path may have no immediate effect on the amount of goods and services hard-path fuels can produce, but we can assume that they would reduce our quality of life.

The other problem with GNP as an indicator of living standards is one that was raised in Chapter 3. A drive in the country—which involves an "unnecessary" increase in household fuel consumption and a consequent decrease in the amount of nonfuel goods and services the nation can produce—may make someone happier than the goods and services that could have been pro-

Figure 4–17.   The Fraction of per Capita GNP Accounted for by Energy Extraction

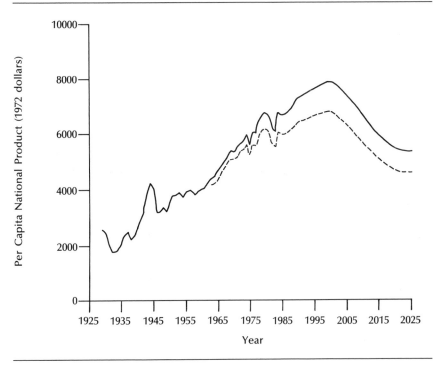

Note: Solid line is historical data and the reference scenario. Dotted line represents the per capita "nonfuel national product"—per capita GNP minus fuel extraction activities.

duced with that gasoline. In other words, individuals are not always interested in maximizing the dollar value of goods and services they receive. If everybody were forced to cut household fuel use to the bare bone, the amount of goods and services available would be increased, but the added goods and services might provide less enjoyment than the fuel-consuming activities that would have to be sacrificed. Many people *like* big cars, frost-free refrigerators, and year-round 72°F indoor temperatures, even though having them reduces the availability of other things. Thus, when a model, whether ours or anyone else's, shows that a massive fuel conservation and curtailment effort will increase per capita GNP, it should be recognized that that strategy may reduce the real living standard for many people, at least in the short term. For such a strategy to be successful, people must be convinced that the rewards are worth the sacrifices.

A "Best-Case" Scenario

It is always possible that our reference projections for the availability of the fuels discussed in our scenario analysis could be excessively conservative. Many readers are probably wondering why we couldn't obtain greater and more prolonged growth with a crash program to develop greater supplies of most or all fuels. The answer lies in the finite supplies of energy we have now to invest in future sources. Developing new fuel supplies takes time and energy. It takes time and energy to explore for new oil and gas; to build coal gasification or oil shale processing plants; to design, test, and install photovoltaic cells; and to construct alcohol or biogas production facilities. The same is true for conservation, which often entails buying new, expensive, but energy-efficient capital. To pursue alternative fuels and conservation means diverting fossil fuels from the production of consumer goods. The more aggressively we pursue alternatives and conservation, the more consumer goods will have to be sacrificed—probably disproportionately more, given the inefficiencies inherent in crash programs. And the limited returns on these investments, due to the low energy profit ratios of all of these alternatives and long payback times of energy efficiency capital, means that the U.S. economy simply will not have enough net energy to maintain living standards in the next fifty years *and* to intensify efforts to develop many new energy sources and replace its capital.

Nevertheless, several of the "optimistic" scenarios described above could occur simultaneously. It's possible, for instance, that the United States will realize the Census Bureau's low-growth population projection, steady growth in efficiency driven by rising fuel prices, and a substantial contribution from the soft path. We put these three projections into a single scenario (also including the reference projections for other fuels), the results of which appear in Figure 4–18.

This "best case" is indeed good, even great: real per capita GNP approaches $10,000 in 1972 dollars, and it avoids the post-

Figure 4–18.   Results of a Best-Case Scenario in Which the Soft Path and Low Population Growth Are Achieved Simultaneously and in Which Energy Efficiency Is Maximized through Rising Fuel Prices

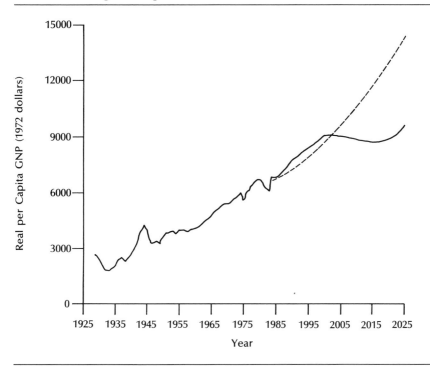

Note: Solid line is best case. Dotted line represents the unreachable target of 2.5 percent annual growth in real GNP per capita.

2000 decline that plagued the other scenarios. However, it should be remembered that, at present, both the total fertility and immigration are substantially higher than the Census Bureau low-growth projection; that fuel prices have stopped rising and energy efficiency is no longer widely considered important; and that the development of renewable fuels is not now proceeding quickly enough to realize the SERI forecast. The United States *might* come close to realizing this best case—but only if it acts immediately to bring it about.

There is one plausible way in which the U.S. economy may have access to more high-quality energy than our scenarios projected. The Hubbert curve for world oil, which shows world oil production peaking in about fifteen years, presupposes that developing nations will be using more oil. But right now they aren't, and the likelihood that they will soon is diminishing. Many nations on the brink of industrialization are beset by huge foreign debts, payments on which are consuming much of their output. With rapidly expanding populations, these nations must scramble merely to meet their people's basic needs; few resources are available to build the fuel-intensive industrial base that defines "development." If this pattern continues to hold true, world oil production may rise more slowly than predicted by the Hubbert method. The peak in world oil production might not occur until 2010 or 2015, allowing the United States (and other industrial nations) to consume more oil than even our "high imported oil" scenario allowed. Of course, as we pointed out in Chapter 1, such a course would not be an unmitigated benefit to the United States: it would further broaden the already enormous gap between rich and poor nations, and it would make the United States more dependent on foreign sources of energy.

FOSSIL FUELS: THE NATION'S PATRIMONY

Increasingly constricted supplies of net energy have an enormous bearing on strategies for the future. That means that the decision regarding which set of alternatives to pursue—to follow the hard path of synthetic fuels or to commit to solar-based renewable fuels—must be weighed carefully. High quality oil and gas are our patrimony, and, if we make the wrong choice as to what to do with them, we won't have enough net energy with which to repair the damage. Synthetic nonrenewable fuels now have relatively poor energy profit ratios, and they can only get worse as we deplete our stocks of coal and oil shale. When these fuels approach exhaustion, we will not have large supplies of net energy, as we do today with oil and gas, to cushion the transition to other fuels. The energy profit ratios of most solar-based fuels are currently not very good either; but there is a reasonable hope of improvement with research and the assurance that, if demand remains constant, their energy profit ratios will not drop.

There is a third option, which many conservatives, including the Reagan administration, are advocating. That is to let the "free market" decide what energy path to follow. This is an extremely perilous course: the current "free market" is anything but free, given the economic, tax, and legal structures that favor certain kinds of resource use over others. A true free market depends on everybody's receiving complete, accurate information about the costs and benefits of their actions, which is certainly not the case today. If we leave these fetters on the "free market" by pursuing the Reagan administration option, as Chapter 7 will show, we may expect a very severe fuel crunch, high unemployment, and grossly expanded government responsibilities to aid the needy. If we want to avoid these problems, the market must be restructured to accomplish society's true aims: specifically, players in the market need to receive complete and correct information about the implications of various options in both the short and long terms. Chapter 7 describes the choices the United States will have to make in the next few years.

CONCLUSIONS

Assuming steady depletion of domestic petroleum; rising and then falling importation of foreign oil; accelerating coal use; a somewhat increased contribution from hydroelectric power; no new nuclear plant orders, but no early shutdowns of existing facilities or cancellations of reactors well under construction; a contribution from soft-path fuels growing to 19 percent of the national energy budget; rising fuel prices; and a continuation of current population growth trends, *per capita GNP will rise until the turn of the century, when it levels off and then drops until again leveling off in 2025.*

Increasing the supply of any of these fuels by a reasonable amount does not avert the decline in per capita GNP, although the absolute level of per capita GNP in 2025 improves somewhat.

Alternative fuels cannot be developed fast enough to compensate entirely for declining oil and gas production as projected by the Hubbert analysis—but an effort must begin soon to develop the most efficient ones quickly if a really precipitous decline in per capita GNP is to be avoided.

If fuel prices fail to rise and increases in energy efficiency stop coming as a result, short-term economic growth will be choked off and the subsequent decline will steepen.

If low population growth, price-driven increases in energy efficiency, and aggressive development of alternative fuels occur simultaneously, per capita GNP rises substantially by the turn of the century and stays there.

Intensified energy-extraction activities swell GNP without improving the quality of life proportionately. Thus, as low-quality alternative fuels begin to offset the decline in oil and gas, per capita GNP will overestimate "true" living standards.

Because net energy supplies are limited, and because it takes fuel to make fuel, the United States can't boost the supplies of more than a few of the fuels available to it. Thus, the decision as to which fuel sources to invest in should be made carefully.

Although this vision of the future falls short of the expectation of steadily increasing affluence that most of us were brought up with, we don't think it is altogether gloomy. After all, the projections that included high levels of alternative fuels led to a per capita GNP in 2025 equal to its 1970 level (though only the soft path is sustainable at this level). We don't believe that a decline in per capita GNP will necessarily entail a parallel decline in the quality of life, any more than rising GNP indicates necessarily a better quality of life. It may be argued that the quality of life today is lower than it was in 1960, even though per capita GNP is 70 percent higher. But, undeniably, a fall in material living standards and, more important, in expectations for the future will probably provoke political unrest and real psychological discomfort. Soon, we will have to decide which aspects of our current lifestyles we most want to preserve, given that we can't preserve them intact. The crucial decisions and tradeoffs in an energy-limited future are examined in Chapter 7. Before that, however, we will illustrate how these broad aggregate trends are being played out in one sector of the economy, a sector that for several reasons may be the most important—the agricultural system.

5 AGRICULTURE: THE EXHAUSTIBLE CORNUCOPIA

Food should be grown. But this food being sold on the tube has not been grown; it has been manufactured.

—Russell Baker

In the opening pages of *The Path to Power*,[1] the first volume of Robert Caro's biography of Lyndon Johnson, Caro called the Hill Country of central Texas in the 1850s "a trap baited with grass." The rolling hills west of Austin were clothed in thick, lush grass, which led the first settlers—mostly poor farmers fleeing the worn-out soils of Georgia, Alabama, and Tennessee—to believe the Hill Country was a fertile paradise. But the grass "had grown not over a season but over centuries," Caro wrote. "It had grown slowly because the soil beneath it was so thin." Once the grass was stripped away by plows and cattle, nothing was left to anchor the soil. The first few crops were very bountiful, but then the white limestone bedrock began to appear through the soil. Dense brush, previously held in check by prairie fires and the grass, spread over much of the remaining soil. Within a few years, the land that at first had supported huge herds of cattle and bumper crops of corn, wheat, and cotton was a virtual desert. Most of those who thought the Hill Country would make them rich instead were condemned—they and generations of their descendants—to lives of grinding poverty. As Caro said, "the Hill Country was hard on dreams."

Today, as government warehouses bulge with surplus food that must be given away or left to rot, it is hard to think of the

147

Texas Hill Country as a microcosm of U.S. agriculture—yet that is not far from the truth. Evidence is amassing that indicates that the U.S. agriculture system cannot be sustained in its current form much longer.

There are two reasons that a study of the carrying capacity of the United States should look in detail at its agricultural system's sustainability. First, we all need to eat. A sustainable society must be able to provide enough food for itself without jeopardizing its ability to continue doing so. It need not grow all its own food so long as it has something else to trade for food, but for a long time the United States has exported more food than it imported. Besides, where else could the United States go to buy large amounts of food? We take it for granted that a sustainable U.S. economy must be able to grow enough food to feed its population.

The second reason is that agriculture is extremely important to the U.S. economy and to the world at large. In this book we use the word *agriculture* to include every aspect of the system that puts dinner on the table—the manufacture of farm machinery and chemicals, the transport of food by rail and truck, food processing and packaging industries, supermarkets and restaurants, the production of ovens and refrigerators—not only the simple growing of food. When defined this way, agriculture is the economy's largest industry, accounting for about one-sixth of GNP. Moreover, U.S. agriculture is an important actor on the global stage: nearly 40 percent of harvested acres in the United States is devoted to export production, and the United States provides more than three-quarters of the corn and soybeans, over 40 percent of the wheat, and nearly a quarter of the rice traded in world markets. A U.S. export capacity also holds down world crop prices; its loss would drive food prices way up, causing shortages and famines even among people who don't buy U.S.-grown food. And, as an assistant secretary of agriculture in the Ford administration, Richard Bell, said in 1975, "Agridollars have gone a long way toward offsetting our petrodollar drain."[2] High foreign demand for U.S. food will continue to be important in paying for imported oil.

But while the agricultural system helps us bring energy into the economy, it also takes energy to run. Energy is needed at every step of the journey of food from field to table. Because agriculture is so necessary to the United States, almost as necessary as fuel, we can extend the analysis begun in Chapter 4: we can ask, How much energy will be available in the future to produce nonfuel and *nonfood* goods and services? In an era of limited energy supplies, can the United States continue to have a large and varied diet for a growing population, produce food surpluses for export, *and* provide cars and computers and health care at something like current levels?

To facilitate the search for answers, we broke down the agriculture system into two components: the on-farm sector, which involves the growing and harvesting of raw crops and animal products; and the off-farm sector, which is responsible for everything that happens to this raw food—transportation, processing, packaging, storage, and cooking—after it leaves the nation's farms. The two components are quite different. The off-farm sector is very much like other industries; food is just another industrial product. The on-farm part of agriculture, however, is unique in many ways, not the least of which is its intimate relationship with the environment.[3]

FARM OUTPUT AND ENERGY

Three distinct periods have marked the development of farming in the United States. During the first, an *expansionist* period, total crop output was increased by increasing the land area in cultivation. This period began early in the nineteenth century. In it, natural resources were abundant, with land often free for the taking. Prairie and forest were turned into cropland almost as fast as people came forward who would withstand the rigors of frontier life, although barbed wire and the steel plow also helped. This period ended in about 1920 (Figure 5–1), when the wave of expansion broke against the wall of the Rocky Mountains. By then approximately 380 million acres were planted, compared to about 390 million today.

Output per acre was generally constant during the expansionist period, as measured both in real dollars (that is, gross farm product) and in bushels or pounds. This changed when farming entered its second phase, *intensification*; total farm

Figure 5–1. New Cropland in the United States from 1850 to 1860 (a), 1880 to 1890 (b), 1900 to 1910 (c), and 1910 to 1920 (d).

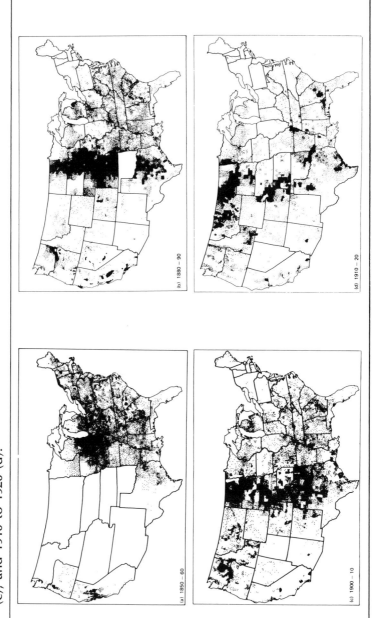

(a) 1850 – 60

(b) 1880 – 90

(c) 1900 – 10

(d) 1910 – 20

Source: D.B. Grigg, *Agricultural Systems of the World: An Evolutionary Approach,* Cambridge Geographical Studies 5 (London: Cambridge University Press, 1974).

Note: One dot on the map represents 5,000 acres of new cropland converted from forest or unimproved prairie.

Figure 5–2. Farm Output Index and Total Cropland, 1860 to 1980

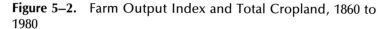

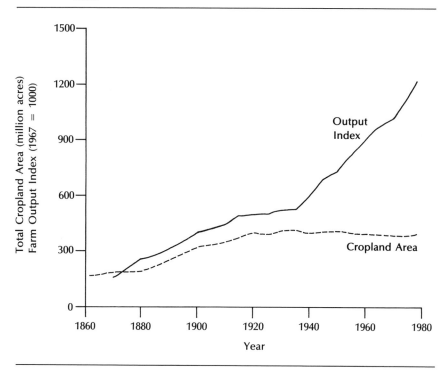

Source: Economic Research Service, USDA, *Economic Indicators of the Farm Sector: Production and Efficiency Statistics,* Statistical Bulletin 657 (Washington, D.C.: USGPO, 1979).

Note: 1967 = 1000. Dotted line is total cropland area; solid line is output index.

output began to rise even faster than it had during the expansionist period (Figure 5–2), even though cropland area stabilized. This trend really took hold just before World War II and continued through the 1970s. Intensification was made possible by an array of technical and social changes that allowed farmers to use huge quantities of fossil fuels to increase crop yields. The widespread availability of tractors and other machinery, fertilizers, pesticides, irrigation systems, and new crop strains, and of government programs to help farmers pay for them, doubled or tripled the amount of food grown on each acre of land. These fuel-based inputs were so effective at supplementing the labor of human beings that fewer people were needed to work the farms. This is the story of the industrialization of farming—the replacement of human and animal labor with fossil fuels. Just as in the general economy, farm workers have been subsidized with spiraling quantities of energy, both directly and indirectly. As a result, productivity (output produced per worker-hour) climbed more than sevenfold between 1940 and 1979. During the expansionist period, labor limited crop production, and all subsequent improvements in technology sought to raise worker productivity. The idea that labor limited production was so strong that, to this day, a great deal of agricultural research is aimed at increasing worker and land productivity even further—despite abundant evidence (such as falling crop prices, continued surpluses, and soaring farm bankruptcies) that further such increases are expensive and unnecessary.

Today, many people believe that the U.S. agricultural cornucopia is practically limitless. Virtually everyone credits the technology flowing from the nation's agricultural research labs and farms with making the United States the world's breadbasket. The almost exponential historical rise in total and per-acre crop production (Figures 5–3 and 5–4) seems to bear this out. Since the march of technology is assumed to be inexorable, many people then conclude that these curves will continue to rise—or, if they don't rise, it will be because economic factors or government meddling got in the way.

There is a fundamental weakness with this interpretation of agricultural performance that is often ignored. The growing output is tacitly assumed to have resulted *only* from hybridization, ingenuity, and the mere passage of time; that physical inputs were also involved is forgotten. Comparing per-acre crop production to energy use (including energy used to produce chemicals and machinery as well as direct fuel use) instead of time provides a quite different perspective. As shown in Table 5–1, although the U.S. Department of Agriculture's (USDA) composite crop production index increased steadily from 1940 to 1979, output per unit of energy input actually declined. Recent increases in production have not kept pace with increasing energy use; from 1970 to 1978 farmers used 50 percent more energy to grow 30 percent more crops. Moreover, the growth rate in yields for some crops has slowed considerably (Figure 5–5). Time doesn't drive crop produc-

Figure 5–3. USDA Index of Total Crop Production, 1940 to 1979

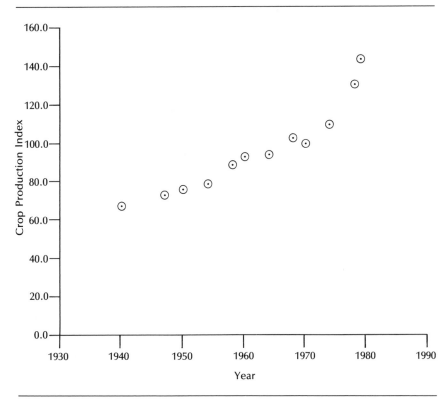

Source: Economic Research Service, USDA, *Economic Indicators of the Farm Sector: Production and Efficiency Statistics,* Statistical Bulletin 657 (Washington, D.C.: USGPO, 1979).

Note: 1967 = 100.

tion upward; the ingredients behind it do—and historically at declining output/input efficiencies.

Moreover, agriculture's economic performance may be slowing down. The USDA's output indexes (as in Figures 5–3 and 5–4) are the most common indicator of agricultural productivity and well-being. But they're partly based on the cost of inputs used to grow crops as well as on the value and physical quantity of output. It's possible that a rise in the output index could solely reflect rising inputs. The output measure is also not necessarily a good measure of the economic health of producers—

Figure 5–4. USDA Index of Crop Production per Acre, 1940 to 1979

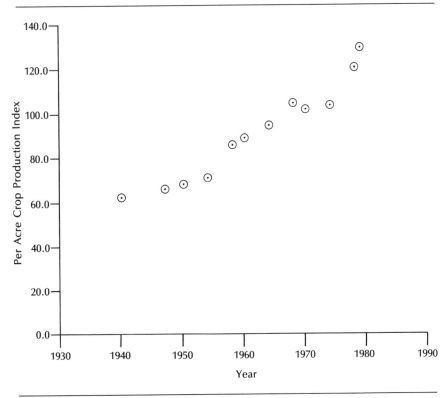

Source: Economic Research Service, USDA, *Economic Indicators of the Farm Sector: Production and Efficiency Statistics,* Statistical Bulletin 657 (Washington, D.C.: USGPO, 1979).
Note: 1967 = 100.

that is, farmers. A more useful indicator is gross farm product, which is the value added in crop production. Because it excludes the value of inputs used to grow crops, it is a better composite measure of aggregate crop production. It has been lagging with both time (Figure 5–6) and energy input (Figure 5–7). It's clear that, using the energy-based definition of resource quality given in Chapter 2, the quality of the agricultural resource base in the United States is declining.

As a result, farming appears to have entered a third phase, *saturation.* But how long will this phase last? Might it be sim-

Table 5–1.   USDA Crop Output Index, On-Farm Energy Use Index, and the Ratio, 1940–1979 (1968 = 100)

Year	Output Index	Energy Index	Output/ Energy
1940	65	21	3.1
1947	71	48	1.48
1950	76	53	1.43
1954	77	56	1.38
1958	86	65	1.32
1960	90	69	1.30
1964	91	87	1.05
1968	100	100	1.00
1970	97	106	0.91
1974	107	153	0.70
1978	127	159	0.80
1979	140	172	0.81

Sources: Economic Research Service, USDA, *Economic Indicators of the Farm Sector: Production and Efficiency Statistics,* Statistical Bulletin 657 (Washington, D.C.: USGPO, 1979); J.S. Steinhart and C.E. Steinhart, "Energy Use in the U.S. Food System," *Science* 184 (1974):307–316; U.S. Department of Commerce, Bureau of the Census, *Annual Survey of Manufactures* (Washington, D.C.: USGPO, various years); U.S. Department of Commerce, Bureau of the Census, *1978 Census of Agriculture,* Vol. 5: 1979 Farm Energy Survey, Special Reports pt. 9 (Washington, D.C.: USGPO); David Torgerson and Harold Cooper, *Energy and U.S. Agriculture 1974 and 1978,* USDA Statistical Bulletin 632 (Washington, D.C.: USGPO, 1980)

ply a transient breathing spell in the overall upward trend toward higher crop yields? Won't new technologies like genetic engineering find ways to squeeze more production from the available inputs?

Many agricultural researchers believe that further increases in yield are not only possible, but probable. Iowa State University's widely respected CARD (Center for Agricultural and Rural Development) models usually assume an annual increase in per-acre yields of about 1 percent, caused by an unspecified combination of technological improvements and intensification of inputs.[4] Some projections are even more optimistic, predicting crop yields as much as 50 percent higher than today's by the year 2000 (that is, at least a 2.5 percent annual increase).[5] These anticipate new advances in nitrogen fixation, insect resistance, and other problem areas, but they also implicitly

Figure 5–5. Yield per Acre of Four Important Crops, 1925 to 1980

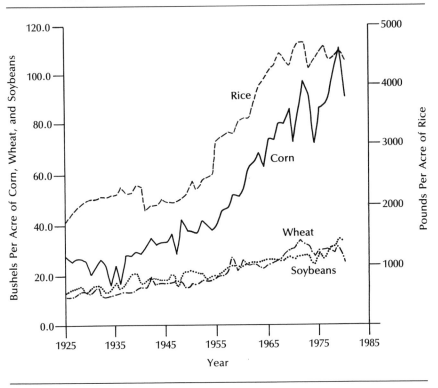

Source: USDA, *Agricultural Statistics* (Washington, D.C.: USGPO, various years).

assume that inputs can be effectively intensified further. Several dozen agricultural scientists contacted in a recent survey indicated that annual increases in corn yields of from 1 to 2 percent are likely due to biotechnology alone, with no increase in inputs.[6] *Biotechnology*, as defined by these experts, is the development of better crop strains through genetic engineering, cell or tissue culture, use of synthetic or natural growth regulators, and enhancement of photosynthesis and nitrogen fixation. Other kinds of technology, not considered in the survey but important nevertheless, include better weather forecasting and better on-farm information management to allow farmers to anticipate pest outbreaks and to time irrigation and fertilizer applications more finely.

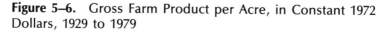

Figure 5–6. Gross Farm Product per Acre, in Constant 1972 Dollars, 1929 to 1979

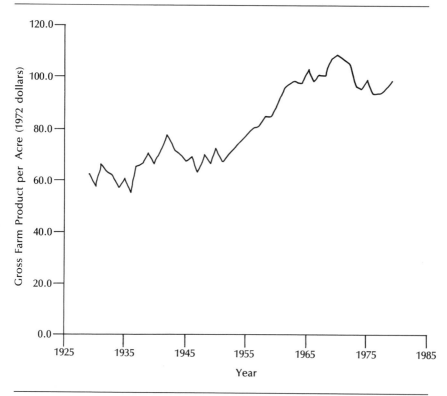

Sources: U.S. Department of Commence, Bureau of the Census, *Statistical Abstract of the United States 1984* (Washington, D.C.: USGPO, 1983); U.S. Department of Commerce, Bureau of the Census, *Historical Statistics of the United States: Colonial Times to 1970* (Washington, D.C.: USGPO, 1975); USDA, *Agricultural Statistics* (Washington, D.C.: USGPO, various years).

But there are compelling reasons to believe that technology will be less effective than customarily anticipated in the future. Not the least important is that gains in crop output have slacked off in recent years. Crop output, as reported by the USDA, has increased by an average of 1.2 percent per year since 1965; this is considerably lower than the average 2.5 percent annual rise experienced from 1950 to 1965.[7] To a great extent, the side effects of previous technological advances may be responsible for this falling off in new advances. Current prac-

Figure 5–7.   Gross Farm Product per Acre in Constant 1972 Dollars, versus On-Farm Fuel Use per Acre, 1940 to 1979

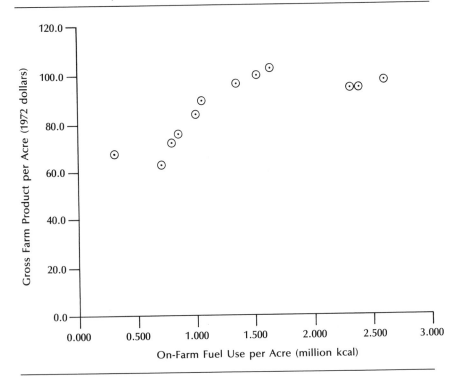

Sources: U.S. Department of Commerce, Bureau of the Census, *Statistical Abstract of the United States 1984* (Washington: USGPO, 1983); U.S. Department of Commerce, Bureau of the Census, *Historical Statistics of the United States: Colonial Times to 1970* (Washington, D.C.: USGPO, various years): J. S. Steinhart and C. E. Steinhart, "Energy Use in the U.S. Food System," *Science* 184 (1974) 307–316; U.S. Department of Commerce, Bureau of the Census, *Annual Survey of Manufactures* (Washington, D.C.: USGPO, various years); U.S. Department of Commerce, Bureau of the Census, *1978 Census of Agriculture,* Vol. 5: 1979 Farm Energy Survey, Special Reports pt. 9 (Washington, D.C.: USGPO); David Torgerson and Harold Cooper, *Energy and U.S. Agriculture 1974 and 1978,* USDA Statistical Bulletin 632 (Washington, D.C. USGPO, 1980)

tices regarding tillage methods, fertilizers, irrigation, pesticides, farm size, and the kinds of foods farmers grow are progressively reducing the amount of food we obtain with a kcal of fuel. Right now it appears that these degradations of the resource base are negating improvements in efficiency due to technology.[8] Alternatively, technology may be seen as masking the effects of degradation.

The Process Of "Management"

Undisturbed natural ecosystems show very little net productivity—that is, the amount of plant and animal material usually doesn't increase very much from year to year. Most of the solar energy captured by the *biota* (an ecological term for all the plant and animal life in a region) is used to support its day-to-day metabolic needs, and little remains for new growth. If some of the biota is removed, such as by humans for food, it grows back slowly. Moreover, very few species in undisturbed ecosystems are edible by humans. As a result, the human carrying capacity of such ecosystems is quite small. Ecologist Howard Odum has estimated that a square mile of unmanaged forest can support only one or two people.[9]

About 10,000 years ago people began what is called *sendentary* agriculture, in which the same patch of ground is farmed permanently or in rotation with fallow. With this so-called Neolithic Revolution, people began to manage ecosystems extensively to increase the amount of food on a piece of land. The simplest way to do that—in theory, if not in practice—is to grow only the useful species and to keep the rest out. This has meant reducing a natural ecosystem to bare earth, sowing seeds of desirable plants, and weeding out the native vegetation as it tries to return. These management strategies haven't changed since the Neolithic Revolution, although the tactics have.

But while the process of management usually raises the amount of food obtained, it usually raises the amount of effort needed to obtain each unit of food as well. Management, by its very nature, disrupts the normal cycles of nutrients among plants, animals, earth, and air. To establish new cycles that allow the perpetual growth and harvest of crops requires substantial investment of human effort. For instance, clearing land leaves the soil vulnerable to erosion, which carries nutrients away permanently.[10] Taking crops off the field also takes nutrients away. Manure and crop residues may be returned, but they don't contain all the nutrients contained in the original crop material. Furthermore, the mere act of tillage, continued over many years, reduces the soil's organic matter content, which is critical for retaining moisture and resisting erosion.[11] If the land is to remain fertile, these nutrients must be replaced "artificially": with commercial fertilizers or manure obtained elsewhere, or with nonfood cover crops, all of which take energy to manage. Similarly, farmers must invest energy in plowing, seeding, weeding, and all the other aspects of sedentary agriculture. It has been calculated that for every kcal of energy invested in a slash-and-burn or other nonsedentary farming system, between 13 and 67 kcal of food are produced.[12] (A kilocalorie of food energy is what most of us know simply as a calorie; that is, a teaspoon of sugar contains 18 kcal of food energy.) In an unmechanized sedentary system, in which most farm work is done by people and domestic animals, a kcal invested yields between 2 and 12 kcal of food. In a modern, mechanized system, a kcal invested brings in between 0.67 and 3.33 kcal of food. The total amount of food produced is vastly increased by mechanization, of course, but at the cost of decreasing energy efficiency (Figure 5–8). The falling efficiency is unimportant as long as fuels are cheap and plentiful, but it is worrisome as fuels become scarce.

It has been argued that sedentary agriculture is never sustainable, since it requires the use of fertilizers, which are usually nonrenewable or of agricultural origin themselves. Whether or not this is true, we can say for certain that many of the techniques of industrial farming accelerate the decline in the quality of the resource base. Further intensification of farming will not only become increasingly ineffective, it may even be counterproductive. Mechanization poses a special twofold threat to the agricultural resource base: farming is in danger of being dependent on nonrenewable fuels, and the fundamental ingredient of farming, soil, is being destroyed.

Recently, some farmers have recognized the drawbacks of industrial farming and have abandoned some aspects of it. Others, like some of the Amish, never adopted them, or at least adopted them selectively.[13] These farmers have done very well financially by growing food in old-fashioned ways: shunning chemical fertilizers and pesticides, avoiding or minimizing the

Figure 5–8   On-Farm Energy Output/Input Ratio, 1940 to 1979.

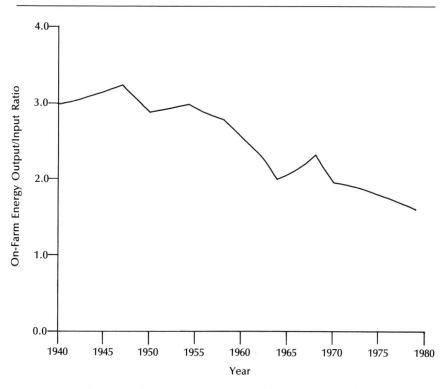

use of mechanized equipment, planting windbreaks and plowing along the contours of hillsides to reduce erosion, and planting soil-regenerating cover plants in rotation with food crops. Some of these practices may reduce yields somewhat, but more often than not the reduction in the farmers' costs is even greater, increasing profitability.[14] These practices also increase the energy efficiency.

Still other farmers have maintained the foundations of industrial farming but have tried to apply the techniques more intelligently and efficiently. New fertilizer, irrigation, tillage, and pest control technologies have been developed that are nearly as effective as conventional ones but that reduce or eliminate the unpleasant side effects. For example: a small amount of fertilizer or irrigation water applied at certain times during a crop's growth cycle may be much more effective than a much larger amount at other times; tillage methods that leave crop residues on the field, instead of plowing them under as most farmers currently do, can reduce erosion by as much as 80 percent[15]; reliance on natural predators to control pests may be more effective, less expensive, and less environmentally dangerous than chemicals. These techniques allow farmers to maintain crop yields at high levels, but reduce their costs and the damage to the resource base.

Nevertheless, conventional industrial farming is probably with us to stay for a long time because most farmers still feel they can't practice the more benign strategies. They have already invested in expensive land and machinery, and they need to keep their incomes up just to service their debts. Said Chip Struckmeyer, a California rice farmer interviewed on the PBS television program "Nova," "We are in a position where we have to produce for the highest yield potential every year, per acre, to stay in business."[16] U.S. farmers consistently grow more food than they can sell; yet farmers with huge debts cannot afford to cut back on their production. Industrial farming, for most farmers, is the only way to keep their incomes high enough to stay afloat. Yet eventually industrial farming will put many of them out of business. Already farm foreclosures and forced sales are at their highest levels since the Depression, as farmers are squeezed between stagnant crop prices and escalating costs for equipment, seed, chemicals, and, most important, loan money. Absent a technological or economic miracle, these trends can only get worse. The following sections examine the ways energy is used on the nation's farms and show why industrial farming degrades itself.

Tillage

Planting and harvesting crops require that soil and plant material be moved around. These tasks involve physical work and therefore require energy. At first, humans did most of this work. Later, after the invention of the harness, domestic animals extended farmers' power, increasing the acreage each farmer could cultivate. As recently as 1910, animals still provided a significant portion of the energy used in the U.S. economy (Figure 3–1). The development of internal combustion engines and electric motors increased the power at farmers' disposal even more (Figure 5–9), so that, following World War II, the bulk of work done on-farm was derived from fossil fuels. A dramatic increase in the horsepower of the average tractor in the early 1960s led to another spurt in fossil energy use. Most ominously, advancing technology has also changed the effect of tillage on the soil.

Soil erosion has been a problem as long as people have practiced sedentary agriculture. Usually, eradicating undesirable

Figure 5–9.   Index of the Contribution of Human Labor and Mechanical Power to On-Farm Agriculture, 1920 to 1980

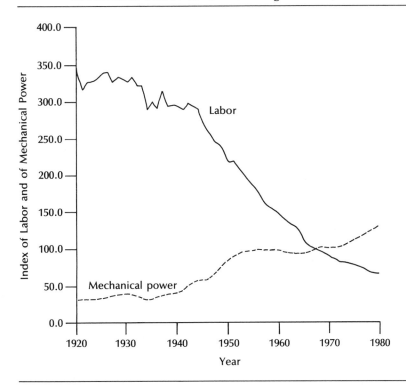

Source: Economic Research Service, USDA, *Economic Indicators of the Farm Sector: Production and Efficiency Statistics,* Statistical Bulletin 657 (Washington, D.C.: USGPO, 1979).
Note: 1967 = 100.

plant species also means leaving the soil bare and unanchored. (Not always, however; so-called no-till and low-till farming techniques, which are growing in popularity, leave residues from the previous crop on the fields to protect the soil from wind- and rain-induced erosion.) Croplands are especially vulnerable in the spring, when the crops are still seedlings, and in the fall, after the harvest—seasons when the weather is often very rainy and windy and the soil is nearly bare. The practice of planting in rows compounds the problem by providing ready-made channels through which rain runoff can carry loose soil. Furthermore, the roots of crop species are generally less effective at holding soil in place than natural plants. Unmechanized farming suffered from erosion, of course, but machinery exacerbates it, to the point where soil erosion in the United States today is again comparable to the Dustbowl of the 1930s.[17]

The advantage provided by machinery is that it enables farmers to prepare their fields, sow their crop, and harvest it much faster than with animals or their own backs. But the way in which the machines are used also worsens erosion. A horse-drawn plow is easier to steer if the furrows follow the land contours; a large tractor operates more efficiently on straight rows. Larry Kay, an Iowa farmer, told interviewers from "Nova" that "large equipment doesn't adapt itself well to contouring. And you end up with a lot of short rows, and we don't like to waste time turning. And it's harder on equipment to turn. So we semi-contour, we lay out a contour line at the top of the hills, and just let them fall on down the hill. If we start going up and down the hills after a while we don't worry about it." But furrows running straight down a hillside leave the field wide open to erosion. These attributes of machinery (as well as the desire to maximize tilled acreage) also led to the removal of windbreaks, worsening erosion by wind.

The USDA estimates that some 23 percent of U.S. cropland suffers erosion rates greater than is considered "tolerable."[18] ("Tolerable" is defined in a rather complicated way, taking into account such factors as absolute soil loss, soil formation rates, the value of what is grown on it, and others. The usefulness of this definition is in some dispute; we cite the USDA figure here simply to give an idea of the general scope of the erosion problem.) The plain fact is that soil is being mined: it is being lost faster than geological processes replace it. Nutrients carried into the Gulf of Mexico are then only partially replaced by fertilizers that take fossil fuels to make and transport.

Commercial Fertilizers

No amount of commercial fertilizer can replace lost topsoil. There are two reasons for this: synthetic fertilizers are significantly less effective on soils that don't already contain some organic matter, and they actively promote the degradation of existing organic matter and increase the future need for fertilizers.

Soil is classified into two layers, a surface layer (topsoil) and a subsurface layer. Subsurface soil consists of very small bits of rock that were laid down by water or glaciers or were formed on the spot by the breakup of underlying bedrock. This subsurface soil is essentially dead, containing little that can be used for food by plants or animals. The topsoil is made of subsurface soil mixed with decomposing organic material called *humus*. The humus is what allows topsoil to support a variety of microbial and higher plant and animal life.

In industrial farming, humus has another, possibly more important, function: it holds fertilizers in the soil. At the heart of the tremendous increases in per-acre crop output that occurred in the period of intensification—the Green Revolution—are new, high-yield, hybrid crop strains. And one of the principal advantages of these strains is that they can use higher levels of commercial fertilizers more efficiently than the old crop varieties. The fertilizers, not the original nutrients in the topsoil, supply the bulk of modern crops' additional nutritional requirements. But the topsoil is still needed because it helps keep the fertilizers from being washed out of the soil. The active ingredients in commercial fertilizers—nitrogen, phosphorus, and potassium—are often electrically charged, which binds them to oppositely charged areas of humus particles. These crucial nutrients (except nitrates, which are easily leached) are thus anchored in the soil, in storage until the crops need them, and prevented from being flushed away by rain or irrigation water.

But fertilizers cause microbes, as well as crops, to bloom. Some of these microbes also use humus as food, and, as their growth is spurred by fertilizer, they may break down the humus much faster.[19] In the absence of humus to hold them in the soil, the fertilizers are likely to be washed away. In this way, the fertilizers sometimes actually degrade the fertility of the topsoil *and* reduce the effectiveness of future applications of fertilizer. Consequently, to maintain yields, farmers may have to use more and more fertilizer. Of course, increasingly intense use of fertilizers accelerates the degradation of topsoil, and farmers may find themselves trapped inside a vicious circle. An additional unpleasant side effect of humus destruction is that, since humus acts as a sponge for water, its loss also increases the amount of water needed to maintain crop yields and increases the threat of erosion. If the land is irrigated, farmers will need to irrigate more—which aggravates erosion further and creates another vicious circle.

As more fertilizers are applied, factors other than the amount of nitrogen, phosphorus, or potassium in the soil begin to limit plant growth. Additional fertilizer induces progressively smaller increases in yield; eventually, additional fertilizer actually reduces yield (Figure 5–10). As more and more fertilizer continues to be applied, to lesser and lesser effect, the energy cost of a unit of food is increased. (Nitrogenous fertilizers are particularly energy intensive because one of the basic chemicals used to make them is natural gas.) We interpret this as a decline in the quality of the agricultural resource base—and it may not even increase the total amount of food produced.

Irrigation

Another important ingredient in modern farming is irrigation. By turning arid shrubland into cropland, irrigation increased the land area under cultivation. Colorado, Arizona, and California have greatly benefitted from irrigation. It has also allowed farmers to grow more profitable crops; in the Great Plains, for example, irrigation has enabled farmers to switch from wheat, which fetches about four dollars a bushel and has a national

Figure 5–10. Yield per Acre of a Typical Modern Hybrid Wheat Strain versus That of a Traditional Variety as a Function of Nitrogen Input

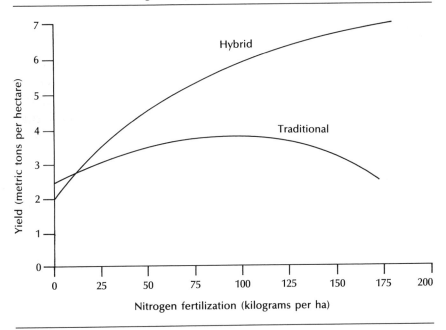

Source: W.S. Clapham, Jr., *Human Ecosystems* (New York: Macmillan, 1981), p. 162.

average yield of about thirty bushels per acre, to corn, which sells for roughly three dollars a bushel but which yields around a hundred bushels per acre.

Just as important, irrigation can increase the per-acre yield of individual crops. An irrigated acre in the Great Plains typically yields three or four times more wheat or sorghum than a nonirrigated acre.[20] In climates with irregular rainfall (like much of the Grain Belt), irrigation is insurance against water shortages at critical periods of a crop's growth cycle. Even slight shortages of water at certain times can damage corn yields significantly. In other words, irrigation offers a buffer against the vicissitudes of nature. The advantages of irrigation, despite the high fuel and capital costs it involves, have convinced farmers to increase the amount of irrigated cropland from 20 million acres in 1944 to 51 million in 1978. This 12 percent of total U.S.

cropland is especially productive: it accounts for 25 percent of the total value of crops produced.

Irrigation, however, may have been *too* effective. Although water, like soil, is usually thought of as a renewable resource, in many places it is being used faster than it is being renewed. Water is being mined.

Approximately two-thirds of the 90 billion gallons of groundwater pumped in the United States each day is used for irrigation.[21] As this water is pumped from the ground, often at the rate of inches or feet per year, it is replaced by rainfall that percolates through the soil into deposits of groundwater called *aquifers*. The rate of this recharge, however, may be as little as tenths of an inch per year in the West, where most of the nation's irrigation takes place. The frequent disparity between use and recharge rates means that the nation as a whole uses 21 billion gallons a day (BGD) of groundwater (for all uses, not just irrigation) in excess of local recharge rates.

The key word here is *local*. When one looks at national averages, the problem of groundwater overdrafts seems negligible: the United States could mine 21 BGD for more than 4000 years.[22] Only when the focus is narrowed to sections of individual states does the true severity of the overdraft problem become clear. Unlike surface waters, water in aquifers moves slowly, generally no more than a few hundred feet per year. Rapid pumping may lower the water table drastically in one part of an aquifer, yet leave the water table of the same aquifer five miles away unaffected for years. Different parts of the same aquifer may also contain widely varying amounts of water.

As a result, areas a short distance apart may face completely different situations regarding their groundwater supplies. For example, in a rare county-level study of an entire region, the High Plains Study Commission, a consortium of private consulting firms and federal and state agencies, projected agricultural trends from 1975 to 2020.[23] In Nebraska, the High Plains aquifer is so rich that irrigation can be expanded; in neighboring Kansas, however, irrigation water will be effectively exhausted for 75 percent of existing irrigated cropland by 2025. This will not spell the end of farming in Kansas, of course: farmers there will switch from irrigated corn to dryland wheat. But their profits will probably be smaller, and they will no longer have recourse to irrigation in case of severe drought, since they will have exhausted their cushion of groundwater.

The problem is not just that groundwater supplies may be exhausted sometime in the future. Falling water tables leave shallow wells high and dry. Deeper wells must then be drilled, and they will cost more to operate. The dollar and the energy costs of food production are therefore raised. In some areas, the expense may become too great: in more than one area of the country, formerly irrigated land has been withdrawn from cultivation. In addition, farmers must compete with municipal and industrial users of water. If irrigation leads to depletion of aquifers, the energy costs of *all* activities—not just food production—are increased.

Finally, irrigation itself often degrades the quality of soil. Much irrigation water is high in sodium, which bonds to humus particles in place of the beneficial phosphorus and potassium in fertilizers. The soil's holding capacity for nutrients is therefore reduced, and more fertilizer must then be applied to maintain fertility. Sodium—a constituent of ordinary table salt—also damages plant roots outright, which is why the Romans sowed the fields of their arch-foe, Carthage, with sea salt after Rome's victory in the last Punic War.

Insectides and Herbicides

Insect and weed control used to be conducted with crop rotation and the farmer's two hands and a hoe. Today, farmers have access to a vast arsenal of machines and chemicals to keep competing plants and animals out of their fields.[24] These armaments contributed significantly to the increased per-acre output of the intensification period.

There is substantial evidence, however, that the use of these chemicals is not sustainable. After years of use, many pest species develop immunity to pesticides. Thus, existing pesticides have become less effective. As resistance to pesticides grows, farmers must use greater quantities to achieve the same effect. In the face of this trend, agricultural researchers are under constant pressure to create new pesticides.

Also, many chemicals are not very selective regarding the species they kill: sometimes pesticides are self-defeating.[25] Normally, wasps control 70 to 90 percent of the olive parlatoria scale, a destructive pest species in California olive groves.[26] In an attempt to eradicate the remaining 10 to 30 percent, the groves were sprayed with DDT. Unfortunately, the DDT was more effective on the wasps than the scales, resulting in an explosion in the scale population and serious damage to the olive crop.

Again, as with tillage, fertilizers, and irrigation, the net long-term effect of industrial methods of weed and insect control is an increase in the energy cost of food, with little or no increase in total output. Furthermore, this leaves aside the question of the negative effects these chemicals may have on human health. Because of the generally low levels of exposure, very little is known about the degree to which routine use of pesticides causes cancer or other diseases in people. The total cost of pesticides may thus be much higher.

Animal-Based Foods in the Diet

Consumer preferences for animal-based foods also contribute heavily to the mounting energy cost of food. About 35 percent of the average U.S. diet, in calories, consists of animal products: red meat, poultry, fish, eggs, dairy products, and animal fats.[27] Almost 60 percent of these animal foods are derived not from unimproved pasture or rangeland but from crops harvested to feed animals.[28] U.S. grazing and pasture lands are grossly inadequate to meet today's demand for animal products. Most experts agree that most of the approximately 650 million acres used to graze livestock are being degraded through overuse: the U.S. Forest Service has estimated that almost 70 percent of this land is in fair to poor condition due to overgrazing.[29]

Therefore, to produce the meat and other animal products that we in the United States want, farmers use industrial farming methods to grow food for animals. For example, 85 to 90 percent of the U.S. corn crop used domestically is fed to animals. (Indeed, when one considers that much of the food the United States sells abroad is also used for animal feed, it may be more appropriate to refer to this country, not as the world's breadbasket, but as its feedbag.) The conversion of this crop energy to the energy contained in the animal foods we ultimately eat is remarkably inefficient. It takes almost 11,000 kcal of crops to produce the 700 kcal of crop-fed animal products in the average daily diet, a ratio of more than 15:1.[30] Much of this inefficiency stems from the national fondness for beef. Cows are ruminant animals, whose original advantage for humans was that they could thrive on grass, shrubs, and other plants that people couldn't eat themselves. Ruminants pay a price for this flexibility, however: their conversion ratios for meat are about five times poorer than those of chickens or swine.[31] Thus, when feeds for beef cattle are grown on land that could support crops edible by people, or when the feeds themselves are edible by people, the original advantage of cattle has been sacrificed.

Because we feed so much of our crops to animals, crop production has had to increase far faster than population growth just to keep pace with the demand for food. In a sense, then, much of the impetus to make heavy use of fertilizers, irrigation, and pesticides comes from consumers' preference for animal products. It is difficult to predict what might happen to consumer preferences in the future. Increasing concern about obesity and heart disease seem already to be affecting people's eating habits (the fraction of the average diet suppied by animal products has decreased from 40 percent in 1960 to 35 percent in 1979), and food prices also influence diets strongly. But population growth and the 15:1 lever effect of animal products in the diet probably mean that the demand for animal feeds will continue to increase. Such an increase will then push farmers further out onto the flat part of their production curves and will raise the energy cost of food even further.

AGRICULTURE OFF THE FARM

Industrialization of agriculture has not been restricted to the nation's farms. Unlike earlier forms of agriculture, industrial food production features extensive fuel-powered networks of off-farm processing and distribution. In a seminal study of U.S.

agriculture published in *Science* in 1974, Carol and John Stein-hart examined the system's behavior from 1940 to 1970, break-ing it down into a network of energy inputs—an energy budget for industrial agriculture (Table 5–2). Today, only about 4 per-cent of the nation's energy budget is used to grow food, while 10 to 13 percent is needed to put it on our plates.[32] Think of the hands our wheat must pass through before we actually eat it: once it leaves the farm, it must go to a mill where it is ground into flour, then to a baker to be turned into bread, then to a wholesaler, then to a retailer, and finally into our homes. Of the 22 million people employed in the entire agriculture system, only about 4 million actually work on farms. And of the $260 billion paid by consumers for food products in 1980, farmers saw less than a third: the remainder went to the middlemen who make up the food processing, packaging, and distribution industries.

In contrast to the situation on the nation's farms, there doesn't seem to be anything peculiar to off-farm agriculture that makes it particularly unsustainable; its current form is unsustainable only to the extent that it is part of the general economy, which uses large quantities of fossil fuels. It is becom-ing progressively less energy-efficient, in terms of the energy used to produce a kcal of edible food: between 1950 and 1970 off-farm energy use (excluding home cooking and refrigeration) increased by 85 percent, while total food consumption in kcal rose by less than 40 percent. But consumer preferences are responsible for the decline in efficiency. The off-farm sector may have used less energy in pre-industrial days, but the amount of time individual consumers spent preparing food was much greater. Indeed, as is true of industrialization in general, the growth of off-farm agriculture stems from the replacement of human energy and time with fossil fuels. Fossil fuels make it possible for us to take a frozen entree from the refrigerator, pop it into the microwave oven, and have dinner ready in less than fifteen minutes. Similarly, fossil fuels allow us to bring live lob-sters to Nebraska and fresh artichokes to New Hampshire. Many of these conveniences represent a real advance in living standards. Nevertheless, we can expect that these conveniences will become increasingly costly to maintain as net fuel supplies fail to keep pace with population growth. We can sustain off-farm agriculture in its present form as long as we like—but, to do so, we will have to divert a growing share of a static energy budget to this aspect of food production, and away from the rest of the economy. In the next chapter, we will present a model, similar to the one in Chapter 4, that shows how much energy would have to be diverted.

Undoubtedly, some across-the-board energy savings could be achieved in the off-farm sector. However, savings that involve no changes in consumers' habits are likely to be small: there is no evidence to suggest that off-farm agriculture is particularly inefficient compared to the rest of U.S. industry. As Chapter 3 argued, the net energy savings achieved by substituting new capital equipment or additional labor for direct fuel use are not likely to be very large, when the energy cost of the new capital or labor is considered.

On the other hand, as in the on-farm sector, there are certain aspects of the off-farm sector that, if expanded greatly, could increase the amount of edible food produced per kcal of fuel. These largely involve altered consumer preferences. They could, by scaling back the size and scope of off-farm agriculture, result in substantial reductions in energy use. U.S. diets, which used to vary markedly from place to place and from season to season, have become increasingly homogeneous. Fossil-fuel-powered technology made this possible by enabling us to move fresh food across the country in a matter of days and by allowing us to store it for months or years. A partial return to regional diets, which consist of food grown locally, could substantially reduce the amount of energy needed to transport food. Similarly, diets composed of in-season food could cut back on the fuel needed to refrigerate, freeze, or otherwise process food. Home gardens offer additional opportunities to reduce off-farm energy needs. Produce grown in the backyard eliminates all the middlemen—truckers, wholesalers, retailers—who spend energy without changing the food in any substantive way. Of course, in the past all diets were regional, seasonal, and/or home-grown, and people deliberately changed them. Such diets restrict consumers' choice of foods and increase the amount of time that must be spent on eating, so a return to them would involve some tradeoff of consumer convenience for lower food prices and more fuel for other purposes. Moreover,

Table 5–2. Energy Budget for the U.S. Agriculture System, Both On-Farm and Off-Farm, 1940 to 1970

Component	1940	1947	1950	1954	1958	1960	1964	1968	1970
On farm									
Fuel (direct use)	70.0	136.0	158.0	172.8	179.0	188.0	213.9	226.0	232.0
Electricity	0.7	32.0	32.9	40.0	44.0	46.1	50.0	57.3	63.8
Fertilizer	12.4	19.5	24.0	30.6	32.2	41.0	60.0	87.0	94.0
Agricultural steel	1.6	2.0	2.7	2.5	2.0	1.7	2.5	2.4	2.0
Farm machinery	9.0	34.7	30.0	29.5	50.2	52.0	60.0	75.0	80.0
Tractors	12.8	25.0	30.8	23.6	16.4	11.8	20.0	20.5	19.3
Irrigation	18.0	22.8	25.0	29.6	32.5	33.3	34.1	34.8	35.0
Subtotal	124.5	272.0	303.4	328.6	356.3	373.9	440.5	503.0	526.1
Processing Industry									
Food processing industry	147.0	177.5	192.0	211.5	212.6	224.0	249.0	295.0	308.0
Food processing machinery	0.7	5.7	5.0	4.9	4.9	5.0	6.0	6.0	6.0
Paper packaging	8.5	14.8	17.0	20.0	26.0	28.0	31.0	35.7	38.0
Glass containers	14.0	25.7	26.0	27.0	30.2	31.0	34.0	41.9	47.0
Steel cans and aluminum	38.0	55.8	62.0	73.7	85.4	86.0	91.0	112.2	122.0
Transport (fuel)	49.6	86.1	102.0	122.3	140.2	153.3	184.0	226.6	246.9
Trucks and trailers (manufacture)	28.0	42.0	49.5	47.0	43.0	44.2	61.0	70.2	74.0
Subtotal	285.8	407.6	453.5	506.4	542.3	571.5	656.0	787.6	841.9

Commercial and home								
Commercial refrigeration and cooking	121.0	141.0	150.0	161.0	176.0	186.2	209.0	241.0	263.0
Refrigeration machinery (home and commercial)	10.0	24.0	25.0	27.5	29.4	32.0	40.0	56.0	61.0
Home refrigeration and cooking	144.2	184.0	202.3	228.0	257.0	276.6	345.0	433.9	480.0
Subtotal	275.2	349.0	377.3	416.5	462.4	494.8	594.0	730.9	804.0
Grand total	685.5	1028.6	1134.2	1251.5	1361.0	1440.2	1690.5	2021.5	2172.0

Source: J.S. Steinhart and C.E. Steinhart, "Energy Use in the U.S. Food System," *Science* 184 (1974): 307–16. © 1974 AAAS

such diets have energy costs of their own: for New England to grow more of its own food, for example, might require it to clear forests that now provide fuelwood or to build and power a hothouse agriculture system. But as the nation's energy budget becomes increasingly constricted, some tradeoffs *must* be made.

6 A MODEL OF AGRICULTURE AND THE U.S. ECONOMY

In all abundance there is lack.

—Hippocrates

Agriculture's heavy dependence on fossil fuels in the United States is on a collision course with three current trends: rising demands for fuel by other sectors, falling per capita supplies of fuel, and a degrading of the resource base. But it is difficult to determine whether a collision will actually take place or, if it does, what the aftermath will look like: there are too many uncertainties about the important determinants of future crop productivity. For instance, the precise rate of resource degradation is the subject of active debate. Some experts believe that soil erosion, compaction, degradation, and pollution will soon reduce yields drastically; others discount such effects and believe technological improvements will actually increase crop yields. Some analysts think that aggressive soil-conserving practices can conquer erosion; some think that recombinant DNA techniques in genetic plant breeding will revolutionize farming; others disagree completely.

There are three ways to deal with this confusion: simply pick a set of projections as the "best" (the usual solution); throw up one's hands and walk away; or accept the uncertainty and see if anything useful may be said in spite of it. We chose the third. We developed a computer model that does not attempt to settle the above disputes but rather examines all sides of them, each

177

in its turn, through scenario analyses. This technique both highlights those areas of uncertainty that most need to be resolved and identifies trends that are common to all scenarios.

The agriculture model, like the general economic model described in Chapter 4, is what is known in the trade as *highly aggregated*—that is, it reduces disparate kinds of outputs and inputs to a single common term. In Chapter 4, inputs were reduced to energy and outputs to dollars. Here, the inputs are land and energy, and outputs are expressed in energy. Based on the historical record of how land, energy, and energy-based inputs have been used to produce food, the model can calculate (1) the amount of land and energy needed to meet a specified level of food demand, depending on assumptions regarding erosion, technological change, and so on, or alternatively (2) the amount of food that can be produced from a specified amount of land and energy, which are likely to become scarcer as population grows and as oil and gas run out. In this *aggregated* view of U.S. agriculture, then, three quantities must be determined: crop demand, the efficiency with which fuel energy is converted to food energy, and the supply of fuels and land. Crop demand, in kcal, is a function of the population size, the caloric content of the average diet, the composition of the diet (animal- versus vegetable-based foods), the average efficiency with which crop-fed livestock convert crops to edible meat, milk, eggs, and fats, and export demand. In the first kind of calculation, crop production is simply set equal to demand, and the model calculates how much energy and land is needed to meet it under various scenarios of efficiency. In the second, the model is told how much land and energy is available, and it calculates how much crop production is possible, again under the different efficiency scenarios.

Briefly, the results are as follows. The amount of energy that will be needed to produce a unit of food is the most important determinant of the system's future, but it is also the least predictable. If, as some analysts warn, land continues to be degraded rapidly, and if technology is unable to boost on-farm energy efficiency to compensate, the United States may have to double its harvested cropland area and double its farm energy use in the next forty years to feed its citizens a large, meaty diet and maintain a large export capacity. And if the United States should be unable to increase its cropland area and on-farm energy use by that much—as virtually everyone would concede—we will be unable to meet domestic demand, let alone to export any food.

Taken as a whole, the scenarios show that the agricultural successes of the last forty years—increasing crop yields and bigger diets from a relatively constant fraction of the nation's land and fuel—can be sustained in the future *only* if the ongoing decline in resource quality is reversed quickly. If the decline is not reversed, the United States will face a dwindling food export capacity and/or substantially higher food prices.

THREE AVENUES OF INVESTIGATION

The objective of our model is to find out how much energy and land agriculture may demand in the future and what the effect of constraints on their supply will be. We also wish to know the effect of resource degradation and declining energy efficiency on crop production. And we want to gauge the effect of possible increases in the efficiency with which energy is used to produce food for domestic consumption and export trade. To do this we have organized our analysis along three avenues of investigation.

A Demand-Driven Approach

First, we calculate the amount of energy and land that would be used if population growth, food consumption, exports, soil erosion, and other factors were to continue their trends of recent years. Food demand, both domestic and foreign, determines crop production, which in turn solely determines land and energy use. A demand-oriented approach has been taken by other studies that assume that crop production will increase due to rising per-acre yields. However, these studies usually ignore the role of energy in agriculture and the decline in crop yields per unit of energy input, both of which are central to our analysis. We use as key indicator variables the fraction of all U.S. energy (based on the Chapter 4 reference projection of total energy supply) demanded by agriculture, the amount of land required to meet production goals, and the ratio of energy outputs to inputs. This avenue is unrealistic, insofar as it allows agriculture to swallow unlimited amounts of land and energy, but it serves an important purpose. That this constraint-free avenue, a purely demand-driven one, does not reflect reality is in fact its principal strength: a finding that current production and efficiency trends lead to absurd levels of energy and land use highlights the unsustainability of those trends.

A Supply-Constrained Approach

The second avenue is really a reversal of the first: it determines the effect of resource constraints on crop production. Because most prime farmland is already in production, any additional land would probably be substantially less fertile, and very little of it would be worth the trouble to farm. The financial difficulties that beset many farmers also restrict their ability to spend more on fertilizers, machinery, and other fuel-based inputs. With rising population and declining supplies of fossil fuels, particularly oil and gas, even devoting the *current* fraction of U.S. energy to agriculture will likely constrain production. Thus, in this approach the model calculates the amount of crops that would be produced from plausible levels of land and energy use and efficiency. Our chief indicators of the system's health in this second approach are crop production, export capacity, and the output/input efficiency ratios.

A "High Technology" Approach

Last, we model the effect of technologies, policies, and management practices that could increase the energy efficiency of crop production. When there is a shortfall in the supply of resources, the system may adjust to increase the amount of crops that can be produced with the same unit of energy input. Such things as organic farming, no-till and minimum-till cultivation, crop rotation, and the wise application of fertilizers are examples of practices that reduce farmers' energy costs but generally maintain production levels. Moreover, biotechnologies may have an important role in boosting crop productivity in the future. In this third approach we test how important and effective these potential efficiency-raising factors may be by extending the supply-constrained analysis. Two paths toward higher efficiency are modeled in the context of land and energy use fixed at current levels.

The model in all scenarios begins its projections in the year 1980 (the last year for which we could obtain adequate data being 1979) and continues them to 2025.

DATA AND ASSUMPTIONS

All three forms of the model calculate an "ideal" crop demand, based on projections of population size, dietary composition and size, and export demand (projections that are not explicitly constrained by prices or resource limits). This "ideal" crop demand is set equal to crop production in the demand-driven analysis; in the supply-constrained and high-technology approaches, it constitutes a target that may or may not be met. All three parts of the model also relate crop production to energy inputs, on a national average, by means of a *yield curve* (see Figure 6–1 and accompanying box), although the scale and shape of the curve changes in the various scenarios. The yield curve shows the response of an average acre of cropland to various levels of energy (in the form of fuels, machinery, and fertilizer) at a single point in time.[1] Thus, in all three of its forms, the model requires projections for crop demand, resource supplies, and the efficiency with which these resources are converted into food.

We have collected the data for our model from the Census Bureau, USDA, Iowa State University's Center for Agricultural and Rural Development (CARD), the National Academy of Sciences, several specialized studies and symposia, and the scientific journals. The task of selecting data from these sources was confounded by many uncertainties on basic issues. For instance, estimates of potential crop yields by the year 2000 range from a 20 percent increase to a 100 percent increase over current yields.[2] Many of the sources are vague about whether these gains in yield are to be realized through intensified use of

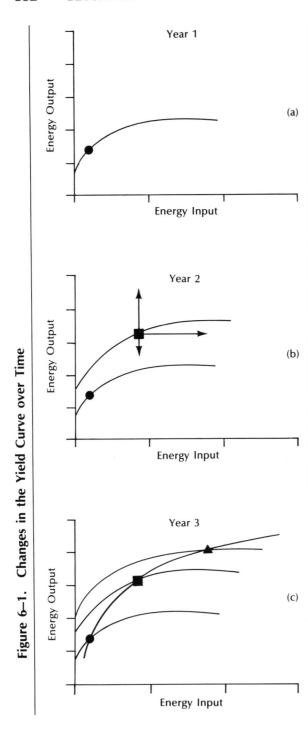

Figure 6–1. Changes in the Yield Curve over Time

Figure 6-1a shows the yield curve for a given year; that is, it shows how much crop output can be obtained from a given level of energy input at a single point in time. The average energy input actually used, however, assumes a single value signified by the solid circle.

Neither the level of energy input nor the yield curve itself remain static from one year to the next. The curve is subject to three vectors represented by arrows in Figure 6-1b. Improving technology pulls the curve upward, increasing the amount of crops grown with a unit of energy input and raising the maximum level of crop output. Technology also moves the curve to the right, increasing the energy input needed to reach the maximum crop output. Finally, erosion and degradative forces drag the curve downward, reducing the amount of crops grown with a unit of energy input and cancelling out some of the technological gains. And historically farmers have used more energy inputs each year than they did before, represented by the square in Figure 6-1b.

In the past several years, however, the yearly net gain in efficiency (technology's upward push minus degradation's downward pull) has been smaller than before. Figure 6-1c illustrates this effect: the yield curve for year 3 is much closer to year 2's curve than year 2 was to year 1. The triangle represents the actual level of energy input. Because the increase in energy input from year 2 to year 3 does not raise crop production very much, the historical yield curve—obtained by connecting the circle, square, and triangle—flattens out as time passes and as energy inputs climb.

inputs, gains in efficiency, or both. Estimates of reductions in potential crop yields due to erosion by 2030 vary from 5 percent to 30 percent.[3] Furthermore, projections made by the agricultural community ignore constraints in the supply of basic inputs such as energy. As a result of this confusion, which plagues nearly every aspect of agriculture, the model's many scenarios cover the ends as well as the middle of the spectrum of possibilities. The following sections provide an overview of the data and assumptions we used.

Energy Availability

In Chapter 4, we predicted the total availability of energy. In the demand-driven analysis presented below, we assume that agriculture can draw any fraction of this pool of energy (including alternative fuels) to meet the demand for food production. Thus, we assume initially that farmers are unconstrained in their use of energy and that the agricultural sector is allocated energy in preference to other sectors. Then, in the supply-constrained and high-tech analyses, we set the amount of energy allocated to agriculture at three levels: (1) 2.5 percent of total domestic energy, (2) 5.0 percent (approximately equal to the current fraction), and (3) 7.5 percent. When energy use is limited, per acre crop production will be restricted unless efficiency can be raised to alleviate the restraint. The high-tech analysis examines the effects of different kinds of efficiency improvement.

Cropland

The current land area in harvested crops is about 350 million acres; we assume that all of this land is receiving fossil energy inputs. In the demand-driven analyses the total cropland base grows as much as necessary to meet production demands. For simplicity, we've assumed that the amount of available cropland is unlimited and that producing a unit of food on this new cropland requires neither more nor less energy than on existing cropland.[4] Under some conditions in the model, though, no amount of energy would be sufficient to grow enough food on existing cropland to meet the demand that is calculated from the yield curve; even assuming technological improvements, the yield curve still flattens at higher levels of energy input. Since raising per-acre energy use will not substantially increase yields in these circumstances, the model will bring more land into production.

However, it is probably unrealistic to add more than 127 million additional acres. The USDA has identified that amount of currently uncultivated land as having "high" or "medium" potential for conversion to active cropland; this is enough to increase the current cropland base by about one-third.[5] Most studies of cropland availability suggest that only 45 to 50 million acres of land are likely to be brought into cultivation.[6] Indeed, erosion and shortages of irrigation water may soon force the removal of some of today's cropland from cultivation, and urbanization will definitely do so. In the supply-constrained and high tech approaches, therefore, we took account of these uncertainties by running the model with three levels of cropland use: (1) 300 million acres, (2) 350 million acres (the current level), and (3) 400 million acres.

Domestic Food Demand

In all three analyses, the "ideal" demand for food is the same, although the ideal may not always be satisfied. Domestic food demand is determined by population size and the total kcal in the average diet. As in our energy model, population growth rates are taken for all analyses from the Census Bureau's middle-of-the-road scenario, which estimates a population of 301 million by 2025. The per capita caloric content of the ideal average diet is also the same in all analyses; based on CARD/USDA studies, we project it to grow from the current 3,500 kcal per person per day (including waste and spoilage) to 3,700 kcal in 2000 and to a high of 3,800 kcal in 2025.[7]

Crop Demand

The amount of crops grown to meet this ideal demand is mostly a function of diet composition, particularly the proportion of animal-based foods, and of exports. About 65 percent of the average diet (in kcal) consists of grains, vegetables, fruits, legumes, and other plant matter, while 20 percent come from red meat, poultry, eggs, dairy products, and fats derived from animals fed on crops.[8] The remaining 15 percent of the diet consists of animal products derived from pasture and rangeland. Hay, alfalfa, and other harvested forage are considered "crops" insofar as energy is expended in pasture improvement and harvest, and the USDA routinely classifies areas devoted to such use as cropland. These percentages are assumed to remain constant throughout the time period in question. Currently, mostly because of the large proportion of beef, crop-fed animal products in the average U.S. diet collectively require a 15.1:1 conversion factor. Based on USDA/CARD projections, by 2000 this ratio drops gradually to 14.2:1 as animals are bred to become more efficient converters.[9] Regarding exports, we adopt current USDA projections, which show a 2.3 percent per year increase (not compounded) until 2000 and a 0.8 percent per year increase thereafter.[10] Under energy and land constraints these export goals (and even the ideal domestic demand) may not be met; the model reports the shortfall.

Technology, Degradation, and the Yield Curve

As noted above, the yield curve determines the amount of crops that can be grown on an average acre from a given amount of energy-based input, at any single time. But the scale and shape of the yield curve changes from year to year because of two opposing forces: technology and resource degradation. Advancing technology has several components, including improved farm management practices, such as better timing of irrigation or selection of fertilizers; improved crop strains from traditional hybridization; or, in the future, better strains from biotechnologies (defined in Chapter 5 as genetic engineering and other novel technologies). Past technological advances have raised the curve (increasing the efficiency with which a unit of fuel is converted to crop output and increasing the maximum amount of food that can be grown on an acre) and shifted it to the right (raising the amount of input energy that must be applied to reach the maximum). Figure 6–2 shows this effect for one major energetic input into farming—nitrogenous fertilizer. In practice, since farmers have generally tried to produce the most food possible on each acre, the amount of input energy used has increased with advancing technology.

At the same time, resource degradation and other sources of inefficiency have tended to pull the curve downward, *decreasing* the amount of food obtained with each unit of fuel. The deterioration of the resource base has decreased technology's effectiveness. For the past several decades technological gains have generally exceeded resource losses. The net result has been rising outputs and lowered food costs. As discussed in Chapter 5, the historic response to increasing per-acre inputs has been increased per-acre yield and decreased energy efficiency (see Figures 5–7 and 2–10). More recently, however, the flattening of the historic per-acre energy yield curve (Figure 6–3) indicates that the overall effects of degradation or poor management have cancelled gains from technological enhancement. Most agricultural experts believe that both technological advances and land degradation will continue; it is their respective future rates that are the subject of debate. We sum up this interplay between technological advancement and land degradation with the term *resource quality*, since together they determine the amount of energy needed to obtain a unit of output— in this case, food.

In the demand-driven and supply-constrained analyses, we use two levels of resource quality. The first, a *moderate resource quality* scenario, is an extrapolation of current estimates of land degradation rates and technological advancement. The second, a *low resource quality* scenario, is based on the assumption that technology will not improve crop output efficiency and that land degradation is more serious than most people believe. Finally, in the *high tech* analysis we examine two types of high resource quality in the context of limited land and energy.

Our appraisal of recent studies sets the rate of yield growth at 1.2 percent per year in the last few years, and we assume that half of this increase is due to efficiency improvements alone,[11] the other half coming from more intense application of inputs. Other agriculture sources expect that the recent slowing of annual increases in efficiency (as discussed in Chapter 5) will continue.[12]

Figure 6–2. Corn Yields in Six States as a Function of Nitrogenous Fertilizer Input, 1950 and 1960

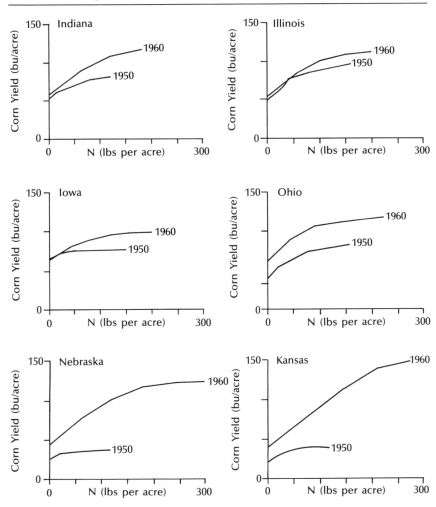

Sources: USDA, *Fertilizer Use and Crop Yields in the United States*, Agriculture Handbook 68 (Washington, D.C.: USGPO, 1954); USDA, *Crop Yield to Fertilizer in the United States*, Statistical Bulletin 431 (Washington, D.C.: USGPO, 1968).

In the moderate resource quality scenario the efficiency gain from technology begins at a rate of 0.6 percent per year and declines continuously to a zero percent gain in 2025: this is what would happen if biotechnology fizzles completely and if conventional

Figure 6–3. Per-Acre Yield versus Energy Input per Acre, 1940 to 1979

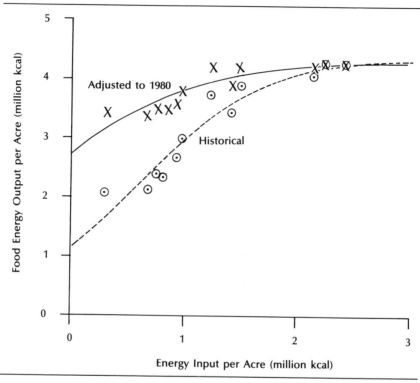

Sources: J.S. Steinhart and C.E. Steinhart, "Energy Use in the U.S. Food System," *Science* 184 (1974): 307–16; U.S. Department of Commerce, Bureau of the Census, *Annual Survey of Manufactures* (Washington, D.C.: USGPO, various years); U.S. Department of Commerce, Bureau of the Census, *1978 Census of Agriculture*, vol. 5: 1979 Farm Energy Survey, Special Reports pt. 9 (Washington, D.C.: USGPO); David Torgerson and Harold Cooper, *Energy and U.S. Agriculture 1974 and 1978*, USDA Statistical Bulletin 632 (Washington, D.C.: USGPO, 1980).

technological improvements continue to become smaller and less frequent. For the lower resource quality scenario we have assumed that only increased energy use will push crop yields higher and that new developments will not raise output without increases in inputs: technological advancements of all kinds come to an abrupt halt. Since the per-acre production of crops would remain close to saturation, increases in overall crop production would necessarily involve the expansion of cropland area. On the other hand, biotechnology may well deliver on at least some of its promises and raise the energy efficiency of farming. In the chapter's final section, we examine two ways in which these advances might be used: (1) alone, with farmers continuing to use high levels of inputs and not attempting to control land degradation, and (2) in conjunction with structural changes in farming, with erosion control and restraints on energy use.

The other half of resource quality, land degradation, may erase some or all of the gains from technology. Most experts agree that erosion is the most serious threat to agricultural productivity, although documentation of its impact on crop yields is not conclusive. USDA/CARD studies project a 15 to 30 percent loss in potential per-acre crop yields between 1980 and 2030 if erosion continues at current rates; others project the loss at 5 to 10 percent.[13] Our moderate resource quality assumption lies in the middle of this range: yields drop by 0.3 percent per year between 1980 and 2025 for a total loss of 14 percent by the end of the simulation. Our low resource quality assumption lies at the extreme end of the range: a 0.6 percent annual loss in yields per acre, for a total yield sacrifice of 27 percent by 2025. In the high tech approach, we examine the effect of a reduction in erosion to a 0.06 percent annual yield loss.

Historical Verification

As we did for the energy model, we tested the demand-driven agricultural model to see how well it could reproduce the historical record of agricultural energy consumption, given food demand and yield curves. (The supply-constrained and high tech analysis use the same equations, but turn them around to calculate food production based on energy use and yield curves.) The assumptions, data, and calculations that will be used to make projections must at least work well enough to use historical data and to be verified against a particular output variable. Figure 6–4 shows the close fit between historical trend in total on-farm energy use from 1940 to 1979 and the trend that the model calculated from data on food production and the yield curve. Figure 6–5 shows the correlation between actual data and the model's estimate of the record for off-farm energy use from 1940 to 1970 (the last year for which there are reliable data). Of course, this bootstrap methodology doesn't prove that our assumptions are correct, but it does demonstrate that the model provides an accurate empirical description of energy use in agriculture.[14]

ENERGY, RESOURCES, AND U.S. AGRICULTURE: 1985–2025

Demand-Driven Analysis

Figure 6–6 projects the effect of unconstrained demand on agriculture's share of the total U.S. energy budget (calculated from

Figure 6–4. Historical Use of Energy On-Farm and the Energy Use Predicted by the Model, 1940 to 1979

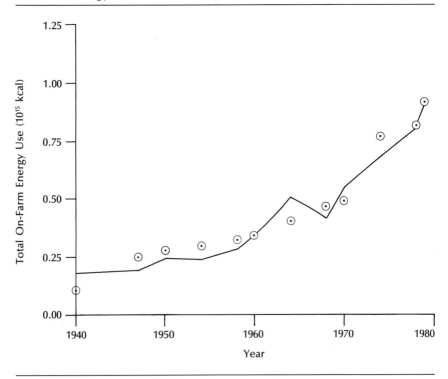

Note: Circles are historical use; solid line is projection.

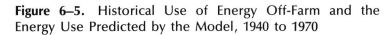

Figure 6–5. Historical Use of Energy Off-Farm and the Energy Use Predicted by the Model, 1940 to 1970

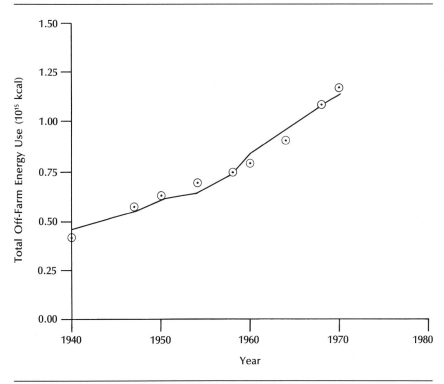

Note: Circles are historical use; solid line is projection. Includes all food processing and commercial refrigeration and cooking, as given in Table 5-2.

Chapter 4's reference projection of fuel supplies), under the moderate resource quality assumptions described above. The on-farm and off-farm shares are calculated separately. From 1985 to 2000 the share of U.S. domestic energy used by agriculture (both on and off the farm) grows from 13 percent to 16 percent, and then to 19 percent by 2025. The fraction used on-farm rises by almost two-thirds, from about 4.7 percent to 7.5 percent by 2025. These are very large increases: at no time in the last forty-five years did on-farm agriculture use even 5 percent of the energy budget. To make matters worse, such increases in agricultural fuel needs would occur at a time when more energy will also be needed to mine fossil fuels. The rest of the economy would suffer accordingly.

Figure 6–6.   The Fraction of the U.S. Energy Budget Used by Agriculture under the Demand-Driven, Moderate Resource Quality Scenario

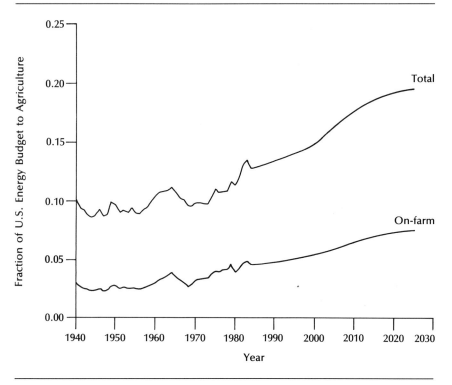

Note: The difference between the total and the on-farm fractions represents the off-farm fraction.

One cause of this growth is increasing demand. Total crop demand rises by 40 percent by 2025 (Figure 6–7). The main source of the rise in domestic demand is illustrated in Figure 6–8. This figure compares the total nonexported crop with the amount used to feed humans directly in the form of bread, vegetables, fruit, and other plant matter. The difference is the amount used as animal feed. Almost all the increase in domestic crop demand is needed to feed animals. Recall that more than 80 percent of crops grown for domestic use goes to supply the 20 percent of the average diet made up of crop-fed animal products. This proportion remains relatively constant even

Figure 6–7. Total or "Ideal" Crop Demand, Including Domestic Consumption and Exports, 1940 to 2025, in Quadrillion kcal

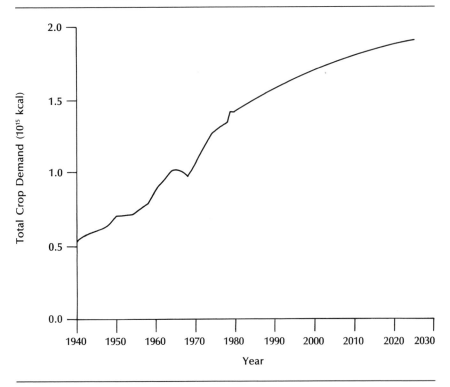

though the conversion efficiency improves. Export demand is projected to rise even more rapidly: it is 48 percent higher than current levels by the year 2000 and 63 percent higher by 2025. This may not seem very realistic, given the generally flat export market of the last few years, but the nation's long-term export policy still calls for major food sales abroad, and our approach here is to take the official forecasts at face value.

The effect of these increases in crop production, under the assumptions of this scenario, would be a consistent decrease in energy efficiency (Figure 6–9). Efficiency declines steadily over time at all stages of food production: raw crops, after animal feeding, and finally after off-farm processing. In the coming decades, meeting the "ideal" demand would require farmers to use considerably more energy: 30 percent more in 2000 and 78

Figure 6–8.   The Domestic Disposition of Crops in Demand-Driven, Moderate Resource Quality Scenario, 1940 to 2025, in Quadrillion kcal

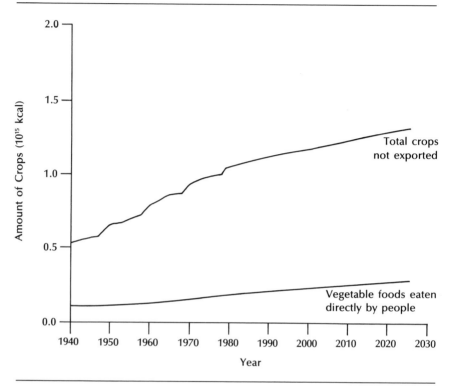

Note: The difference between vegetable foods eaten by people and total crops represents crops used as animal feed.

percent more in 2025 (Figure 6–10). As a result, crop output per acre begins to decline after reaching a peak in 2005. In 2025 per-acre production is only 1 percent higher than current levels. This is largely a result of declining, and eventually negative, returns for each unit of additional energy used on farms. Mounting food demands send per-acre energy use upward at the same time as the cumulative effect of land degradation begins to outweigh the incremental effect of technological improvement (Figure 6–11).

However, it must be remembered that in this first avenue of investigation the system is, by definition, not constrained by

Figure 6–9.   National Agricultural Energy Efficiency in Terms of the Ratio of Food Energy Output to Fuel Energy Input (Including Chemicals and Machinery), in Demand-Driven, Moderate Resource Quality Scenario, 1940 to 2025

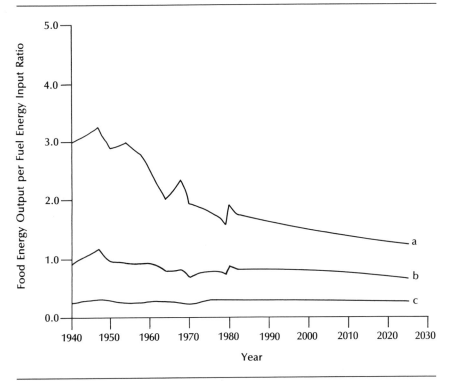

Note: Three levels of food output are considered: (a) raw crops in the field, (b) after crops have been converted to animal products, (c) after food has undergone off-farm processing.

supply. As a consequence, the model allows the cropland base to increase dramatically. By 2000 the model adds approximately 50 million acres of new cropland to the current base of 350 million acres (Figure 6–12), and by 2025, more than three-quarters of all potential cropland is utilized. The new cropland, as explained in note 4 for this chapter, would probably be of lower quality and would require substantially larger than average energy inputs to achieve an average crop yield; but we did not include this effect in the model. We also neglected energy costs due to water depletion, pests, and other nonerosional losses of

Figure 6–10. Absolute Quantity of Energy Used by Agriculture in Demand-Driven, Moderate Resource Quality Scenario, 1940 to 2025 in quadrillion kcal

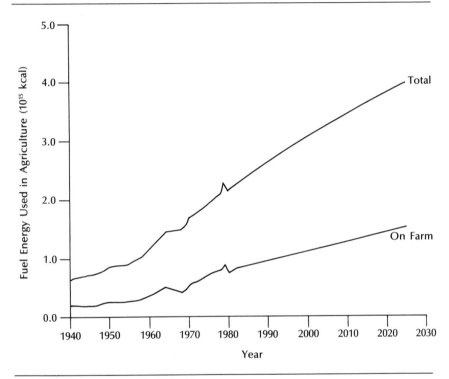

Note: Difference between total and on-farm represents off-farm energy use.

fertility. Thus, bear in mind that the model overestimates the output/input ratio and underestimates its energy needs. Even so, meeting the projected demand for food would require cultivating virtually every patch of reasonably arable land—a very different result from that anticipated by the USDA/CARD estimates—and would be clearly impossible.

If rapid erosion *and* no technological advancement take place simultaneously as demand for food rises—the low resource quality scenario—the amount of energy needed to grow a unit of food would markedly increase. Then even more serious problems would appear. In this scenario (still demand-driven and not supply-constrained), on-farm energy consumption

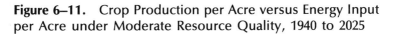

Figure 6–11. Crop Production per Acre versus Energy Input per Acre under Moderate Resource Quality, 1940 to 2025

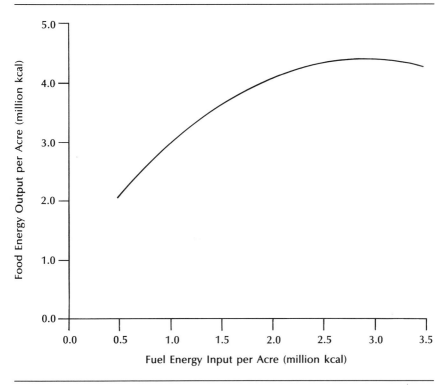

needed to meet demand by the year 2000 is about 20 percent higher than in the moderate resource quality scenario, and it steadily builds to 40 percent more by 2025 (Figure 6–13). Even as early as 2000 on-farm energy use is up 46 percent over today's use. By 2025 on-farm energy use more than doubles its current level, consuming 10 percent of all domestic energy (Figure 6–14). When the off-farm component is included, agriculture in this country would require 22 percent of all domestic energy. About 40 percent more land is also needed under low resource quality than in the moderate resource quality scenario. In fact, a staggering 643 million acres would have to be harvested in 2025 to meet projected demand (Figure 6–15) if the low resource quality scenario comes true—nearly double the amount of land harvested in 1985.

Figure 6–12.   Cropland Area Required to Meet Demand in Demand-Driven, Moderate Resource Quality Scenario, 1940 to 2025

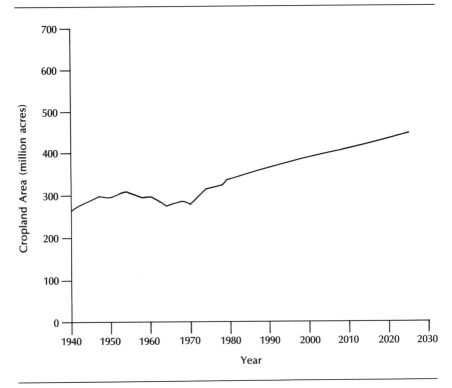

It's clear that, if the future resource quality of agriculture should follow the more pessimistic estimates, U.S. agriculture—indeed, the entire economy—will be in serious trouble. We will need to double the fraction of the nation's fuel budget devoted to on-farm activities (Figure 6–14). In summary, the demand for agricultural production examined in this section seems difficult to achieve unless farmers use much more energy than they do today. This increase in energy use translates into very large increases in agriculture's share of all domestic energy during a period when there will be very severe competition for energy with manufacturing and household sectors. Increased use of energy by agriculture results in consistently lower energy efficiency even while total output rises.

Figure 6–13. Absolute Quantity of Energy Used in Agriculture both, On-Farm and Off-Farm, in the Demand-Driven, Low Resource Quality Scenario, 1940 to 2025, in Quadrillion kcal

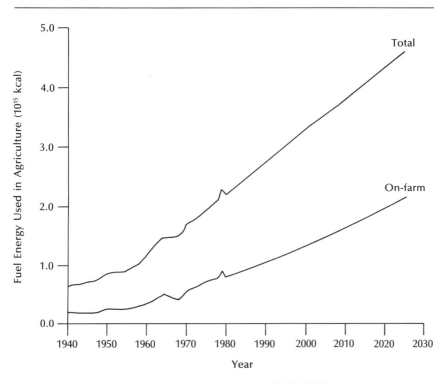

In the past this process translated into relatively low food prices (due to the increased output) but rising production costs (due to rising prices for energy-based inputs); if it continues in the future, the farm sector would face much more difficult economic conditions than today's, which are bad enough. The difference between the prices that farmers receive for their products and the prices they pay for inputs (the parity index, a reflection of farmers' profit margins) has decreased steadily in recent years, with an especially sharp fall during the period of the first oil crisis, from 1973 to 1975. The decrease in parity is a symptom of increasing stress in the farm sector; a healthy agriculture system is not just highly productive, but it must also keep its producers solvent. Farmers' net income in constant dol-

Figure 6–14. The Fraction of the U.S. Energy Budget Used in Agriculture in the Demand-Driven, Low Resource Quality Scenario, 1940 to 2025

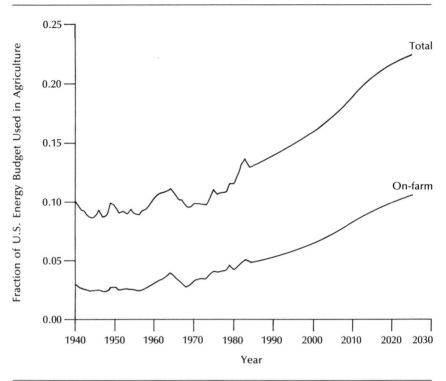

lars has also been dropping. Indeed, one reason that U.S. farmers grow so much food is that they need to maximize their gross income to stay in business. Moreover, declining efficiency doesn't just hurt farmers economically; it can also lead to more rapid land degradation. Some conservation practices pay for themselves in short-term gains, but most are long-term investments, and most use energy and cost money. When faced with rising production costs and the need to produce more food and hence more income, farmers will be pressured by economic factors beyond their direct control to put off implementation of conservation practices.

It is reasonable to conclude that agriculture will soon be in a period of transition, that demand projections can be met only

Figure 6–15. Cropland Area Required in the Demand-Driven, Low Resource Quality Scenario

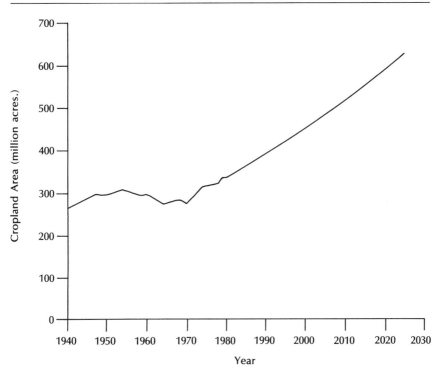

with a massive infusion of energy and new land. But what would happen if the amount of available energy were limited because of constraints like rising energy prices? What would occur if the cropland base were to be limited or reduced by poor quality, urban sprawl, and other factors? To what degree can conservation and other adjustments to limits on land and energy help ease these constraints? We explore these questions in the next two sections.

Supply-Constrained Analysis

The U.S. agricultural system depends heavily on energy, especially in the form of natural gas and petroleum; in fact, much cropland today could not be farmed at all without the use of fossil energy. Agriculture uses energy for three basic purposes: (1) to increase crop production, (2) to replace human labor, and (3) to reduce the variability of crop production and the risk of crop failure. It is obvious that changes in the supply of energy to agriculture will, over time, alter crop production. Many studies since the oil embargo of 1973 have suggested that energy supply constraints and energy price increases would have serious effects on agricultural output. For instance, commercial nitrogenous fertilizer use would be reduced, and some areas would be taken out of grain production and placed into fallow. Likewise, a reduction in the use of energy for irrigation, crop drying, frost control, pest control, and other means of buffering agriculture from the variabilities of nature would result in increased crop failure and crop loss.[15] Given this, and the results of the demand-driven analysis, it is important to understand the implications of land and energy constraints for agriculture.

In the previous scenarios, we allowed the amount of land to increase as needed to meet food demand. But there are obviously some restraints on the amount of land available for farming: much of the land considered "potential cropland" by the USDA is already used to graze animals, is in forests or other uses, and/or would be bad for growing crops. It would be very expensive, in terms of fertilizers, irrigation, and so forth, to turn much of it into active cropland. Moreover, some cropland has been and will continue to be lost permanently to urban development. The rate of urbanization has slowed from its peak in the 1950s and 1960s but will continue to be a factor of some importance in the future.[16]

In the demand-driven analysis, domestic and export food demand were calculated first, and then the model determined how much land and energy would be needed to meet that demand. For this part of our analysis we calculated the amount of food produced at several levels of constraints on land and energy utilization, described in the "Data and Assumptions" section. First we restrict the cropland base alone; then energy alone; and, finally, both land and energy. All of these calculations are conducted with yield curves reflecting both low and moderate resource quality.

Figure 6–16 shows how much food can be produced at two future dates, 2000 and 2025, at three different levels of land use using moderate resource quality (top) and low resource quality (bottom), and compares the resulting crop production to the projected "ideal" demand. This demand target is shown in Figure 6–16 as solid horizontal lines representing domestic and total crop demand, the difference being exports. In these scenarios, energy use is allowed to rise until every acre is "saturated" with inputs— that is, until additional inputs produce essentially no additional crop output.[17] A shortfall in meeting the demand target indicates either that export capacity would have to be reduced, domestic demand and eating habits would have to be adjusted, or both. Nonetheless, in the case of the low resource quality situation neither domestic nor export demand could be met in 2025.

The effect of reduced energy consumption with low or moderate resource quality is a significant erosion of production capacity (Figure 6–17). In the year 2000 a farming system with a low resource quality could not meet demand using 5.0 percent of the nation's fuel, approximately the same fraction allocated currently. By 2025 export capacity disappears under low resource quality conditions, regardless of energy supply. At moderate resource quality, however, the system meets or almost meets production targets except when energy use is fixed at 2.5 percent.

When constraints are applied to both land and energy, the situation naturally becomes worse. We assumed that cropland area would remain at its current level of 350 million acres, and then ran the model with the three different levels of on-farm energy use employed previously, again under both moderate and low resource quality. Figure 6-18 shows the effects of these constraints on crop production at the turn of the century and in 2025. Simply stated, export targets become unattainable. With low resource quality, an added problem emerges: the 350-million-acre cropland base is barely adequate to meet domestic demand in 2000, even with 7.5 percent of the nation's fuel, and by 2025 a domestic shortage occurs. Our model also indicates that it is senseless to attempt to solve the problem by throwing energy at it: with saturating yield curves and a fixed land base, only so much food can be produced. Under these conditions, food pricing and dietary adjustments are inescapable.

Figure 6–16. Crop Production Given Various Limits to Cropland Area, under Moderate and Low Resource Quality Conditions, 2000 and 2025, in Quadrillion kcal

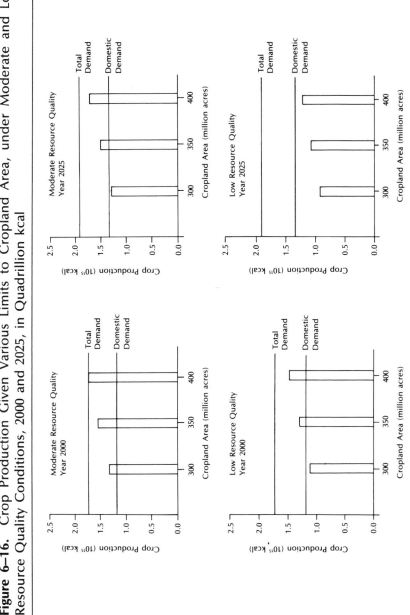

Note: Current cropland base is 350 million acres. The "ideal" demand targets are indicated by the horizontal lines.

Figure 6-17. Crop Production When On-Farm Fuel Use Is Capped At Various Levels, under Moderate and Low Resource Quality Conditions, 2000 and 2025, in Quadrillion kcal

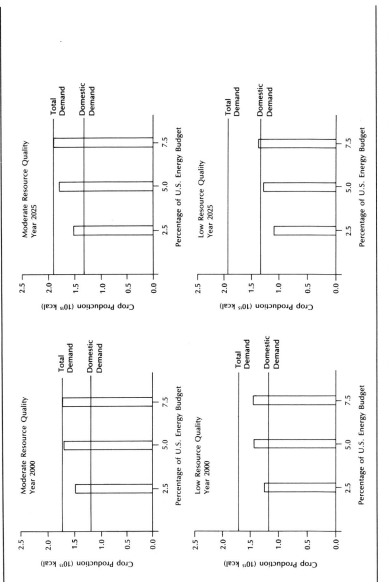

Note: Current on-farm fuel use is about 4.7 percent of U.S. fuel consumption. The demand targets are indicated by the horizontal lines.

Figure 6–18. Crop Production When Cropland Area Is Limited to 350 Million Acres and On-Farm Energy Use Is Capped at Various Levels, 2000 and 2025, in Quadrillion kcal

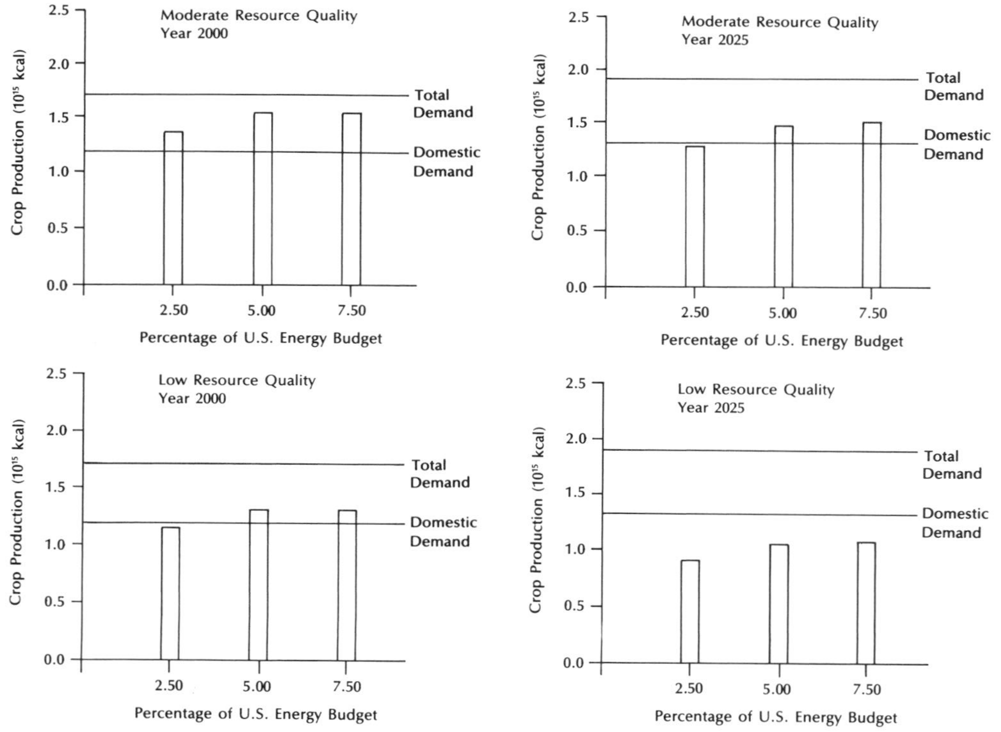

Note: The demand targets are indicated by the horizontal lines.

Figures 6–16 to 6–18 show essentially two snapshots in time (the years 2000 and 2025), and although they represent important milestones in the long-term trend, they don't tell the entire story. When exactly does export capacity fail to meet targeted goals, for instance? Consider a quite possible case in which we use the current proportion of total U.S. energy consumption on-farm (5 percent) and the current cropland base (350 million acres) along with a low resource quality condition. We would lose all export capacity by the year 2007 (Figure 6–19). With moderate resource quality we would experience a less severe decline in export capacity, although export capacity still falls off markedly by 2025. Under these conditions drastic economic decisions would await us.

If the average citizen's eating habits and agriculture's share of energy do not change, it is unlikely that export goals could be met without an additional bonus from an unforeseen technological breakthrough. When, in the 1970s, the USDA launched a program to encourage export production, the message was that "exports are good for all Americans," and the policy was to "plant fencerow to fencerow." In recent years this policy has been in eclipse, as the hoped-for markets failed to develop. Some of the USDA's latest data indicate that the quantity of exports has now begun to fall. From our analysis, we see that in addition to such market forces, resource scarcities may have equal or greater impact in restricting the United States' once-heralded surplus capacity in the future.

In summary, the demand-driven and supply-constrained analyses show that, if the expected big increases in crop-growing efficiency fail to materialize, farmers will have to draw a good deal more energy and land to meet production goals. On the other hand, any restriction in the availability of energy or land will place severe burdens on agriculture in the United States: increased efficiency (or changed diets) would become *absolutely necessary* to maintain an export capacity through 2025.

"High Tech" Analysis

To compensate for detrimental trends, the agricultural sector will have to choose between diminished productivity and struc-

Figure 6–19. Export Capacity with Cropland Area Held at 350 Million Acres, On-Farm Energy Use at 5 Percent of the U.S. Fuel Budget, and Both Low and Moderate Resource Quality, 1940 to 2025, and USDA Projected Target

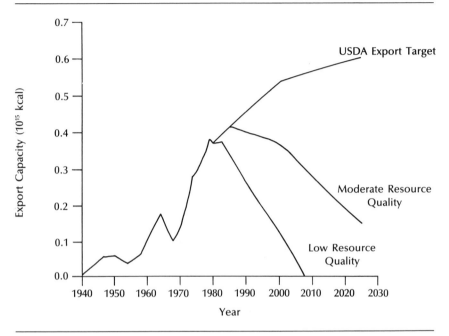

tural changes within the farming system. We have already demonstrated the consequences of pursuing the first strategy. It's reasonable to suppose that the agricultural establishment will try to guide U.S. farming away from the unpleasant course described by the previous scenarios.

U.S. agriculture developed in response to a series of resource constraints—first on available labor, then on land, and now on energy. Technology has been used to remove constraints in the past, and many will argue that it will be pivotal in removing constraints in the future. If this is true, there are two ways in which technology could be used to help farmers avoid the problems caused by resource constraints: (1) a "hard path," in which innovation would be channeled strictly into maximizing yields while leaving alone the current custom of applying lots of energy-based inputs, and (2) a "soft path," in which farmers adopt different goals as well as different cropping methods. This final step in our agricultural analysis investigates how technology and efficiency gains can be applied to move farming toward a more sustainable future.

By elevating the level at which saturation occurs on per-acre yield curves, yield-enhancing technologies provide a tempting opportunity for farmers to continue on the path of energy intensification. Genetic improvements through hybridization have accounted for about half of the total increase in yields for our major crops since the 1940s, and many experts expect the emerging field of biotechnology to increase yields at a rate rivaling that of the past.[18] The introduction of "more efficient" crop strains, whether through biotechnology or anything else, will not *by itself* increase the energy efficiency of agriculture; it certainly hasn't in the past. If improved strains are the only adjustment, they will encourage higher production from each acre and even higher use of inputs, since there is no reason to believe that such improvements would change the shape of the yield curve.

Besides, a whole suite of other forces, such as economic structures and institutional inertia, discourage farmers from modifying current energy input practices. For example, direct fuel purchases remain a relatively minor portion (10 to 15 percent) of farm costs, subduing farmers' sensitivity to rising fuel prices. One CARD study estimates that a quadrupling of fuel prices would reduce on-farm direct fuel use by a mere 5 percent.[19] Another mechanism discouraging energy conservation is national policy, reflected in legislation such as the Emergency Petroleum Allocation Act of 1977 and the National Gas Policy Act of 1978. These laws ensure that farmers will obtain all the oil and gas they need in times of shortage, thereby removing one more incentive to lessen dependence on fuel. Still another impediment to less intensive agriculture is the obvious reluctance of commercial farm suppliers, who are major information sources to farmers,[20] to advocate input-reducing farming techniques. Furthermore, the recent decline in public funding for agricultural research makes it difficult to implement a radical and widespread departure from current patterns of energy use. Recent economic conditions have forced farmers to seek high yields in the hope of overcoming their enormous debt burden.

But this deepens their commitment to intensification. Thus, there are powerful forces at work to promote the hard path to increased efficiency, defined as raising the efficiency of crop strains while making no other changes in the farming system.

On the other hand, we can imagine that the coming period of energy scarcity may encourage new rules of behavior, transforming current industrial farming into a far more efficient endeavor. Because of their versatility, oil and natural gas have become particularly valuable inputs to industrial agriculture. The basic structure of industrial farming requires mobile fuels and fertilizers; adequate substitutes (both in quantity and utility) for them do not now exist. As oil and gas run out, the impact will fall especially hard on farmers. Legislation may insulate farmers against oil embargoes, but they're still vulnerable to rising prices insofar as they raise the price of all inputs. Another incentive for farmers to conserve energy is their poor financial situation, which paradoxically is the very factor that now forces farmers to intensify their cropping techniques. Farmers who are willing to take slight losses in crop yield, simply by cutting back on fertilizers and pesticides, can compensate the reduction in gross income through even greater reductions in their costs. Widespread adoption of such strategies would simultaneously increase the energy efficiency of production and reduce the chronic surpluses that constitute much of the "farm problem." Farmers might also, if the proper data can be obtained, cut costs without sacrificing income through the wise use of on-farm information resources such as computerized crop management systems and access to large data banks. The cost of computer-aided farming should continue to decline relative to the costs of physical resources, and so foster its acceptance within the farming community. Finally, erosion is of great concern to policymakers, the public, and farmers alike and will likely evoke a series of control measures. By their very nature, erosion control practices maintain and enhance long-term yields, and for this reason they will increase the energy-efficiency of farming. That is, they will if this yield enhancement can be achieved at stable or decreasing energy consumption rates. The soft path, then, includes these sorts of modifications in farming practices in conjunction with continued improvement in crop strains.

In our simulation of these uses of improved technology, both the hard and the soft paths benefit by a 1.1 percent yearly gain in real energetic crop efficiency. The hard path is unrestricted in its per-acre energy application rate. However, it continues along at the 0.6 percent annual land degradation rate of the earlier scenarios. In contrast, the soft path reduces the land degradation potential to one-tenth the level of the hard path. In addition, the soft path scenario is forced to sacrifice crop yields by a total of 12 percent by year 2000, which should reduce energy use even more substantially.[21]

The analysis shows striking differences between the two approaches. Figure 6–20 depicts total U.S. crop production as a result of four contrasting scenarios. It first demonstrates the wide disparity between the USDA target and the supply-constrained condition with low resource quality, energy capped at 5.0 percent of total consumption, and land limited to 350 mil-

Figure 6–20. Crop Production under Three Contrasting Assumptions Regarding Resource Quality and Technology , and USDA Projected Target, 1940 to 2025, in Quadrillion kcal

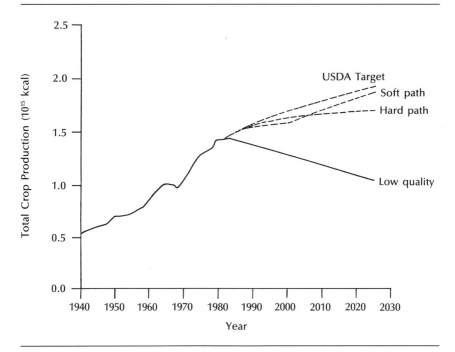

lion acres. The chart also shows, interestingly, that although neither the soft- nor the hard-path strategy hits the demand targets, they at least reverse the troublesome trend depicted for the supply-limited, low resource quality condition.

But viewing total production hides important dynamics. Figure 6–21 shows how the more sensitive export capacity might be affected by the two strategies. From 1985 through 2005 there appears to be relatively little difference between the two approaches, with the hard path doing slightly better. After this twenty-five-year readjustment period, however, the soft path resumes expansion in export potential, while the hard path falters and declines. The reason for this is that the soft path's sacrifices in yield cause its energy efficiency to rise by 2000 to a level similar to that of the 1950s (Figure 6–22). In contrast, the efficiency of the hard path continually declines despite liberal gains in technology. As expected, improved crop strains unac-

Figure 6–21. Export Capacity under Three Contrasting Assumptions Regarding Resource Quality and Technology, and USDA Projected Target, 1940 to 2025, in Quadrillion kcal

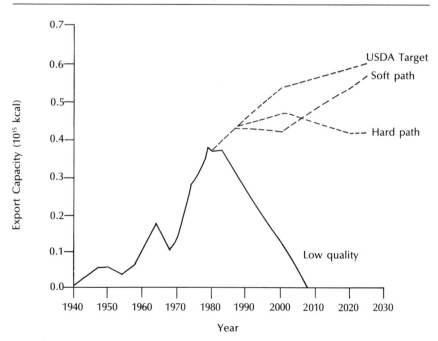

companied by structural changes in farming practices solve nothing. Moreover, the increasing inefficiency translates into increased overall fossil energy use. By shortly after the turn of the century, the hard path runs into the 5 percent cap on energy use. For roughly the same level of total crop output, the soft path uses about 50 percent less fuel than the hard path. Soft-path agriculture would be using only 2.7 percent of total U.S. energy use in 2025.

This analysis demonstrates that a policy that hopes to mask the effects of degraded resources and unfavorable economics simply through genetic improvement of crops is probably doomed to failure. In the context of energy scarcity, the soft path is clearly more sustainable.

Figure 6–22. National On-Farm Ratio of Food Energy Output to Fuel Energy Input under Three Contrasting Assumptions Regarding Resouce Quality and Technology, 1940 to 2025

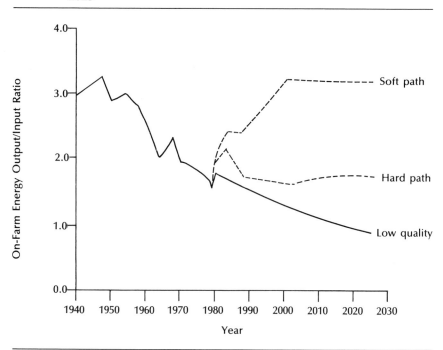

CONCLUSION

Are current trends sustainable? Of course, the answer depends on what one defines as "current trends." To the average person, the most important trends are a large diet that includes a lot of animal products; a large export capacity to help the nation's trade balance; and stability in the size of the cropland base, in the portion of the nation's fuel used in agriculture, and in the organization of the off-farm sector. The analysis described in this chapter indicates that all these trends can be sustained simultaneously only under very special and unlikely circumstances. The United States can maintain these trends through 2025 only if it can both achieve a high rate of growth in technologically based improvements in on-farm efficiency and also avoid most of the negative effects of land degradation. Both of these circumstances involve the reversal of significant agricultural trends. When one thinks about the probabilities of such good luck, the most reasonable judgment is that current trends are *not* sustainable and that either the agricultural system or the rest of the economy will, starting soon, enter a painful period of adjustment to resource scarcities. Indeed, the United States will have to work hard just to avoid becoming a net food importer over the next forty years. As suggested at the beginning of Chapter 5, the loss of a U.S. food export capacity would be a global as well as a national catastrophe.

Moreover, a shrinking per capita fuel supply, and an even more rapidly shrinking supply of oil and gas, puts much heavier pressure on the nation's farmers than our highly aggregated analysis has suggested. Nitrogenous fertilizers are made almost exclusively with natural gas; crop drying is done primarily with liquid propane gas; and tractor fuels, herbicides, and insecticides are all petroleum products. If the nation's farms had to use the same mix of fuels as they do today, according to the reference scenario's projection of on-farm energy needs, about 10 percent of all oil and 60 percent of all natural gas consumed in the United States would have to be used on-farm by 2025. Coal, on the other hand, is currently almost useless in agriculture— and coal is widely viewed as the most likely successor to oil and gas. Of course, technological changes could allow coal to replace oil and gas for some uses, and synthetic fuels could replace them entirely. Nevertheless, it's clear that if farmers' needs differ markedly from the rest of the economy's, and if an energy infrastructure must be designed to accommodate farmers special needs, it will place an added and unprecedented burden on the whole economy. It also should force the agricultural research establishment to shift its emphasis from boosting crop yields to finding ways to reduce oil and gas needs. In the past, agricultural research allowed farmers to raise their productivity dramatically; in the future, research efforts may increasingly have to be aimed at keeping farmers' heads above water.

Our analysis also indicates that future research efforts might best be aimed at alleviating the most worrisome effects of land degradation. Only the paucity of good data prevented us from treating any degradational effect besides erosion. In the long run, the side effects of industrial agriculture may be the most significant threats to the system's and our society's sustainability. The fact that we can't say for certain should serve to heighten, not lessen, concern about this issue.

7 CHOICES AND TRADEOFFS

If you do not think about the future, you cannot have one.
—John Galsworthy

No longer can the United States have a growing population *and* a growing average material living standard *and* food surpluses *and* the assurance that future generations can have a material living standard like ours. Until recently we had (and thought we could always have) all of them; now we must decide which to forgo. The choices are hard: Do we want to make the inevitable switch to renewable energy sources now or postpone it by replacing oil and gas with other nonrenewable but familiar-looking fuels? Would we rather use fuels in the household or in producing nonfuel goods and services? Do we wish to discourage or encourage childbearing or aggressively control immigration? Are a high average wage and low employment preferable to low wages and high employment? Would we prefer to reduce agricultural energy use by cutting surplus production or by striving for technological solutions?

Furthermore, these economic questions bear on two other, more profound issues: to what extent is the current generation morally obliged to leave resources to succeeding generations, and how should our society treat the unequal distribution of material wealth, nationally and internationally? One cannot take a stand on, for example, which kinds of fuels to use in the future without also taking one on these moral issues, too. This

217

chapter will describe some strategies available to implement these choices, and the costs and benefits and value judgments underlying each strategy.

It is natural to view the existing economic structure as neutral to these choices, as simply part of the landscape. But it is not neutral at all: today's market was constructed over centuries to encourage the consumption of apparently inexhaustible resources. For instance, extractive industries get depletion allowances, tax breaks that lower the cost of using up their deposits of natural resources. If society's best interests now lie in conserving resources, then the existing market works *against* those interests. In that case, those structures that encourage the consumption of resources need to be altered or removed. Leaving the system alone, making no changes in the way we do business or in government policies, is to make a choice—a choice to use resources as rapidly as possible, a choice to perpetuate the present distribution of wealth.

SOCIAL EQUITY AND THE SHRINKING PIE

The dilemmas described in this chapter are relatively new for the United States. So long as high-quality resources were abundant, we didn't have to choose between household fuels and other goods, or between population growth and individual affluence, or between high productivity and high employment, or even between present and future consumption. In all cases, we assumed that economic growth would allow us to have both.

But soon—in ten or fifteen years—we'll be facing a long period of decline in per capita material wealth. This is something that the United States has never before experienced. The implications of such a reversal of history go well beyond the economic sphere and threaten the nation's basic social and political fabric.

A stagnant or shrinking economy will have a major effect on society's expectations. With few exceptions, each generation in the United States has become materially better off than the preceding one. This pattern of increasing wealth has become an indelible part of the American Dream; a higher standard of living than our parents is practically a birthright. These expectations are the standard against which actual performance is judged. During times of failed expectations, a society is especially vulnerable to a person or philosophy promising to restore it to its former glory. The fall of Weimar Germany is probably the best example. It is important for everyone to understand that many of our economic problems stem from a deteriorating supply of fuels and other resources—which may be equivalent to stating that our economy has matured—and that the clock may not be turned back. Society needs to adjust its expectations and strategies.

Moreover, certain issues that have been swept under a rug— a rug labeled "Economic Growth"—will have to be faced squarely. The United States has done little specifically about unequal distribution of income and economic opportunity; rather, we have relied on general economic growth to better the lot of the poor. With a growing economic pie, the poor have been told, everyone can have a larger slice. Thus far, we have managed to appease most disadvantaged groups with this promise. But when the pie stops growing and the number of hungry mouths does not, the disadvantaged will make increasingly strident demands for social justice, demands that will have to be answered.

Thus, the declining resource base will not only force us to choose between economic alternatives; it will also make us address issues of social equity head on and make yea-or-nay decisions. Perhaps this necessity will give us the courage to achieve real justice.

FUTURE FUEL SOURCES: THE HARD VERSUS THE SOFT PATH

According to the most respected estimates of petroleum resources, the United States has already exhausted two-thirds of all the domestic oil and gas it will ever produce. Production of these fossil fuels has been declining since 1971, and so have their energy profit ratios: the energy profit ratio of domestic oil and gas fell from 22 in 1967 to 8 in 1982 (the latest year for which data exist), and the energy profit ratio of imported oil dropped from 23 in 1971 to 6 in 1981. Domestic exploration for new oil and gas for use as fuel (as opposed to chemical feedstocks) will become fruitless within twenty years.

Two alternatives have been proposed to replace oil and gas—the solid coal, synthetic liquid and gaseous fuels, and nuclear power that make up the hard path, and the renewable solar-based fuels and conservation of the soft path. The two paths seem nearly equivalent in the effect they would have on near-term economic production. The advantages of the soft path are not evident until after 2020. Their energy profit ratios are now about the same (Table 2–2), and they could be developed at about the same rate. But there are differences between the two paths that involve the moral issues of social equity and present versus future consumption.

For instance, hard-path fuels are physically and functionally similar to oil and gas, while most soft-path fuels are not. Consequently, a wholehearted commitment to the soft path would also entail an expensive up-front restructuring of the economy. Take transportation, for example. Our fleet of cars, buses, trucks, trains, ships, and airplanes is almost entirely dependent on gasoline and diesel fuel. To convert it to the soft path we would have to start over almost from scratch, drastically reducing the need for transportation and developing a vehicle fleet that uses soft-path fuels like solar or hydroelectricity (or hydrogen electrolyzed from water) and an ability to service it. We could try to use alcohol or other renewable liquid fuels, but the energy profit ratio of alcohol isn't much greater than 1, and we would have to convert much agricultural land to biomass production.

This sort of restructuring would consume resources that could otherwise be used both now and in the future to create goods and services. Even when soft-path fuels are similar to existing ones, there are problems: windmill and photovoltaic electricity, for example, is generated on a schedule that is only as predictable as the weather. It would be difficult to satisfy electrical demand entirely from soft-path technologies.[1]

The hard path presents a different set of problems. The huge expense associated with individual synthetic fuel facilities and nuclear power plants requires that they be owned by large corporations and/or the federal government. Although this is consistent with current patterns of ownership—only fifteen companies accounted for two-thirds of the nation's production of crude oil in 1980[2]—this highly centralized system places the responsibility for making policy decisions in the hands of a small group of owners and managers. And the hard path's centralization leaves it vulnerable to disruption by saboteurs and terrorists, as Amory Lovins and others have pointed out.[3] Successful attacks could create economic chaos and actual physical destruction. For example, plutonium need not be made into a bomb to be deadly: a person carrying ten billionths of an ounce of plutonium dust in his or her lungs has a one out of eight chance of getting lung cancer.[4] A hundred pounds of plutonium dust dumped from an airplane could cause thousands of deaths. Essential parts of a synfuel- and nuclear-based energy system would have to be heavily guarded. People seeking jobs in them would have to undergo exhaustive security checks. The hard path could therefore erode the privacy rights and freedom of travel that we now take for granted.[5] The dispersed nature of the soft path renders it practically immune to these problems.

There is yet another big difference between the hard and soft paths. The hard path is nonrenewable, while the soft path can yield essentially unending energy. As the coal, oil shale, and uranium of the hard path run out, the United States will have to make yet another transition: to fusion, solar, or perhaps something entirely different. This may not occur for another hundred years or more, but we can predict a few aspects of that transition with confidence. The energy profit ratio of hard-path fuels is already much lower than that of oil and gas today, and it will keep falling as the best deposits of coal, oil shale, and uranium are used up. A decision to follow the hard path, therefore, condemns people in the future to a more painful transition than the one we face now.

Finally, although the soft path would not be entirely pollution-free, the hard path would be far more disruptive. The problems with coal—whether in solid, liquid, or gaseous form—are legion and include every step of the process from mining to disposal of combustion wastes. These problems are not insoluble, but the solutions reduce the energy profit ratio. The same is true for oil shale and nuclear technologies.

The net effect of the hard path, then, is to sacrifice goods and services (and some measure of personal happiness) in the future in exchange for more goods and services in the short term. Following the soft path means sacrificing some goods and services now to make things easier in the future. The soft path would also greatly decentralize the ownership and control of energy sources, putting greater power, as well as greater responsibility, in the hands of consumers.

In addition to these choices, there is one objective criterion for judging various fuel sources: their energy profit ratios. As this book has argued repeatedly, net energy is a more relevant indicator of fuel supplies than gross energy: net energy is what we use to heat our homes, power our cars, and run our factories. We shouldn't throw energy away by investing it blindly in low-quality fuel sources if better alternatives are available. The energy profit ratio is therefore a vital consideration in choosing the next generation of fuels.

In fact, an existing federal law, P.L. 93-577, codifies this principle with regard to federal support for new energy sources: "The potential for production of net energy by the proposed technology at the stage of commercial application shall be analyzed and considered in evaluating proposals." Since the government directly or indirectly supports much of the energy research and development in the United States, this law could be a significant guard against the waste of energy resources.

Unfortunately, the government is not heeding its own advice. The government's auditor, the General Accounting Office, reports that the Department of Energy "has not made much use of net energy analysis as an aid in overall planning of this nation's energy R&D efforts or in evaluating and assigning relative priorities to proposed R&D."[6] Clearly we can't predict at the point of initial research which fuels will have the highest energy profit ratios, but if we follow the progress of energy profit ratios during research, we can use that information to decide whether to stop or to intensify development of a potential fuel source. For example, the energy profit ratio for photovoltaic cells has risen dramatically in the past decade, with further increases likely,[7] which should make photovoltaics a prime target for research money. On the other hand, nonrenewable fuels by definition will have falling energy profit ratios; concentration of research money on these fuels is therefore questionable.

The U.S. nuclear industry is a sobering example of what can happen when energy profit ratios are ignored altogether. It now appears that the United States will be lucky if the nuclear industry eventually produces as much energy as it has consumed. Although individual plants have an energy profit ratio of approximately 4, the energy profit ratio of the whole industry is lowered by two additional energy investments: federal subsidies, which aren't included in the energy (or dollar) investment in individual plants, and the energy invested in the 22 unfinished nuclear plants that have been cancelled.[8] When these costs are included, the energy profit ratio of nuclear power turns out to be no greater than 3.4 over the lifetime of all plants now on line and under construction,[9] which is much lower than that of many fuels the United States could have exploited with far less controversy. And this estimate doesn't include the substantial (and probably monumental) energy costs associated with decommissioning or permanent waste storage. Of course, the experts could not have foreseen all the problems that ultimately beset the nuclear industry, but to a great extent the experts allowed themselves to be swept along by the general euphoria of the Atomic Age. Confident of their ability to overcome all problems with the new technology, policymakers simply *knew* that nuclear power would ultimately be "too cheap to meter." Thus, the United States needs to scrutinize proposed alternatives far more closely than it did nuclear power. Energy profit ratios, and how we expect them to change in the future, are an indispensable tool in that scrutiny. It is especially vital that the energy costs associated with government subsidies, pollution, environmental degradation, and other "externalities" be included in the calculation of energy profit ratios.

But it is not enough to know the advantages and disadvantages of potential alternative fuels; we also need to know whether the existing market system will lead to timely decisions to invest in alternative fuels. Many observers point to the increasing importance of wood, wind, and other nonfossil fuels as an indication that the market is already making the transition away from oil and gas. Perhaps all we need to do is let the existing market handle the transition without interference. But a decision to give full rein to the existing market should be made carefully, for the stakes are high.

Since none of the hard-path or soft-path fuels (except for solid coal and small-site hydro) has an energy profit ratio as great as oil and gas, the aggregate energy profit ratio of the nation's fuel mix is bound to drop. The only way to keep net energy production from falling as rapidly as energy profit ratios is to develop more fuel sources and obtain more gross energy. However, there is a long lag between the expenditure of energy on capital and the flow of energy from the new source: fourteen years may intervene between the decision to build a nuclear fission plant and its commissioning, and the schedule for building synthetic fuel facilities is even longer. Thus, the decision to invest needs to be made well before the need for new sources becomes tangible.

In the case of the United States, this decision must be made very soon. Increasing production from Alaskan oil fields has partially masked the decline in production from the lower forty-eight states. But Alaskan production is expected to peak in 1986 or 1987; the already-declining total U.S. production will then fall off sharply. If we wait to begin developing alternatives until we actually feel the pinch from this decline, the lag between investment and fresh fuel supplies will prolong and deepen the necessary cuts in consumer goods and services.

This lag effect can be demonstrated starkly with the aid of our model. At the end of Chapter 2, when we used it to examine some of the effects of falling energy profit ratios, it showed that the economy could not obtain a constant level of net energy, no matter how much gross energy was available. This model made the unrealistically optimistic assumption that society invested in new fuel sources the instant that fuel quality began to decline and that that investment began to yield energy within a year. If we impose the slightly more realistic assumption that five years elapse between the initial investment and first flow of new energy, a different picture emerges. If we start investing in capital five years before energy profit ratios decline, the energy available for producing consumer goods is squeezed slightly at first (Figure 7–1). But if the investment doesn't begin until fuel quality actually drops, the total loss of energy available for producing consumer goods is enormously larger (although the drop is postponed by five years) (Figure 7–1). Thus, the lag between investment and fuel flow presents the United States with a choice: a small sacrifice of net energy now, or a much larger sacrifice in the future.[10]

If we want to minimize the trauma associated with declining fuel quality, then investment in alternative fuels should begin well before society actually needs them. But in the real world such farsighted investment is rare. The return on investments is usually spread out into the future, and the present value of a dollar expected to be earned ten years from now is much lower

Figure 7–1. Comparison of Net Energy Production If Society Invests in Fuel-Producing Systems before Fuel Quality Declines versus Investing When Fuel Quality Actually Starts Declining

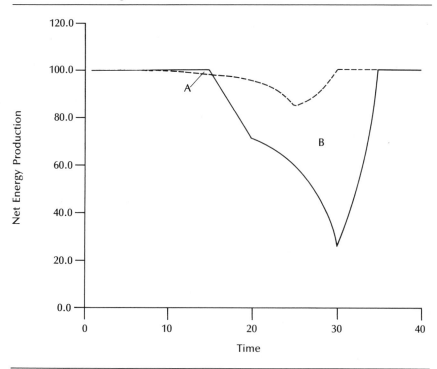

Note: Dotted line is production if investment begins before decline; solid line is production if investment begins during decline. In the short run, society loses some net energy (area A) if it invests early but avoids a much larger loss (area B) soon after.

than that of a dollar in hand today. There are a number of reasons why. For one thing, people (both as individuals and as corporations) need money today, since some expenses can't be put off. Moreover, promises are not always kept. This ineradicable uncertainty reduces the present value of dollars promised in the future—and not even the bravest economist would claim certainty about the future trajectory of fuel prices. The recent behavior of fuel prices has been so erratic that even short-term forecasts have looked foolish. Neither the sudden jumps in oil prices in 1973–74 and 1979–80 nor the recession–induced price slide in 1982–85 was anticipated. Some analysts have speculated that OPEC has acted shrewdly and deliberately in causing price oscillations. Each of its major price hikes was followed by a smaller reduction, allaying much of the hysteria bred by the sudden price rises and, more important, discouraging investment that might have reduced U.S. dependence on oil.

Adding to this uncertainty is the history and future possibility of government price controls on energy. The federal government officially controlled the price of oil from 1971 to 1981, and it still sets prices for some natural gas. These controls have kept fuel prices low and have discouraged development of alternative fuels. Although the current climate in Washington favors deregulation, it is far from clear that this sentiment will prevail for the next forty years as various parts of society feel the squeeze from declining energy supplies.

Yet another discouragement to timely investment in alternative energy sources has been the real interest rate—the difference between the nominal interest rate and the rate of inflation—which has been unprecedentedly high during the last four years (almost 8 percent in 1982). High interest rates raise the cost of capital purchases directly, since usually the money must be borrowed. Moreover, as interest rates climb, some investments in capital equipment will look increasingly unattractive when compared to other, safer investments like Treasury bills. Uncertainty about future fuel prices makes government securities even more attractive.

In short, because of high interest rates and uncertain returns on fuel-related capital investment, the market is not likely to make a timely response to dwindling supplies of oil and gas. The necessary incentives are just not there. To avert the problems that a delay would cause, then, some government pump-priming is in order. The government doesn't necessarily have better foresight capability than private businesses (it may in fact be worse), but the government is uniquely capable of changing the rules of the economic game to make long-term investments in energy systems economically justifiable for private firms.

For example, the federal government could help develop alternative energy sources by offering tax credits or low-interest loans. Such assistance could be awarded for the construction and installation of energy-producing or energy-saving devices that met certain criteria, not the least of which should be the energy profit ratio. The loans or credits would reduce the capital costs of projects and encourage people to purchase insulation or solar water heaters that consumers would otherwise see as "bad" investments. Such programs are already in effect, but on a very limited scale: the Solar Energy and Energy Conservation Bank was set up in 1979 to subsidize research into renewable fuels and the installation of certain fuel-producing and fuel-conserving devices, only to have its budget slashed by the Reagan administration. Also, corporations doing research and development on various synthetic fuels are eligible for loans from the government-owned Synthetic Fuels Corporation (SFC). To be effective, however, such programs must have enough money behind them for everyone to participate—which the Solar Bank did not—and need to be directed at the best long-term energy investments—which the SFC was not. Future such programs must be thought out more carefully than the SFC, and supported more than the Solar Bank. Of course, the cost of these programs, effective or not, is passed on to taxpayers.

To reduce the uncertainty surrounding future fuel prices, the government could guarantee the price of fuels produced by new fuel systems. The government would assure owners of electricity-generating windmills, or other systems producing energy for sale, that they will receive a certain price for the energy they produce. This certainty would encourage investment in new fuels. These incentives are already in effect, although again on a very limited scale. Investors in synthetic fuel plants have received price guarantees for fuels they will produce, and the Public Utilities Regulatory Policies Act of 1978 requires utilities to pay the going market rate for electricity generated by private generating systems (such as small-site hydro and windmills). If market prices don't reach the guaranteed level, the financial burden of these programs would be carried by the public as taxpayers.

The government could also address the problem of uncertainty by improving its data collection procedures. Knowledge of what is happening in vital parts of the economy is a prerequisite for reliable economic forecasts. In addition to its decennial population census, the Census Bureau conducts thorough censuses of agriculture, mineral industries, and manufacturers every five years, and the results are usually not published until at least two years later. Thus, the most recent data may be seven years out of date. Yet the Reagan administration, in the name of deficit reduction, has cut the budget of the Census Bureau and other departments charged with collecting such data. It would probably be to the public's advantage, and certainly to the advantage of businesses, if these agencies were given enough personnel and money to conduct more frequent surveys and to release the data more quickly.

No matter what is done, the need to develop fuel sources with energy profit ratios much lower than those of oil and gas will engender tremendous expense—expense that the public will eventually have to pay either as taxpayers or as consumers. One implication of this choice will be its effect on equity: Should the burden fall on consumers of energy according to the amount of fuel they consume, or should it be apportioned according to the ability to pay? Poor people spend a much higher proportion of their incomes on fuel than wealthier people do: according to a 1982 DOE study,[11] families making less than $5,000 per year spend about 15 percent of their income on fuel, while families with incomes greater than $35,000 typically spend about 3 percent on fuel. The ability of low-income groups to reduce fuel use on their own without endangering their health is already quite limited. If people pay the cost of developing new fuel sources as consumers—which is what making no changes in government policy will entail—poor people will bear the brunt of it. If the government were to give financial support to conservation policies and the development of alternative fuels now, the short-term costs (and taxes) would be increased, but the nation could be spared a trauma that would be wrenching for everyone.

Another implication of the need to invest in new fuel systems is that such investments are all the more difficult when the government is soaking up every spare dollar (and then some) to pay for the Reagan administration's military buildup. The trillions of dollars that the administration would like to spend on space-based defense, new generations of missiles, and other hardware could instead be used to build photovoltaic cells, windmills, and other fuel systems, which would go a long way toward providing the United States with a secure economic foundation for the future. Thus, the debt incurred to pay for the weapons buildup doesn't merely burden future taxpayers with heavy interest payments; it also reduces the future size of the economic base from which to make the payments. Furthermore, the production of armaments decreases the overall efficiency with which energy is used to support the quality of life here and now, insofar as weapons, although adding to GNP, don't measurably increase the nation's standard of living. It's cruelly ironic that these grotesque expenditures for weapons are meant at least partly to prevent the disruption of energy imports. Is the impoverishment of our future really the appropriate response to Islamic fundamentalism and the Soviet threat?

HOUSEHOLD FUEL USE VERSUS NONFUEL GOODS AND SERVICES

Chapter 3 described a tradeoff between the use of fuel in the household sector and the availability of nonfuel goods and services—a tradeoff that is not one-to-one. When energy supplies limit economic production, using a dollar's worth of gasoline in a private car may mean that several dollars' worth of other goods cannot be produced. Even a slight reallocation of fuel from the household sector to manufacturing or other intermediate sectors can increase GNP substantially.

But an ideal society is not necessarily one in which households ruthlessly minimize their fuel use. At some point a few gallons of gasoline for the family car may contribute more to consumer satisfaction than does another television set or cosmetic surgery or some other purchase. When consumers spend their money, they strike a balance between their desire for fuel and their desire for other goods and services. And the use of fuels now—whether directly in the household or indirectly in making consumer products—reduces the amount available in the future for either purpose.

Individual consumers decide how much fuel to buy on the basis of fuel prices relative to the price of other things. Although this may not be the only consideration, it is the most important. Since historically the United States has been blessed with an abundant supply of cheap energy, we have developed energy-intensive habits and tastes. These can be traced back to early colonial times, when vast timber stands made energy almost as free as air compared to what the colonists were used to in Europe. According to one writer,

> All cabin dwellers gloried in the warmth of their fireplaces, exploiting their world of surplus trees where a poor man, even a plantation slave, could burn bigger fires than most noblemen in Europe. . . . In the dead of winter, a family kept warm, not by buying "sich uppish notions" as blankets, but by putting more wood on the fire and sleeping in their clothes.[12]

The abundance of coal and then petroleum allowed these fuel-intensive lifestyles to continue, even as the demand for fuel for manufacturing and other intermediate uses soared. Centuries of perceived abundance have ingrained in many people a sense that consumption of natural resources for one purpose has no bearing on the availability of resources for other purposes.

This unconscious assumption of perpetual abundance has affected our settlement patterns, our transportation system, and our housing stock. Compared to Europe and Japan, where resource limitations have been a fact of life for centuries, U.S. society is extremely fuel intensive. For example, as was described in Chapter 1, the United States has one of the lowest population densities of any industrial nation, which imposes a high level of household fuel use because more energy is needed to move people and goods between homes, workplaces, and recreation areas, and which discourages mass transportation. Our fuel-intensiveness is also related to consumer tastes that are less rigid, such as our preference for big cars with big engines and for spacious houses with thin walls. According to Lester Brown in *The State of the World 1984*,[13] the average fuel economy of the U.S. auto fleet was 17.9 mpg in 1978, compared to 25.9 mpg in Europe and Japan. And the average U.S. home loses two to three times as much energy per square foot as the average Swedish home,[14] since until recently the effort (that is, the dollar cost) required to insulate U.S. homes was perceived to be greater than the cost of the extra fuel.

Part of these differences in fuel use can thus be attributed to cheap-resource-inspired settlement patterns with which the United States is stuck for the next forty years. But some of it stems from habits that we *could* change more quickly if we wished. This flexibility is important because we must make some choices about the allocation of fuel. Do we wish to maintain our fuel-intensive lifestyles until there is no longer enough fuel to support them? Or do we wish to divert some fuel from the household sector to the production of consumer goods and services?

Probably this choice would require us to curtail some of our fuel-using activities. However, there are also many opportunities to carry on the same activities with less fuel—what was called, in Chapter 3, conservation *per se*. For example, studies have shown repeatedly that insulation saves more money than it costs. Frost-free refrigerators now sold in Japan need less than half as much electricity as otherwise similar domestic models, and air conditioners are available that are half again as efficient as 95 percent of the air conditioner "fleet."[15] In most cases, consumers can save money on their fuel bills while getting the same or better service from their purchase.

But the popularity of insulation and energy-efficient appliances has been much lower than their economic advantages would suggest. For example, David Goldstein of the Natural Resources Defense Council reports that less than 5 percent of central air conditioners sold in 1981 had energy efficiency ratios (the ratio of the air conditioner's cooling power, in BTUs per hour, to its electric requirement, in watts) higher than 9.5, even though cost-effective models with efficiencies as high as 14 were available. National and local surveys have revealed that, contrary to the common perception, very few people have invested in energy conservation measures.[16] Why would people fail to take actions that would increase their own material welfare?

Certainly, some people simply don't care about saving money; some don't care about the future. Most, however, would like to save money and resources for themselves and the future but don't. Many consumers are unaware of differences in energy efficiency, while others hesitate to buy energy-efficient appliances because they think the savings too small. Morever, a low income will discourage extra investment of any sort; people with little spare cash don't want to tie it up in appliances that will pay them back over several years. Finally, psychological studies have shown that consumer decisions are colored by noneconomic considerations that may outweigh the dollar costs and benefits.[17]

Clearly, it isn't enough just to put energy-efficient appliances on store shelves. Even though such appliances are cost-effective, the market is not inducing many people to buy them. If it is in the national interest for people to buy them, as seems reasonable, then the incentives to buy them need strengthening, and the obstacles to buying them should be removed.

A number of analysts have pointed out the relatively poor information people receive about their uses of fuel: for instance, most people grossly overestimate the amount of electricity used by lights and television sets and underestimate that used by refrigerators and water heaters. Absolutely perfect information is obviously out of reach, but it may be improved enough to allow consumers to make more informed decisions. Cars and most heavy appliances now carry a label with some kind of energy-efficiency rating. However, many consumers distrust or are unaware of these labels, and, according to David Goldstein, appliance salespeople tend to downplay their significance, telling potential buyers that the labels are unreliable. In fact, Goldstein cites a study by Pacific Gas and Electric Co., which showed that 70 percent of appliance salespeople do not even discuss energy efficiency. Therefore, appliance dealers and manufacturers may wish to sponsor an advertising campaign to publicize and build confidence in the rating system. There is no apparent reason why fuel economy could not be a prime selling point for refrigerators or air conditioners, as it was until recently for cars.

Home energy audits are perhaps homeowners' only source of specific information about the usefulness of insulation, weatherstripping, and storm windows. Some utilities will, at no charge to the customer, send an auditor to a home to recommend various improvements and to estimate the resulting savings. Unfortunately, people don't always trust such audits—and without reliable information, few people will spend the hundreds or thousands of dollars required for such improvements. The distrust is not without foundation. A follow-up of eighteen professional energy audits, comparing the auditor's predicted energy savings to the actual savings, showed that only four audits were within 20 percent of actual savings.[18] Five underestimated actual savings, and nine overestimated them. One homeowner's bad experience may, by word of mouth, lead whole blocks to doubt the validity of energy audits. This unreliability could be reduced either through vigorous industry self-regulation or through the government: energy auditors could be licensed after demonstrating competence.

Utilities may also find their financial interests are served by helping consumers reduce fuel purchases. As the energy profit ratio of fuels has dropped in recent years, new capacity has become very expensive. Utilities could forestall having to build additional capacity and increase their profit margins by using their financial resources to limit consumer demand. David Goldstein estimated that an extra $50 paid to buy an efficient refrigerator would avert the need for utilities to spend $600 on new generating capacity, assuming all refrigerator buyers spent the extra money. Utilities could, for example, lease energy-efficient furnaces, heat pumps, water heaters, refrigerators, and air conditioners to customers at below-market rates, or the utilities could help consumers buy these appliances outright. Eric Hirst of the Oak Ridge National Laboratory found that the availability of low-interest loans (whether from utilities or elsewhere) was the most effective way to encourage household fuel savings.[19] Several utilities around the country, such as Pacific Gas and Electric, have already instituted programs to help people buy insulation and energy-efficient appliances.

Low-interest loans by utilities could help eliminate two other obstacles to household energy efficiency. Many consumers would like to buy efficient appliances but can't because they are too poor. And many observers have identified an apparently intractable problem with rental housing in which tenants pay for fuel: neither landlord nor tenant has much incentive to buy insulation or efficient heavy appliances. If tenants make the investment, it's lost when they move; if the landlord makes it, it may not raise the value of the property enough to justify the improvement, especially in poorer neighborhoods. But it may very well be in the interest of local utilities to finance the renovation of such buildings.

Utilities can't solve these problems by themselves. Appliance manufacturers and dealers may find that a special effort to sell energy efficient appliances, perhaps with rebate programs and low-cost financing, will benefit their public images and their overall sales. The government could also lend a hand with retrofitting existing buildings and with construction of new, efficient housing. It already gives tax credits for insulation and other energy-saving devices installed in existing houses, but these are quite limited and do not yet help poor people. These programs could be expanded to include all major appliances and to cater to low- and middle-income households. In some cases— for example, people who are too poor to take advantage of tax credits—direct grants or loans would be far more effective. It is important to remember that special provisions will have to be made in any program for the needs of low-income households. Poor people are more likely to use fuel inefficiently because they often live in poorly insulated buildings with cheap, inefficient appliances. And, because they are poor, they can't buy insulation or efficient appliances. If society wants to save energy, society helps itself by helping low-income households save, too. Energy that escapes through the walls of a tenement is just as lost as the energy used in a 15 mpg luxury car.[20]

Regrettably, much new housing is as energy-inefficient as old housing—even though well-insulated, passive-solar houses are not much more expensive to build. Architects, contractors, and developers could be very influential in seeing that energy-efficient housing becomes standard.[21] Individual communities may benefit by amending building codes to mandate insulation and intelligent design: money paid to local contractors and building suppliers stays in the community and increases the tax base; money paid to multinational fuel companies leaves the community forever. Plumbing codes were instituted with the comfort and safety of society in mind; if the comfort and safety of people in the future is an important consideration, then "energy codes" may be justified.

Yet another reason why energy efficiency is not a prime consideration in purchasing decisions is that consumers are not perfect calculators. They often put their money into the bank at a much lower rate of return than they could get, in the form of reduced fuel bills, by spending it on a fuel efficient appliance. MIT economist Jerry Hausman found on average that, for air-conditioner buyers to spend the extra money for an energy-efficient model, they must get 26 percent of the extra money back each year in energy savings.[22] Another survey revealed that consumers who spend up to $100 on insulation expect an annual return between 75 and 200 percent.[23] This kind of "nonrational" behavior must be considered in designing incentives for consumers to buy fuel-efficient appliances, cars, and houses.

Rising fuel prices are probably the most effective means of encouraging conservation. Rising fuel prices deter household (and overall) fuel use: the big jumps in fuel prices during the 1970s caused most of the reduction in household fuel consumption. But throughout the 1970s into the 1980s government regulations held the price of oil and gas well below the levels that a truly free market would probably have set. One of the Reagan administration's few actions to discourage resource depletion has been to lift these controls (and this effect was probably unintentional).

But rises in real fuel prices fall hardest on the poor.[24] The heavy impact is especially important because low-income people have very little discretionary fuel use.[25] Rising fuel prices may force many poor people to choose between eating and heating. Recognition of this has prompted some liberals to advocate comprehensive controls on fuel prices. Controls have been supported as well by many middle-income people, who are motivated both by suspicion that profit-hungry corporations have been gouging them and by a desire to protect their own pocketbooks, as well as those of the poor, during a period of scarcity. If fuel prices are controlled so that they lag or merely keep pace with the price of other goods and services, we can expect that consumption of fuel in all households will rise, as it has during other periods of flat or declining fuel prices. Indeed, one of the scenarios in Chapter 4 indicated that price controls would foreclose any possibility of increasing the nation's energy efficiency, and with it the possibility of maintaining per capita GNP near current levels in the face of declining fuel supplies.

Other strategies have been proposed that would allow fuel prices to rise but that would cushion the shock to the poor. Perhaps the most intriguing involves a fuel stamp program similar to the existing food stamp program. In this way, poor people could still afford to buy fuel for survival, and the general price of fuel could still rise enough to discourage discretionary fuel purchases by everyone else. Obviously, this would entail considerable government (taxpayer) expense, as well as a somewhat higher level of household fuel consumption than the unfettered market would allow.

Rising fuel prices will be a powerful disincentive to household fuel consumption in almost every household. Unfortunately, though, the Reagan administration views the end of controls as the *only* change needed to encourage fuel conservation. When Reagan's first budget director, David Stockman, was still a congressman, he wrote that the simple step of allowing prices to rise to their fair market value would reduce fuel purchases to optimal levels.[26] Stockman neglected the other factors that encourage household fuel use: the lack of complete information and the lack of money for the necessary investments.

Even after removing the above-mentioned obstacles to saving fuel and money, we may find that household fuel consumption is still higher than we would like. Stronger measures may be called for. For example, the government could set minimum energy-efficiency standards for fuel-using goods. This approach has already been taken to increase the fuel economy of the automobile fleet. In 1975 the federal government passed a law requiring car manufacturers to increase, on a specified schedule, the aggregate fuel economy of the vehicles they sell: 18 mpg in 1979, 20 mpg in 1980, and 27.5 mpg in 1985. This law could be strengthened by mandating a minimum efficiency for all models, rather than fleet-average standards. Similar laws could cover heavy appliances. California has set minimum standards for many appliances sold there, which, due to the size of the California market, are effectively national standards (at least for refrigerators). The California efficiency requirements, however, are a good deal less stringent than could be met even with current technology. For example, California requires that a 15-cubic-foot self-defrosting refrigerator use less than 1400 kilowatt-hours per year, although models using about half that much electricity have been available for years.[27] (It's worth noting in passing that any such regulations must not be relaxed if they're to be effective. Both Ford and General Motors have asked that mileage standards be relaxed, and the Reagan administration has been sympathetic. If such exemptions are granted routinely, it would completely vitiate the standard.)

Rationing is perhaps the strongest potential strategy. Rationing has worked in the past only when supported by an overwhelming majority of the population, and only for short periods generally acknowledged as emergencies. During World War II, rationing was reasonably effective since people understood that fuel used in the household reduced the amount available to fight the war. More recent schemes—including the rationing of oil at the wholesale level in 1973–74 and the odd/even system of gasoline buying in 1979—were less successful because many people believed the shortages were contrived to raise prices and profits. In the future, only wholehearted general agreement that fuel scarcity represents "the moral equivalent of war" would make rationing a viable alternative.

The United States obviously faces difficult choices. Contrary to what many have claimed, there is no easy way to lessen the amount of fuel used in the household sector: the economic structure built over decades to encourage people to buy and depend on fuel cannot be swept away quickly or painlessly. Reducing household fuel use much beyond current levels will require restructuring the ways in which market influences consumer decisions, which in turn will entail some expense. The alternative is to sacrifice other goods and services instead.

POPULATION GROWTH VERSUS HIGHER LIVING STANDARDS

Assuming that some alternative fuels are developed, the actual supply of fuel to our society as a whole may not decline very much. But continued population growth would reduce per capita energy supplies, with a resultant drop in per capita output of goods and services. While most of the benefits of low growth or of reduction of the size of the United States' population would become evident only late in our energy and agricultural scenarios, in the long run population is a very powerful influence on living standards. No population projection need be accepted as inevitable; the rate of population growth is not fixed. The Census Bureau estimates cover only a narrow range of fertility rates, and the total fertility rate of U.S. women could rise above 2.3 or fall below 1.6. Over the past three decades, since the middle of the baby boom, fertility rates have fallen steadily. If people prefer the economic benefits of low, zero, or negative population growth to the benefits of a large family, how can these trends be encouraged?

Some government policies may already have encouraged lower birthrates. Many states loosened their restrictions on the distribution, sale, and advertising of contraceptive devices, widening their availability. Many school districts introduced sex education into both elementary and secondary schools, helping young people avoid having unwanted pregnancies. And many court and legislative decisions led to the wider availability of abortions.

The effects of these government actions, however, were probably dwarfed by social trends that altered the position of women in society. The increasing entrance of women into the workplace has meant that more women have more options—that they can choose careers other than childbearing and childraising or that, if they have fewer children, they can work outside the home. The sexual revolution removed much of the stigma from sexual activity that doesn't result in parenthood. Many people decided that the personal advantages of having fewer children and the worldwide environmental disadvantages of population growth outweighed other considerations. And the spiraling cost of raising children and reduced real incomes in the 1970s have meant that many people can't afford more than one or two children even with both parents working; one-worker couples and single parents are even less able to afford children.

Additional government actions to encourage lower birth-rates would be neither realistic nor very effective. The federal government and most states allow tax deductions for children, but the pronatalist effect is probably too small to be measured. Other than that, the government programs that share the costs of having children, and therefore encourage more childbearing, cannot be cut without reducing the care that society guarantees to existing children. Public school education, special care for handicapped children, and welfare programs for the children of the poor (such as Aid for Families with Dependent Children) certainly weaken some economic disincentives to childbearing, but these are basic obligations of a modern government.

On the other hand, government advances that have been made over the past three decades are currently besieged. State, local, and federal funding for abortion has been cut back, and the very legality of abortion is threatened. Education of children in the use of birth control devices, and especially the availability of such devices, has been opposed by many groups and individuals, including some school boards. Studies indicate that about one-quarter of all births are unplanned or unwanted. The reduction or abolishment of these governmental programs could result in further increases in this needless contributor to population growth.

Besides birth and death rates, the other determinant of a population's growth rate is net immigration. Federal actions successfully controlling immigration could affect population growth relatively rapidly. For example, assume that the federal government had lowered the level of legal immigration, allocated sufficient resources to enforce immigration laws, and had achieved zero net annual immigration by the end of 1980. In that case, with a fertility rate of 2.0, the U.S. population in the year 2000 would be about 250 million. On the other hand, if current federal policies toward legal and illegal immigration are unchanged, and net annual immigration continues at about a million, U.S. population in the year 2000 will be almost 275 million. However, zero net immigration is probably out of reach for some time: thus far Congress has been unwilling to commit the money needed to enforce existing immigration laws, and many groups are uncomfortable with the prospect of vigorous enforcement. Moreover, political and economic conditions in much of the Third World guarantee that many people will strive desperately to enter the United States, illegally if necessary. The United States thus faces a difficult choice between the costs, both financial and social, of immigration control and the cost of higher population growth.

Economic trends will continue to influence childbearing practices. Should the workforce continue to expand, and should the percentage of women in the workforce continue to rise, it is likely that fertility rates will fall even further. But if unemployment should grow, it could have unpredictable results: young couples faced with an uncertain economic future or with actual unemployment may postpone having children because they cannot afford them; on the other hand, young women who are unable to find adequately remunerative work may find childbearing and childrearing to be their only alternative role.

Social changes may be the most important factor in further lowering fertility rates. Religious organizations in the United States have been the most effective opponents of trends that have lowered birth rates: the Catholic church has strenuously fought contraception and abortion; Jewish religious organizations have expressed dismay over the low fertility rate of Jews; fundamentalist Protestants have led the opposition to sex education for the young. Attitudes are changing, however: some religious leaders of all faiths have begun to join more actively in the population movement, and they are attempting to counter, and even to alter, the pronatalist activities of their churches.

In the end, the fertility rate is created by millions of individual decisions about whether to have children. These decisions are influenced by innumerable factors, but very important among them is the meaning of childbearing within the society, the social attitude toward large or small families or childless couples. Education about the results of population growth—not only by public schools and religious groups but also by advocacy organizations such as the Population Reference Bureau, the Population Council, and Zero Population Growth—will to a large extent determine what factors people weigh when they make those decisions.

HIGH PRODUCTIVITY VERSUS FULL EMPLOYMENT

Through most of the next forty years, the number of people who want jobs will almost certainly expand. Even with declining household fuel use, it will not be possible to provide all these workers with rising amounts of fuel per worker-hour, unless the number of worker-hours is reduced. Therefore, we can no longer expect to have both full employment and high output per worker. Rather, we will have to choose from a spectrum of possible combinations of productivity and employment. At one end, we can have a relatively small cadre of highly fuel-subsidized, highly productive, highly paid workers, who support a large population of unemployed people with their taxes; at the other, we can give everyone a job that produces much less output and that pays correspondingly less. No longer can we have both high employment and high earnings. The total amount of output would be the same with either strategy. The difference is one of distributional equity.

Factory owners and managers decide how much labor, capital, and fuel to use based on what the market tells them is cheaper. Most people are currently unable to participate directly in the choice between high productivity and high employment (although some unions in shrinking industries like steel have negotiated tradeoffs between wage cuts and layoffs). If the strategy the market favors isn't the one most citizens favor, then they need to design government policies to change the signals the market sends to owners and managers. As it happens, existing government policies tilt the market toward the high productivity/low employment solution. On the other hand, rising fuel prices favor the low productivity/high employment strategy. It isn't clear which will win.

We may already be seeing the effect of increasingly expensive fuel on the economy. Between March of 1979 and March of 1984, 2.4 million manufacturing, construction, and mining jobs were lost. Most new jobs, on the other hand, were in the service sector, which use much less fuel per worker-hour but which also produce less (in dollars of output per worker-hour) and pay less. Since the late 1960s two-thirds of all new jobs have been in industries where the average annual payment was $13,600 in constant 1980 dollars; jobs paying an average wage of more than $20,250 in 1980 dollars—almost all of which are in manufacturing—have had the least growth since 1970.[28]

But government policies oppose this trend. The capital depreciation allowance is one of the most important existing policies favoring high productivity and low employment.[29] It allows firms to write off the depreciation of machines on their taxes, usually much faster than the machines actually wear out. This reduces the cost of capital and encourages managers to replace workers with capital (and fuel to run it)—and no such allowance is given to encourage the use of labor or other inputs to production. During periods of declining productivity and output, calls are frequently heard to speed the rate at which owners can write off their capital. When the Reagan administration took office, a speed-up in the capital depreciation allowance was part of its economic recovery program. But while increases in this allowance may indeed raise labor productivity, when fuel supplies can't be expanded they also entail a new cost—unemployment. Thus, society will want to take a long, hard look at new calls for accelerated depreciation allowances. It may even wish to roll them back.

It would be more desirable and less intrusive to maintain labor productivity with less fuel and capital. Fortunately, such a strategy may be possible without having to rely on a technological fix. Evidence is mounting that increasing worker involvement in plant management increases the amount of output workers produce per kcal of fuel used. Part of Japan's success has been attributed to its routine use of worker circles. Profit-sharing and direct worker ownership may be even more effective. In plants where workers benefit or suffer directly according to the factory's output quality and profitability, absenteeism and shirking are usually quite low. Studies indicate that worker-controlled plants are much more efficient than factories managed traditionally.[30]

Finally, it should be noted that, even with the high earnings/low employment economy that a continuation of present policies would produce, wages and living standards for employed workers will probably still fall. As unemployment rose, so too would government transfers to the out-of-work. Taxes would then have to rise as well to pay these benefits, which would reduce the take-home pay of remaining workers. Moreover, political economists argue, the large number of unemployed workers would depress wages: a worker who complained about a wage cut could easily be replaced by an unemployed worker glad to get any job. Massive social unrest would also almost certainly accompany massive unemployment, entailing equally massive social costs.

AGRICULTURE

From the 1940s until the late 1970s U.S. agriculture was a story of rising total output, per-acre yields, and expectations. During this period most research and effort went toward discovering new ways to use more energy to raise yields. Land was limited and labor was costly; but energy was cheap and abundant.

In the last few years, however, neither output nor the number of people supported by an acre of cropland has risen as fast as before. This has been attributed by some observers to weakened government support for agricultural research (although others have complained about the direction of research as well). Consequently, many scientists and policy people have advocated increased funding for such research, most of which would presumably concentrate on raising per-acre yields. At first glance this seems a laudable goal, as population growth is likely to push the demand for food and fiber upward in the near future. However, our study comes to rather different conclusions.

The quality of the U.S. agricultural resource base has been declining. That is, the amount of food produced per unit of energy has been been declining. Three important facts emerge from our analysis: (1) today's methods of farming depend heavily on the use of fossil fuels, especially natural gas and oil products; (2) there are now only very small returns for added energy use; and (3) the amount of oil and gas available domestically is likely to decline before the end of the century.

In the near future farmers will continue to face declining returns on their investment, and in the longer term resource degradation will result in declining absolute returns. If output/ input efficiencies keep declining, farmers will achieve high yields only by continuing to make major sacrifices: they'll have to pay even more for energy and for all other farm inputs, they'll have to accept even lower prices in the market (because of "overproduction"), they'll have to live with even lower net returns, and even more of them will go out of business. It may prove impossible to increase production by increasing the land base or the amount of energy used in farming. It is unlikely that more than 40 or 50 million acres could be added to the current cropland base. Trying to cultivate more land than that would probably reduce the overall average fertility of U.S. farmland, as poorer land would have to be used, and it would reduce the land base available for other vital activities. And using more energy will necessarily reduce the share available to other sectors, which in turn could cause hardships for the agricultural sector because of its links to other sectors. Increasing fuel use in agriculture would also raise the price of fuel. Agricultural policies that emphasize raising production without increasing output/input efficiencies, if they work at all, will be very costly.

It seems certain that new, less fuel-intensive methods for producing food will soon be necessary. As was discussed in Chapter 6, there will be strong institutional and legislative pressures to "adjust" merely by intensifying past practices— technologies that superficially appear to reward higher fuel use—rather than by adopting new rules of management. Change is often hard and painful. These "hard-path" approaches seem easy and may even appear effective in the short run. But in the long run the associated increases in energy use and land degradation will exhaust the hard path's effectiveness. Furthermore, these hard-path options depend heavily on technological solutions that are yet unproven or undiscovered.

The emphasis of policy and research may be better directed toward reducing resource degradation, increasing output/input efficiency, and altering cropping practices so that they need less energy. As domestic energy supplies shrink, maintaining production will be a more pressing problem than finding ways to increase it.

Of course, we aren't the first to advocate increasing the energy efficiency and reducing the degradative effects of modern farming. But many of the methods advanced by other analysts to reach these goals are probably unworkable. For example, one of the more radical suggestions is that farmers go back to pre-industrial farming techniques—that they abandon tractors and chemicals for draft animals, manure, and stoop labor. Such a policy would almost certainly increase the output/input efficiency but also meet with a raft of obstacles, not the least of which would be the problem of breeding enough draft horses and oxen to equip all the nation's farms. According to USDA figures, approximately 23 million draft animals were at work in 1920; by 1960 the number had fallen to less than 3 million. Moreover, the cropland needed to grow food for a big draft animal herd would cut deeply into an already strained land base.

A more frequent recommendation is that agriculture become a producer of energy, through the production of alcohol from crops and crop residues. This approach has some appeal, but it's hardly a panacea. For one thing, alcohol's energy profit ratio is only slightly above 1. For another, current studies point to as much as a ninefold increase in erosion when all crop residues are removed for alcohol production.[31] Only a twofold increase in erosion rates would vastly increase the need for energy. Thus, any net energy that might be derived from alcohol production is likely to be used in counteracting the added erosion. Finally, there is again the problem of the limited cropland base: land used for fuel production is unavailable for food production. And food can be traded, directly or indirectly, for several times as much fuel in world markets as could be produced via alcohol from the same land base.

Fortunately, there are other ways to lower energy use and increase conservation. Studies in organic and regenerative farming, integrated pest management, and similar approaches suggest that there is much promise in these methods and that they present fewer of the problems described above, although much more research is needed. When the *Des Moines Register*, the premier newpaper in the nation's heartland, runs a five-part series on organic farming, it would be difficult to dismiss these methods as radical or "counter-culture." For those farmers who continue to use fertilizers and other energy inputs, better knowledge about the timing and placement of inputs can reduce energy costs. By reducing energy costs while maintaining production levels, farmers can increase profits without having to increase their gross output. Along with cost-cutting policies comes land conservation, which will be another way of limiting the *need* for inputs in the future.

Will agriculture reverse the trend in declining resource quality? The answer to this question largely depends on our ability to implement appropriate policies. Nonetheless, agriculture is an activity that in its best practices links human knowledge and biological processes. Food is a renewable resource; its production, unlike that of fossil fuels, does not necessarily follow a Hubbert curve. It is possible to slow erosion greatly and thereby to stop the decline in resource degradation. It is even possible to build up soil organic matter and to *reverse* the decline. Other examples abound, but it is clear that the closer the system is tied to its fossil fuel resources—and the further it is removed from its biological resources—the more likely it is that food production will continue to decline in quality and efficiency.

Ideally, different farming strategies would be accompanied by shifts in the kinds of foods demanded by consumers. But demand preferences can't be changed by decree. The existing market delivers large amounts of grain-fed beef and highly processed foods because consumers want them and because it can deliver them at affordable prices. We don't want to deny the possibility that education could induce people to buy less meat and heavily processed food. Advertising has certainly played an important role in building consumer desires for such products, and it could be equally effective in reducing them—particularly in conjuction with real price increases. The demand for these foods will not fall very much unless prices rise to the point where consumers won't pay them. Therefore, if society feels that protecting the sustainability of U.S. agriculture is more important than maintaining the easy availability of steaks and potato chips, it must see that people receive the necessary signals from the market. Unavoidably, that means that supermarket prices for these commodities must be raised—preferably, though painfully, through the removal of existing subsidies.

EPILOGUE

We have depleted most of our high-quality resources; the supply
   obtainable from low-quality deposits is largely limited by the
   supply of fuel; and the supply of fuel itself is bound by these
   constraints.
For the past fifty years at least, the efficiency with which the
   United States converts energy to goods and services has been
   primarily determined by the types of fuels consumed and
   household fuel consumption; over the last ten years fuel
   prices have also played an important role. For the future,
   expected changes in the fuel mix will depress the nation's
   energy efficiency, and the ability of households to reduce fuel
   consumption without also reducing living standards will be
   constrained. Rising real fuel prices would encourage greater
   energy efficiency and offset the effects of declining fuel quality but for obvious reasons do not represent a utopian solution. Technology-based, painless ways of increasing the
   nation's energy efficiency are possible but unprecedented.
A substantially reduced rate of population growth in the United
   States would substantially reduce (but not eliminate) the
   pressures on the nation's resource base.
The quality of the nation's agricultural resources is deteriorating at an alarming rate, jeopardizing the United States' ability to continue as a food exporter. The decline is the result not
   only of modern farming methods, but, just as important, also
   of the consumer desires that determine what and how much
   food farmers must grow. As a result, farm bankruptcies are
   accelerating and the rural economy itself is in danger.
Therefore, if we want to be sure that people forty years from
   now will have enough fuel and other resources to maintain
   material living standards at a level near ours, we must either
   cut back our consumption of resources now or achieve some
   unprecedented technological breakthroughs to increase the
   efficiency with which we use resources.

The times we live in are often called the Space Age or the
Atomic Age or the Computer Age. Yet while the technologies
from which these names are derived have often dominated the

headlines, they have had only a peripheral effect on our daily lives. How many of us have ever been in space, or known anyone who has been in space, or even used anything that has been in space? Nuclear reactors supply less than four percent of the nation's energy, and nuclear weapons have changed the daily lives and work of only a handful of people in the United States (although they've changed the way in which many more think about the future). Many people now interact with computers in one way or another, but again, the essence of our lifestyles today is little different from that of thirty years ago.

The substance that has affected the lives of more people in more ways than anything else in history has not yet lent its name to an Age. But, centuries hence, historians (or archeologists) will almost certainly refer to the period of 1900 to 2050 as the Oil Age. Oil has transformed practically everything—our jobs, our homes, our entertainment, our environment. Oil has made the 55 gallon drum probably the world's commonest and most widely distributed object. It is certain that oil has made the United States the world's biggest economic, agricultural, and military power, and the Soviet Union the second biggest. The United States (and Western civilization) *is* oil.[32]

But people who are voters and decisionmakers today (including the authors of this book) will live to see the end of the Oil Age. There are only ten or twenty years of per capita economic growth remaining before declining oil and gas production begins to drag the economy downhill. When that occurs, so much time and effort will have to be spent dealing with the week-to-week contingencies involved in meeting people's basic needs that it will be impossible to plan a post–Oil Age economy. Thus, we have now a small and closing window of continued prosperity during which we enjoy the luxury of deciding, consciously and carefully, what sort of economy we would like to have after the oil runs out. Moreover, this window of prosperity allows us to make long-term investments in fuel-saving and fuel-producing technologies with the least pain. Such investments will have to be made sometime: it would be far better to make them while we're still getting richer instead of while we're getting poorer.

It's probably impossible to overestimate the difficulty involved in making people think about and plan for a lean future during a fat present. The task would be made easier if we knew more about the nation's carrying capacity, if we could say with a measure of certainty, "Here is what the future will look like if we pursue strategy A; this is what will happen with strategy B." This book is an early step toward that goal. Further steps, however, will require far more complete and accurate data than is currently available. It is very difficult to track energy flows through the economy because no one keeps consistent, integrated records. And, unfortunately, the one entity with an explicit mission "to promote the general welfare" has, under the Reagan administration, abrogated its responsibility to keep such records by curtailing its data collection in the name of deficit reduction. This shortsighted policy should be reversed forthwith if the United States is to have any chance of making a smooth, equitable transition away from oil and gas.

There should be little doubt that we will miss the Oil Age. The economic superstructure that has grown up around the exploitation of this resource—the concentration of ownership and distribution—has been widely criticized, and oil has contributed substantially to the pollution problem; but, in its heyday, it was more abundant and more versatile than any other fuel we have or can expect to have in the next forty years. Nostalgia for the hulking, all-steel cars of the 1940s and 1950s that the Oil Age gave us is already evident, and as we give up more and more of the goodies the Oil Age brought us, sighs for the "good old days" will become louder. But there is no doubt whatever that the Oil Age will soon be over and a new age—the Photovoltaic Age, perhaps—will dawn.

AFTERWORD

Carrying Capacity Comments: Saving Energy

Although it appears that much of the energy conservation in past years was due to the shift to higher-quality fuels and the shift from household use to industrial and service use, dramatic new paths now opening up could save a great deal of energy in the future.

• Arthur Rosenfeld of Lawrence Berkeley Laboratories reports that America could save the amount of energy produced from *30* full-sized 1,000 megawatt power plants merely by shifting from typical 1900 kwh (kilowatt hour) refrigerators to 700 kwh refrigerators. (By 1993, all refrigerators sold in California will be *required* to consume less than 700 kwh per year. California figures that that's cheaper than building new power plants.) The new refrigerators are not exotic new technologies; they simply have more insulation, more efficient motors, evaporators, and compressors — which makes them cost about $50 more than an average refrigerator at present. Super-efficient refrigerators that use only 100 kwh per year have moved from out of the research laboratories and are being hand-built for consumers for about $2,000 apiece. Even at that steep price, super-effi-

251

cient refrigerators are more cost-effective than building and operating power plants to provide electricity for less efficient devices.

• Rosenfeld reports that simply shifting to high-efficiency fluorescent lights and high-efficiency ballasts would save as much energy as could be produced by *40* full size 1,000 megawatt power plants if they all operated at peak efficiency. In fact, the 200 billion kwh saved would be equal to *60 percent* of the 325 billion kwh produced in 1984 by all the U.S. nuclear power plants.

• The U.S. automobile fleet average has moved from about 16 miles per gallon (mpg) to about 26 mpg in a decade and could certainly go much higher. The most efficient cars on Amercia's roads, such as the Chevrolet Sprint and the sporty Honda CRX-HF, get around 50 mpg (city plus highway average). The Japanese are even producing a photovoltaic scooter that uses *no* gallons — the power comes from sunlight via photovoltaic (electric) cells on the scooter.

• Amory Lovins reports that the use of modern motor, control, and drive train technology can save about half of industrial-drive power in the United States at an investment level of about 0.5 cent per kwh. How much *is* half of our industrial-drive power? About the equivalent of *70* 1,000 megawatt power plants.

• There are dozens of other energy-saving technologies. The super insulated houses of Saskatchewan cost about $2,000 more than a "normal" house and pay back that $2,000 in a couple of heating seasons. Cogeneration could save as much energy for Americans as it currently saves for Europeans. Gas turbines for "peak power" needs are much cheaper than building huge power plants and then leaving them idle most of the time, Time-of-day pricing, computer-timed shut-offs, integrated appliances — all are part of the enormous potential for conserving energy in the United States. Will we do it? No one knows. Much will depend upon whether the federal government mandates efficiency standards similar to California's and those recently passed by Congress (and vetoed by the President). Much will depend upon the future price of energy. Much will depend on how rapidly we learn and take action.

We are also considerably more optimistic about photovoltaics than Table 2-2 on page 70 indicates. This table assumes that large energy costs would be involved in bringing photovoltaics into commercial production. This has not proved to be the case. The table also assumes that photovoltaics, unlike other energy sources, would require batteries to store the power produced. Again, this has not proved to be the case, and will not be until photovoltaics (PVs) produce 20-30% of our electric output when storage problems will probably develop. Many PV systems simply feed energy into the power grid when the sun is shining, just as wind turbines or water turbines do when the wind is blowing or the water flowing. Robert Aster, at Jet Propulsion Laboratories, calculated the energy/profit ratio for photovoltaic (excluding batteries and future scale-up costs but including all energy requirements of a PV factory plus the energy implicit in the materials themselves plus the energy required for tracking-rigs and other balance-of-systems requirements) and found energy/profit ratios of 4.3 to 8.0 for panels manufactured in the early 1980s and 11.5 to 21.4 for panels manufactured in the late 1980s. Even the lowest of these values compare very favorably to other methods of producing electricity and the numbers for PV seem to keep getting better every year.

Considerable innovative research and implementation of energy-saving techniques and machinery have occurred since the basic research for *Beyond Oil* was completed. However, since many of the energy-saving research, development, and policy initiatives of the Carter administration were either cancelled or severely cut back, valuable years for adequately preparing for the coming transition have already been lost. The short-term advantages of the current low price of oil (under $20 per barrel) will work to the long-term detriment of the United States and other nations because it will encourage both the consumption of rapidly depleting oil resources and the future postponement of energy-saving initiatives. For example, the triple damage being done by rolling back the gas mileage standards for new cars, the abandonment of the 55 mph speed limit at the federal level, and the increase in the sales of larger automobiles will have serious negative repercussions for those living in the late-1990s and beyond.

In the following recommendations, both the positive and negative factors that have come into play since CSRC's research was completed are incorporated. Fortunately, the CSRC model (like other computer models) can very easily be updated as new facts and energy-saving techniques become available. The model will be revised and *Beyond Oil* will be updated as soon as there is enough further data to reassess the long-term advantages of soft path technologies. Meantime, modelers and energy planners should substitute more current figures as they appear.

Sources:

Robert Aster, "Energy Payback of Flat-Plate PV Modules and Arrays," DOE/JPL 1012-58, *Progress Report 18*, Pasadena, CA, July 1981.

C. Flavin, *Renewable Energy at the Crossroads*, Center for Renewable Resources, 1985.

H. Geller, "Energy Saving Potential From National Appliance Efficiency Standard," American Council for An Energy Efficient Economy, July 1985.

A. Lovins, *Brittle Power*, Brickhouse, 1982.

A. Lovins, "Least Cost Electricity Strategy for Wisconsin," Rocky Mountain Institute, September 1985.

A. Meier, J. Wrights, and A. Rosenfeld, *Supplying Energy Through Greater Efficiency*, University of California Press, Berkeley, CA, 1983.

R. Williams and E. Larson, "Steam-Injected Gas-Turbines," Gas Turbine Conference, American Society of Mechanical Engineers, June 1986.

Carrying Capacity Recommendations

Supported by the findings of the CSRC study, Carrying Capacity, Inc., is promoting seven public policy initiatives that together would take some of the trauma out of the transition to a world beyond oil.

1. *Raise Fuel Taxes and/or Impose Import Duties.* A major increase in the taxing of gasoline will postpone the day when it has to be rationed. This tax would have to be high enough to induce conservation and produce significant revenues. Economist Paul Hawken has suggested a tax as high as $1.00 per gallon at the pump, still low compared with Eurpoean and Japanese taxes. The proceeds from an oil tax could be invested in research, development, and the implementation of widespread photovoltaic, wind, and other flow-energy technologies and in implementing conservation nationwide. To be politically

feasible, the full implementation may have to be phased in over several years, but proceeds could also be used immediately to fill the nation's Strategic Petroleum Reserve while the world price of oil remains low.

2. *Develop Cogeneration Capacity.* Cogeneration — utilizing the heat cast off in electricity production — is an old European technique that the United States has only begun to exploit. Most of our large nuclear and coal-fired power plants merely vent the waste heat that they generate, whereas in Europe such heat is channeled to nearby industries and homes. Cogeneration is not only effective for large installations, such as central power plants, but also for small units. For example, the cogenerator at the Hillcrest Junior High School in Edmonton, Alberta, uses 20 percent less energy than a conventional system, and the cogenerator paid for itself in only 5.5 years. Cogeneration can even work at the household level, thanks to a small cogenerator, Fiat's TOTEM, that produces both electricity and heat. The unit, which runs on gasoline, methane, or alcohol, is 92 percent efficient, compared to about 60 percent for conventional furnaces and 20 to 40 percent for power plants.

3. *Conserve Energy Through Efficiency.* The savings from many current conservation efforts have not yet appeared in the data available to CSRC, but they will. Most major energy "consumers," such as automobiles, houses, electric motors, and household appliances have a long way to go to reach their peak conservation potential. Whereas the average new American car now gets around 25 mpg, 55-mpg cars are already on the road, 80-mpg cars soon could be, 100-mpg cars are on the drawing boards, and solar-photovoltaic cars propelled by their own energy are being developed.

New standards in California will double the efficiency of refrigerators and air conditioners over the next few years, and refrigerators in pilot production are about eight times more efficient than the current U.S. average. National minimum efficiency standards for appliances such as refrigerators, furnaces, air conditioners, and clothes washers and driers have been agreed to by environmentalists, consumer groups and appliance manufacturers and (although vetoed in late 1986 by the President) have been passed by both houses of Congress. Equally amazing improvements in light bulbs, electric motors, and window insulation will eventually yield tremendous energy savings. These improvements could result in a substantial drop in energy consumption, reduced air pollution, and billions of dollars in savings to consumers and could save the equivalent of dozens of large power plants by the turn of the century.

If, during the next 20 years, we were to follow a "least cost" investment scenario, buildings would require only about half as much energy as projected by many economists and policy-makers. Meanwhile, more and stronger energy-efficiency provisions should be incorporated into building codes. The key is strict National Energy Efficiency standards such as those already in place in California and Sweden.

Least-cost utility planning — now officially endorsed by the National Association of Regulatory Commissioners — is being promoted by more and more utilities and state regulators around the nation. Such planning will result in tremendous electrical savings and will help obviate the need for new power plants.

4. *Set a Federal Example in Conservation.* During the first oil crunches, when the federal government lowered its thermostats, reduced highway speeds, and increased auto fuel efficiency standards, the nation complied. Our government needs to reinstate these laws and enforce these policies, which were abandoned or reversed during the current administration. Government should also take even stronger steps by using the contracting process to encourage industry to become even more efficient, while at the same time keeping the public better informed about energy problems and energy spending. The Pentagon, for example, commands a vast budget, some of which might more profitably be devoted to energy efficiency. It is also notoriously prodigal in its own use of energy: the Department of Defense alone accounts for 82 percent of all federal energy use. Some of the defense establishment's huge R&D budget should be mobilized to solve the problem of energy depletion rather than contributing to it. (Of course, it is also to the military's advantage to keep its planes, ships, and tanks going for as long as possible and to mute criticism from both Americans and other nations about wasting fuel.)

5. *Promote Low-Input Farming Methods.* The practices of regenerative, sustainable, and organic farming — which boost

net profits by reducing the need for fertilizer, herbicides, and insecticides — are just beginning to snowball. If appropriate conservation and alternative agriculture sections are implemented, the 1985 Agriculture Productivity Act will further encourage these practices. Although some savings often appear immediately, it is usually three to five years before the full benefits show up in higher profits, reduced losses during poor years, lower energy input, higher soil fertility, and less erosion. The effect of these practices will be far more significant than current data indicate.

American farmers could save much traction energy by relying mainly on perennial grains that grow again from their roots each year. A decade of research on perennial grains has begun to show some promising results. Trees are an even better investment than perennial grains since they do not need to regrow a stalk each year. Studies such as J. Russell Smith's *Tree Crops* demonstrate that many pod-bearing and nut-bearing trees have yields equal or superior to current grain yields. Such tree crops reduce sharply the amount of traction energy required; they not only reduce soil loss, but in many cases they also produce an annual soil grain.

6. *Invest in Renewable Fuels.* The 1952 Paley Report (*The President's Materials Policy Commission Report*) concluded that, with a modest government investment, the United States could produce much of its energy by renewable means by the year 1975. It predicted that a nuclear route would cost more. Yet, as Christopher Flavin notes in *Renewable Energy at the Crossroads*, even though Americans embraced atomic energy and spent almost nothing on renewables, by 1984 renewables accounted for 9.4 percent of our primary energy and nuclear only 4.5 percent. If we had channeled into renewable fuels the $88 billion synthetic fuel subsidy ($17 billion of which was actually consumed before the program was abandoned) or the billions invested in nuclear power, we would today be much less dependent than we are on conventional fuels.

Perhaps the most promising development is in photovoltaics — modular, solid-state sources of energy that are enjoying phenomenal success, with world production doubling every sixteen months. These no-moving-parts devices are the only electricity-producing option whose price is falling. More important, they are the only means of producing electricity with a *rising* energy/

profit ratio. From an energy/profit ratio of 1 in 1972 (when it took as much energy to make a cell as the cell could produce), today's *conservative* estimates place the energy/profit ratio for complete single-crystal systems as high as 10. Although their energy profit ratio has yet to be extensively studied, the new amorphous cells are even more promising than the early single-crystal technologies.

7. *Control Population Growth.* With the supply of oil and gas dwindling, industrial-type agriculture cannot indefinitely support the current U.S. population of over 240 million people, much less a larger population, if we hold to our current diets and consumption habits. Per capita income will be substantially higher with slower or negative population growth. The U.S. and world populations cannot long be equitably maintained even at current levels. Not just population stabilization but also population contraction — already under way in several European countries — is needed to bring resources and demand into balance over the long term. Given the tremendous implications of population growth, both through immigration and natural increase, Congress should no longer ignore the issue. In a national population policy, it must establish upper limits on population that reflect the geometric effect of population growth and its pressure on finite resources. We should also regain control of our borders, considering that the legal and illegal immigration rate is estimated to be almost as great as our natural rate of population increase (births less deaths).

* * * * * *

None of these recommendations are easy, but all are realistic and attainable and the sooner we begin, the better off we will be. The United States can no longer purchase a better standard of living by systematically impoverishing the planet. If the American Dream is to remain alive beyond the next ten years, we must conserve our remaining fuel and soil and develop efficient sustainable technologies for a world beyond oil.

NOTES

CHAPTER 1

1. J.E. Stiglitz, "A National Analysis of the Economics of Natural Resources," in V. Kerry Smith, ed., *Scarcity and Growth Reconsidered* (Baltimore: Johns Hopkins University Press, 1979), p. 61.
2. H. Kahn, W. Brown, and L. Martel, *The Next 200 Years* (New York: Morrow, 1976), p. 58.
3. Julian Simon, *The Ultimate Resource* (Princeton: Princeton University Press, 1981), p. 197.
4. D.A. Brobst, "Fundamental Concepts for the Analysis of Resource Analysis," in Smith, *Scarcity and Growth Reconsidered*, p. 114.
5. L.R. Brown, P.L. McGrath, and B. Stokes, *Twenty-Two Dimensions of the Population Problem*, Worldwatch Paper #5 (Washington: Worldwatch Institute, 1976).
6. R. Constanza and C. Cleveland, "Ultimate Recoverable Hydrocarbons in Louisiana: A Net Energy Approach" (Baton Rouge: Center for Energy Studies, Louisiana State University, 1984).
7. Simon, *The Ultimate Resource*.
8. For example, Tony Davis has described in some detail the problems facing the city of Tuscon in "Trouble in a Thirsty City," *Technology Review* 87(6) (1984):66–71.

9. C.S. Hopkinson and J.W. Day, "Net Energy Analysis of Alcohol Production from Sugarcane," *Science* 207 (1980):302–03. Barry Commoner, in a New Yorker article, acknowledges but is unfazed by alcohol's rather poor energy profit ratio. "Ethanol," *New Yorker* (Oct. 10, 1983):124–53. Yet even at the higher end of the potential range, vast acreage would have to be devoted to crops for alcohol production if the resulting net energy were to have any impact.

CHAPTER 2

Data for the population and GNP of the United States were taken from *Historical Statistics of the United States* and *Statistical Abstracts of the United States* (various years). Both of these publications are compiled by the U.S. Department of Commerce, Bureau of the Census.

Data for U.S. fuel consumption were taken from *Historical Statistics of the United States*, *Monthly Energy Review* (various years), and the *Annual Review of Energy* (various years). These last two publications are compiled by the U.S. Department of Energy, Energy Information Administration.

Data for annual production of crude oil and natural gas in the lower forty-eight states were taken from *Historical Statistics of the United States* and *Monthly Energy Review* (various years).

Data for annual production of crude oil and natural gas in Alaska were obtained from *The Basic Petroleum Handbook* (American Petroleum Institute) and *The Oil and Gas Journal* (various years).

Data for fuel consumed by the petroleum extracting sector (SIC sector 13) and the petroleum refining sector (SIC sector 291) were obtained from *Census of Mineral Industries* and *Census of Manufactures* (various years), respectively. Both publications are compiled by the U.S. Department of Commerce, Bureau of the Census. Data for annual production of crude oil by all actions were taken from *Petroleum Facts and Figures* and *Basic Petroleum Handbook* (both published by the American Petroleum Institute, various years) and the *International Energy Annual* (U.S. Department of Energy, Energy Information Administration).

1. D.A. Brobst, "Fundamental Concepts for the Analysis of Resource Availability," in V. Kerry Smith, ed., *Scarcity and*

Growth Reconsidered (Baltimore: Johns Hopkins University Press, 1979).

2. Several measures of resource quality are already used by economists. These measures include the resource's market price, the value of the resource left in the ground, and the cost in worker-hours or dollars of extracting each unit of output. For a more complete discussion of the relative advantages and disadvantages of these various measures of resource quality, the interested reader should consult Anthony C. Fisher's paper, "Measures of Natural Resource Quality," and "The Adequacy of Measures for Signaling the Scarcity of Natural Resources" by Gardner M. Brown, Jr., and Barry Field; both papers are in Smith, *Scarcity and Growth Reconsidered.*

3. The economy has performed relatively poorly since 1973, and the monetary and fiscal (Keynesian) policies traditionally used to stimulate economic growth have not produced the desired results. We have experienced high inflation and low or negative economic growth simultaneously, which conventional economics is hard-pressed to explain. The failure of traditional policies has been recognized by many economists such as P.F. Drucker, who stated, "both as economic theory and economic policy, Keynesian economics is in disarray," in D. Bell and I. Kristol, eds., *The Crisis in Economic Theory* (New York: Basic Books, 1982).

4. This pattern of exploitation is virtually universal. Humans use the deposits that are most easily extracted first, and by definition, these easily extracted resources require the least effort. For example, surface seeps were the first deposits of oil discovered. Later, as demand exceeded the supply obtainable from these seeps, we turned to more sophisticated means for discovering new oil fields, such as surface geology, geophysics, and subsurface geology. These techniques extended our reachable supply but also increased the amount of energy needed to get it. Some wells now are drilled 15,000 ft deep, or almost three miles down.

5. The relation between cumulative demand, instantaneous demand, and the the average quality of domestic copper ore mined is supported by statistical analyses. Since 1906, cumulative copper production accounts for 67 percent of the annual variation in copper ore quality, while the amount of copper produced in a given year accounts for another 20 percent. These factors together account for 87 percent of variation in copper quality since 1906, and the mathematical equation that describes this relation is more than 95 percent reliable in a statistical sense.

6. Copper ore is not the only domestic metal whose declining quality is causing U.S. industry to suffer. For example, the United States has nearly depleted its high-quality hematite (iron) ores and now uses lower-quality taconite ores. These taconite ores are much lower in quality than the ores available from other nations, such as Brazil and Australia. As a result, North American companies that obtain their own ore in the United States, such as Reserve Mining, have experienced economic difficulties despite the technological breakthroughs that allowed them to use taconite ores. Olle Geijerstam, "Iron Ore—A New World Market?," *Raw Materials Report* 1(1) (1981):48–57.

7. D.J. Kakela, "Iron Ore: Energy, Labor, and Capital Changes with Technology," *Science* 202 (1978):1151.

8. The dependence of modern crop strains on fossil fuel subsidies is especially important in the Third World. Use of modern crop strains hurt many poor farmers because they cannot afford the fossil fuels subsidies required. As a result, some Indian scientists considered a return to traditional varieties of wheat because they have greater yields than the hybrids when fertilizer is not available in large quantities (Nicholas Wade, "Green Revolution (II): Problems Adapting a Western Technology," *Science* 186 (1974):1186.

9. The concept of energy profit ratio was developed originally by Howard T. Odum and termed *net energy ratio* in his book, *Environment, Power, and Society* (New York: John Wiley & Sons, 1971). Many different values for the net energy ratio of a particular fuel source can be calculated according to the energy flows included. Three values of net energy ratio were defined by by Charles Hall, Cutler Cleveland, and Mitchell Berger, "Yield Per Effort as a Function of Time and Effort for United States Petroleum, Uranium, and Coal," in which the term *net energy ratio* was changed to *energy return on investment* (in W.J. Mitsch, R.W. Bosserman, and J.M. Klopatek, eds., *Energy and Ecological Modelling* (New York: Elsevier, 1981).

10. For example, see Julian Simon, *The Ultimate Resource* (Princeton: Princeton University Press, 1981).

11. Martha W. Gilliland, *Net Energy Analysis: A New Public Policy Tool* (Boulder: Westview Press, 1978), p. 10.

12. M.K. Hubbert, "Nuclear Energy and the Fossil Fuels," in *Drilling and Production Practice* (American Petroleum Institute, 1956).

13. M.K. Hubbert, "Energy Resources, A Report to the Committee on Natural Resources," National Academy of Sciences/ National

Research Council Publication 1000-D (1962); also Hubbert, "Nuclear Energy and the Fossil Fuels."

14.   M.K. Hubbert, "U.S. Energy Resources: A Review as of 1972," Senate Committee on Interior and Insular Affairs (1974), Serial No. 93-40 (92-75).

15.   We modified Hubbert's original method for calculating yearly oil production. Instead of calculating curves for cumulative discoveries and production and subtracting the two, we used statistical techniques to calculate the "best fit logistic curve" for cumulative crude oil production. The first derivative of this equation gives yearly production rates. This procedure was repeated with data sets for oil production in the lower forty-eight states, Alaska, and the entire world, and for natural gas production in the lower forty-eight states and Alaska.

16.   The Hubbert analysis assumes that cumulative discovery and production of oil will resemble a logistic curve based in the theory of "big numbers" because of the time associated with discovering dispersed oil wells and recovering oil from them. Since all Alaskan oil is found in one field and since significant production had to await the Alaskan Pipeline, the basic assumptions behind a Hubbert analysis were violated and hence its description of Alaskan oil production is less accurate.

17.   According to most analyses, Alaska should yield about 9.6 billion barrels of oil. This is about 4.5 percent of the 214 billion barrels that we estimate, using the Hubbert method, will be produced overall in the United States.

18.   For a good review of the shortcomings of previous predictions concerning the impending exhaustion of domestic oil and gas, see *Presidential Energy Program*, Hearing before the Subcommittee on Energy and Power of the House Committee on Interstate and Foreign Commerce, (Serial number 94-20 p. 643). On the other hand, for a good review of how projections for U.S. oil and gas reserves have converged toward M. King Hubbert's original prediction, see Hubbert, "U.S. Energy Resources."

19.   The lower forty-eight states contain about 4.7 million square kilometers of sedimentary rock, and there have been some 2.9 million wells drilled in the United States, only a small fraction of which are offshore or in Alaska.

20.   R. Lowenstein and G. Stricharchuk, "Mukluk Oil Field Starts to Look Like a Bust as 3 Partners Say Test Well Appears Dry," *Wall Street Journal*, Dec. 6, 1983, p. 3.

21.   Robert Costanza and Cutler J. Cleveland, "Ultimate Recoverable Hydrocarbons in Louisiana: A Net Energy Approach"

(Baton Rouge: Center for Energy Studies, Louisiana State University, 1984).

22. W.F. Weeks and G. Weller, "Offshore Oil in the Alaskan Arctic," *Science* 225 (1984):371–78.

23. Colin Norman, "Interior Slashes Offshore Oil Estimate," *Science* 228 (1985):974.

24. M. Blumstein, "Buying vs. Exploring for Oil," *New York Times*, March 19, 1984, p. D1.

25. R.D. Hershey, "Experts Predict California Oilfield Will Be Biggest Find Since 1968," *New York Times*, November 15, 1982, p. A1.

26. Only 0.6 percent of all known domestic oil fields contain 40 percent of recoverable oil supplies (see R. Nehring, "The Discovery of Significant Oil and Gas Fields in the United States," Rep. No. R-2654/12-USGS/DOE (Santa Monica: The Rand Corp., 1981). Also, see Menard and Sharman, "Scientific Uses of Random Drilling Models."

27. Charles Hall and Cutler J. Cleveland, "Petroleum Drilling and Production in the United States: Yield Per Effort and Net Energy Analysis," *Science* 211 (1981):576.

28. Robert Kaufmann and Charles A.S. Hall, "The Energy Return on Investment for Imported Petroleum," in W.J. Mitsch, R.W. Bosserman, and J.M. Klopatek, eds., *Energy and Ecological Modelling* (New York: Elsevier, 1981).

29. Hubbert did construct some production curves for U.S. coal supplies in his 1974 analysis of U.S. energy supplies (see Hubbert, "U.S. Energy Resources"), but did so only with many assumptions and restrictions and cautioned readers against taking these analyses at face value.

30. Hall, Cleveland, and Berger, "Yield Per Effort..." (see note 9).

31. Cutler Cleveland, personal communication.

32. Energy content of a pound of coal as obtained from *Minerals Yearbook*, U.S. Department of Interior, Bureau of Mines, and from U.S. Department of Commerce, Bureau of the Census, *Monthly Energy Review* (April 1979).

33. D. Osborne, "America's Plentiful Energy Resource," *The Atlantic* 253(3) (1984):86–97.

34. Cutler J. Cleveland and Robert Costanza, "Net Energy Analysis of Geopressurized Gas in the Gulf Coast Region," in W.K. Lavenroth, G.V. Skogerboe, and M. Flug, eds., *Analysis of Ecological Systems: State of the Art in Ecological Modelling* (New York: Elsevier, 1983).

35. Julian Simon, "The Scarcity of Raw Materials," *The Atlantic* (June 1981):33–41.
36. B. Commoner, "A Nearly Perfect Fuel," *The New Yorker* (May 2, 1983):66–95.
37. B. Commoner, "Ethanol," *The New Yorker* (Oct. 10, 1983):124–53.
38. A report by the Rand Corporation states, "Estimates of capital cost of pioneer energy process plants have been poor indicators of actual capital costs. Pre-design and even early design estimates (even in constant dollars) have routinely underestimated definitive design costs or ultimate design costs by more than 100 percent for oil shale, coal gasification and liquefaction, tar sands, solid wastes and nuclear fuel reprocessing plants" (E.W. Merrow, S.W. Chapel, and C. Worthing, "Review of Cost Estimates in New Technologies: Implications for Energy Process Plants" (Santa Monica: Rand Corporation, 1979). We have no reason to think that early cost estimates for soft-path fuels will be any better.
39. M.S. Burnett, "A Methodology for Assessing Net Energy Yield and Carbon Dioxide Production of Fossil Fuel Resources," in W.J. Mitsch, R.W. Bosserman, and J.M. Klopatek, eds., *Energy and Ecological Modelling* (New York: Elsevier, 1981).
40. A.J. Large and L.M. Apcar, "Clinch River Nuclear Project Dies in Congress," *Wall Street Journal*, Oct. 27, 1983, p. 3.
41. L. Lidsky, "The Trouble with Fusion," *Technology Review* 86(7) (1983):32–44.
42. C.S. Hopkinson, Jr. and J.W. Day, "Net Energy Analysis of Alcohol Production from Sugar Cane," *Science* 207 (1980):302.

CHAPTER 3

Data for the U.S. population and for fuels consumed by the U.S. economy were obtained from *Historical Statistics of the United States: Colonial Times to 1970* (1975) and *Statistical Abstracts of the United States* (various years). Both of these publications are compiled by the U.S. Department of Commerce, Bureau of the Census.

Data for fuel consumed, value added, payroll, and production worker-hours were taken from the *Census of Manufactures* and *Annual Survey of Manufacturers*, both published by the U.S. Department of

Commerce, Bureau of the Census (Washington, D.C.: USGPO, various years).

Data for the average wage in manufacturing industries were taken from U.S. Department of Commerce, Bureau of the Census, *Historical Statistics of the United States: Colonial Times to 1970* (Washington, D.C.: USGPO, 1975), and U.S. Department of Labor, Bureau of Labor Statistics, *Monthly Labor Review* (Washington, D.C.: USGPO, various years).

Data for household fuel purchases (1972 dollars) and GNP (1972 dollars) were obtained from the *National Income and Product Accounts of the United States* 1929–1974 and 1976–1979 and *Survey of Current Business* (various years). All of these publications are compiled by the U.S. Department of Commerce, Bureau of Economic Analysis (Washington, D.C.: USGPO).

Data for investment by the petroleum industry were taken from *Census of Mineral Industries* (SIC 13) and *Census of Manufactures* (SIC 29), various years. Both publicatons are compiled by the U.S. Department of Commerce, Bureau of the Census (Washington, D.C.: USGPO, various years).

Data for the income of a family of four with and without employed members were obtained from U.S. Department of Commerce, Bureau of the Census, *Statistical Abstract of the US* (Washington, D.C.: USGPO).

1. For a good example of this line of argument, see A. Manne, "Fable of the Elephant and the Rabbit," in C.J. Hitch, ed., *Energy Conservation and Economic Growth* (Boulder: Westview Press, 1977), p. 139–51.

2. This minimum amount of energy needed to perform a given task is set by the laws of thermodynamics and assumes "ideal" conditions. In our example of lifting a ton of bauxite, 235 kcal represents the amount of energy needed assuming frictionless pulleys, no air resistance, and so forth. Of course, these conditions do not exist, and actual processes only approach these thermodynamic limits, and usually not very closely.

3. Only about 12 percent of the energy in gasoline is actually converted to forward motion of an automobile. About 33 percent is lost with the exhaust, 29 percent is used to cool the cylinders, 6 percent to pump air, 6 percent is lost due to rolling resistance, 6 percent to aerodynamic drag, and so on. John H. Gibbons and William U. Chandler, *Energy: The Conservation Revolution* (New York: Plenum Press, 1981).

4. In *Energy and Society* (New York: McGraw-Hill, 1955), Fred
   Cottrell was one of the first to describe how technological progress could be described as the result of ever more sophisticated
   ways of subsidizing human labor with nonhuman fuel.
5. Data for the amount of work done by humans, work animals,
   and inanimate fuels from 1850 through 1950 were taken from J.
   Frederic Dewhurst and Associates, *America's Needs and
   Resources* (New York: Twentieth Century Fund, 1955). The
   analysis was extended to 1980 by calculating total worker-
   hours, based on average weekly hours worked by those in the
   private sector multiplied by total employment (data from
   Monthly Labor Review, U.S. Department of Labor, Bureau of
   Labor Statistics, various years), to estimate the contribution
   from human workers. Data for animal power through 1970 was
   obtained from *Historical Statistics of the U.S.* and the 1970 value
   was extrapolated to 1980. Finally, the amount of work done by
   inanimate fuels was derived by multiplying the energy value of
   fuels consumed by the conversion efficiencies of the capital
   devices calculated by Dewhurst and his associates. This method
   of updating the original analysis probably underestimates the
   work powered by inanimate fuels since the efficiency of machinery may have risen since 1950.
6. C.J. Cleveland, R. Costanza, C.A.S. Hall, and R. Kaufmann,
   "Energy and the U.S. Economy: A Biophysical Perspective," *Science* 225 (1984):890–97. We measure productivity as the value
   added (as measured in real dollars) per production worker-hour.
   Records of production worker-hours started in 1947. In order to
   extend our analysis back to 1909, we divided the payroll paid by
   manufacturing industries by the average wage paid by manufacturing industries. To check the size of the error introduced by
   this method of estimation, we repeated this procedure for years
   following 1947 and compared these estimates with the recorded
   values. This method of estimation probably does not introduce
   an important error in our calculations of productivity, since the
   average absolute error between the recorded values and the estimates was only 3.1 percent.
7. Because both per capita GNP and fuel consumption have grown
   relatively steadily over the last hundred years or so, many economists argue that the two are independent trends that happen to
   have grown at roughly the same rate. But sophisticated statistical techniques, termed Box-Jenkins analyses, were used to test
   this hypothesis, and they showed that the two indeed are related
   (for more details, see note 30 in Cleveland, Costanza, Hall, and

Kaufmann, "Energy and the U.S. Economy"). Despite this interdependence, a cause-and-effect relation between the two cannot be established using statistical techniques (A.T. Akarca and T.V. Long, "On the Relationship between Energy and GNP: A Reexamination," *Journal of Energy and Economic Development* 5(2) (1980):326–31. See also Eden S.H. Hu and Been-Kwei Hwang, "The Relationship between Energy and GNP: Further Results," *Energy Economics* 6 (1984):186–190.

8. The international relation between energy use and economic production has been the focus for many books and papers. For a good description, see J. Darmstadter, J. Dunkerly, and J. Alterman, *How Industrial Societies Use Energy* (Baltimore: Johns Hopkins University Press, 1977).

9. A recent exhaustive study that reaches this conclusion was summarized by Thomas Johansson and Robert H. Williams at the 1984 AAAS meeting in New York City; it is supposed to appear soon in book form, *Energy for a Sustainable World*, by J. Goldemberg, T. Johansson, A.K.N. Reddy, and R.H. Williams.

10. We recognize that the ratio of output (measured by inflation-corrected dollars) to energy use has shortcomings when used as a measure of energy efficiency. Several considerations induced us to use it anyway. Perhaps the most important reason is that, as an aggregate measure, it includes the indirect energy costs of capital and labor used to produce goods and services. Equally important, this measure of energy efficiency is used by a wide range of people and agencies to measure the effectiveness of conservation measures and project future levels of energy demand. For example, see "Drop in U.S. Energy Use in 1979 Hints at a New Era of Efficiency," *New York Times* May 18, 1980, p. 1; or the *1982 Annual Energy Outlook*, U.S. Department of Energy, Energy Information Administration.

11. For a detailed argument along these lines, see Amory Lovins, *Soft Energy Paths: Towards a Durable Peace* (Cambridge, Mass.: Ballinger, 1977), and Robert Stobaugh and Daniel Yergin, eds., *Energy Future: Report of the Energy Project at the Harvard Business School* (New York: Random House, 1979).

12. R. Kaufmann, "Factors Affecting the Energy/Real GNP Ratio" (in preparation).

13. R. Turvey and A.R. Nobay, "On Measuring Energy Consumption," *Economic Journal* 75 (1965):787–93.

14. F.G. Adams and P. Miovic, "On Relative Fuel Efficiency and the Output Elasticity of Energy Consumption in Western Europe," *Journal of Industrial Economics* 17 (1968):41–56.

15. M. Slesser, *Energy in the Economy* (New York: St. Martins Press, 1978).

16. Warren D. Devine, *An Historical Perspective on the Value of Electricity in American Manufacturing* (Oak Ridge, Tenn.: Institute for Energy Analysis, Oak Ridge Associated Universities, 1982).

17. Nuclear and hydroelectricity are sometimes called primary electricity to distinguish them from electricity generated from coal-, oil-, or gas-fired generating stations. The energy in uranium and falling water can't be used to subsidize muscle power in any way other than by generating electricity, except for a few exceptions, like water wheels, made trivial by modern technology. On the other hand, coal, oil, and gas could be used in other ways. When they are converted to electricity, energy is no longer available to power automobiles or make steel. Moreover, at least two-thirds of the energy in fossil fuels is simply lost as waste heat in electric generating plants, unless there is some kind of cogeneration system, and even then a substantial amount of energy is still lost. But the important distinction is that there is an opportunity cost to using fossil fuels to generate electricity: fossil fuels used to generate electricity can't be used directly in other ways. Although nuclear power is often lumped with electricity made from fossil fuels because both involve the use of heat and steam to turn the turbines, nuclear power is distinguishable from fossil fuel electricity because there is no opportunity cost to using uranium. No other important use is sacrificed by using it in nuclear power plants. In fact, electricity generated from wind, photovoltaic cells, or geothermal plants should have the same effect as nuclear or hydroelectricity, since there is no opportunity cost associated with these energy sources.

18. According to M. Slesser, *Energy in the Economy*, primary electricity produces from 2.6 to 14.3 times as much output as fossil fuels.

19. Annual number of heating and cooling degree-days for Honolulu and Duluth were obtained from the Department of Commerce, Bureau of the Census, *Statistical Abstract of the United States* (Washington, D.C.: USGPO, 1983), p. 211. A city registers a heating degree-day for each degree (Fahrenheit) below 65° its mean temperature stands each day. If Duluth's mean temperature on a given day is 40°, it chalks up 25 heating degree-days. Cooling degree-days are calculated similarly, for every degree more than 80°.

20. The real GNP/energy ratio reflects the energy intensity of goods and services consumed in final demand weighted according to

their relative importance in final demand. Household fuel consumption is especially energy intensive. Bruce Hannon ("Analysis of the Energy Cost of Economic Activities: 1963–2000," *Energy Systems and Policy Journal* 6 (1983):249) found that a dollar's worth of fuel purchased by households represented 140,000 kcal, whereas a dollar's worth of nonfuel goods or services purchased by households represented 8,900 to 43,000 kcal. Based on this relative energy intensity, small changes in the proportion of household fuel purchases should have an important effect on the real GNP/energy ratio.

21. R. Howarth, C.A.S. Hall, and R. Kaufmann, "The Energy/Economic Link: An International Assessment" (in preparation).

22. The empirical equation for energy efficiency yielded by our analysis is:

$$
\begin{array}{llll}
\text{Energy/Real} & = 17{,}639.9 & - 164.4 \times P & - 723.3 \times E \\
\text{GNP} & & & \\
\text{(kcal/1972 dollar)} & & (8.5)^a & - (222.2)^a \\
& & (19.2)^b & (3.3)^b \\
& + 2{,}984 \times H & & - 1{,}177.7 \times F \\
& (149.8)^a & & (312.7)^a \\
& (19.9)^b & & (3.8)^b
\end{array}
$$

^{a} standard error
^{b} t statistic

where P, E, H, and F denote the percentage of the fuel budget from petroleum, from primary electricity (nuclear and hydro), personal consumption expenditures on fuel as a fraction of GNP, and the fuel price index (1972 = 100), respectively. The standard error for the entire equation is 361.4 kcal/1972 dollar real GNP, which is 2.3 percent of the energy/real GNP ratio in the base year 1972. The adjusted $r^2 = 0.97$. Coefficients for all three variables are significantly different from zero ($p < 0.001$). A value of 0.10 was used to adjust for autocorrelation (Durbin-Watson statistic = 1.71). To test for heteroscedasticity, Spearman rank correlation coefficients were calculated for the absolute value of the error term ranked with each of the independent variables, the dependent variable, and time. In no case was there a statistically significant relation ($p < 0.1$).

23. To look for structural changes in this relationship, we ran a dummy variable analysis on time and each of the independent variables. In no case were the coefficients of the dummy variables statistically significant at the 10 percent level or higher.

Ideally, we would like to conduct an entirely separate analysis for 1972 through 1981 to see if the same two factors account for the changes in the real GNP/energy use ratio observed in this period. But household fuel consumption and the percentage of fuel supplied by primary electricity have changed nearly in parallel, creating the statistical problem of collinearity and leaving the results inconclusive.

24. Harold J. Barnett, "Scarcity and Growth Revisited," in V. Kerry Smith, ed., *Scarcity and Growth Reconsidered* (Baltimore: Johns Hopkins University Press, 1979); also, Julian Simon, "The Scarcity of Raw Materials," *The Atlantic* (June 1981):33–41.

25. R.H. Rasche and J.A. Tatom, "Energy Resources and Potential GNP," *Federal Reserve Bank of St. Louis Review* 59(6) (1977):10–24.

26. Cleveland, Costanza, Hall, and Kaufmann, "Energy and the U.S. Economy."

27. This figure was calculated crudely by dividing $2.5 billion, the estimated cost of an aircraft carrier in 1981 (according to various newspaper accounts), by the 1981 GNP/fuel use ratio.

28. As reflected by his policies, President Reagan also has ignored the impact of the declining natural resource base. As he said in his 1981 State of the Union address, "There is nothing wrong with our internal strengths. There has been no breakdown in the human, technological, and natural resources upon which the economy is built."

29. Most macroeconomic texts, including those used to instruct graduate students, do not mention natural resources. Those that do, do so only in a cursory manner. For example, the production functions used to locate the equilibrium level of output include only labor and capital, ignoring the contribution made by fuel and other resources (see, for example, William Bransom, *Macroeconomic Theory and Policy* (New York: Harper & Row, 1979).

30. Cleveland, Costanza, Hall, and Kaufmann, "Energy and the U.S. Economy."

31. D.B. Brooks and P.W. Andrews, "Mineral Resources, Economic Growth, and World Population," *Science* 185 (1974):13.

32. For a good discussion of how technological change should reduce the amount of energy needed to produce a real dollar's worth of output and therefore reduce the economy's dependence on fuel, see M.H. Ross and R.H. Williams, "Achieving the Goals of the Employment Act of 1946—Thirtieth Anniversary Review," vol. 2, *Energy* (Joint Economic Committee, U.S. Congress, 1977).

33. For an example of conventional economic views on energy price elasticities, see G. Kouris, "Energy Demand Elasticities in Industrial Countries: A Survey," *Energy Journal* 4(3) (1983):73–94. Our estimate was derived from the following equation:

$$\ln (\text{Energy/Real GNP}) = 10.7 - \underset{\underset{(11.8)^b}{(0.04)^a}}{0.47} \times \ln P - \underset{\underset{(3.5)^b}{(0.02)^a}}{0.07} \times \ln E$$

$$+ \underset{\underset{(14.7)^b}{(0.3)^a}}{0.44} \times \ln H - \underset{\underset{(6.3)^b}{(0.03)^a}}{0.19} \times \ln F$$

[a] standard error
[b] t statistic

where P, E, H, and F denote the percentage of the fuel budget from petroleum, from primary electricity (nuclear and hydro), personal consumption expenditures on fuel as a fraction of GNP, and the fuel price index (1972 = 100), respectively. The adjusted $r^2 = 0.97$. A value of 0.35 was used to adjust for autocorrelation (Durbin-Watson statistic = 1.69). We tested for heteroscedasticity by calculating Spearman rank correlation coefficients, which were never statistically significant. Furthermore, multicollinearity probably did not affect the estimate of price elasticity because dropping any or all of the independent variables did not change it in a statistically significant manner ($p > 0.5$).

Usually, the price coefficient obtained from yearly data is considered an indicator of short-run price elasticity only. To calculate the long-run elasticity, one uses lag methods; we used a Koyck lag. The lag variable had a statistically significant coefficient ($p < 0.05$), but it had a positive value, which is clearly implausible. We don't argue against a long-run price response; rather, our inability to obtain a credible estimate indicates that the long- and short-run components cannot be teased apart from available data. Our estimate of -0.19 probably includes the long-run effect.

34. According to neoclassical economists, plant managers should employ that combination of outputs that produces the desired level of good or service for the least cost. As a result, when the price of fuel rises relative to other factors of production, managers will choose a different combination of productive factors when they revise their plant operations. For a good quantitative

description of this process in relation to energy, see E.R. Berndt and D.O. Wood, "Engineering and Econometric Interpretations of Energy-Capital Complementarity," *American Economic Review* 69 (1979):342–54.

35. D. Pimentel, et al., "Food Production and the Energy Crisis," *Science* 182 (1973):443.

36. J.C. Gibbons, "Energy Prices and Capital Obsolescence," *Energy Journal* 10(10) (1984):29–43.

37. Charles Hall, Cutler Cleveland, and Robert Kaufmann, *Energy and Resource Quality: The Ecology of the Industrial Process* (New York: John Wiley & Sons, 1986).

38. Robert Costanza, "Embodied Energy, Energy Analysis, and Economics," in H.E. Daly and A.F. Umana, eds., *Energy, Economics, and the Environment* (Boulder: Westview Press, 1981); Robert Costanza, "Embodied Energy and Economic Valuation," *Science* 210 (1980):1219–24; and Robert Costanza and Robert Herendeen, "Embodied Energy and Economic Value in the United States Economy: 1963, 1967, and 1972," *Resources and Energy* 6 (1984):129–63.

39. This estimate is based on average earning of a family of four with one member employed, as opposed to no member employed, and the portion of income spent on fuel as opposed to nonfuel goods and services. R.A. Herendeen, "Affluence and Energy Demand" (American Society of Mechanical Engineers, 1973-WA/Ener-8).

40. Ross and Williams, "Achieving the Goals of the Employment Act of 1946."

41. Indeed, curtailed household fuel purchases have not been without serious adverse effects. For example, the *New York Times* (April 26, 1983) reported that outbreaks of Legionnaires' disease have been tied to energy conservation measures that reduced the temperature of hot water tanks. Also, the Yale-New Haven (Conn.) Hospital said that chilblain, a nearly-forgotten syndrome characterized by painful swelling of the hands and feet and caused by prolonged exposure to cold temperatures, has reappeared as people have cut back on home heating (*Yale-New Haven Hospital Report*, January 1983). And rarely does a year go by without deaths of poor and elderly people in the winter in the Frost Belt and in the summer in the Sun Belt because they couldn't afford adequate heating and cooling.

42. R.C. Marlay, "Effects on Investment in Energy Conservation of DOE's Program and of Market Forces," staff working paper, Office of Policy Planning and Analysis (Washington, D.C., 1981).

43.   Marlay, "Effects on Investment."

CHAPTER 4

1.   Data Resources, Inc., *US Long-Term Review* (Lexington, Mass.: McGraw-Hill, Spring 1982).
2.   Workshop on Alternative Energy Strategies (WAES), C.L. Wilson, project director, *Energy Supply to the Year 2000: Global and National Studies* (Cambridge, Mass.: MIT Press, 1977).
3.   These estimates for the depletion of U.S. and world petroleum and crude oil supplies were made based on the Hubbert curves shown in Chapter 2.
4.   As indicated by Figure 3–12, the Hubbert curve has remained very close to actual petroleum production. Indeed, since 1900, the greatest error in the Hubbert curve was 11 percent in 1963.
5.   For example, DOE projections of U.S. energy supplies include no gas imports Department of Energy, "Energy Transitions: The Forecast Through 2020," DOE/EIA-0281, (Washington, D.C.: USGPO, March 1981).
6.   W.A. Loeb, "How Small Hydro Is Growing Big," *Technology Review* 86(6) (1983):50 ff.
7.   In our reference scenario, we assumed that hydro's contribution increased from 1.0 quad in 1982 to 1.27 quad in 2025. This assumption was based on Harvey Brooks and Jack M. Hollander, "United States Energy Alternatives to the Year 2010 and Beyond: The CONAES Study," *Annual Review of Energy* 4 (1979):1–70.
8.   C.A.S. Hall, C.J. Cleveland, and M. Berger, "Yield Per Effort as a Function of Time and Effort for United States Petroleum, Uranium, and Coal," in W.J. Mitsch, R.W. Bosserman, and J.M. Klopatek, eds., *Energy and Ecological Modelling* (New York: Elsevier, 1981).
9.   Brooks and Hollander, "United States Energy Alternatives."
10. Department of Energy, Energy Information Administration, *Monthly Energy Review* (various years).
11. Department of Energy, Energy Information Administration, *Monthly Energy Review* (November 1984).
12. Department of Energy, Energy Information Administration, "U.S. Commercial Nuclear Power: Historical Perspective, Current State and Outlook," DOE/EIA-0315 (Washington, D.C.: USGPO, March 1982).

13. W.J. Dupreed and J.C. Cortino, *U.S. Energy Use Through the Year 2000* (revised) (Washington, D.C.: Bureau of Mines, U.S. Department of Interior, 1975); WAES, *Energy Supply to the Year 2000*; Brooks and Hollander, "United States Energy Alternatives."

14. Solar Energy Research Institute, *A New Prosperity: The SERI Solar/Conservation Study* (Andover, Mass.: Brick House, 1981).

15. T.J. Lareau and J. Darmstadter, *Energy and Household Expenditure Patterns* (Baltimore: Johns Hopkins University Press, 1983).

16. Examination of a wide array of fuel price projections revealed a consensus that real fuel prices will increase at an annual rate of 2.0 to 3.4 percent. The projection of consumer income for a given year was derived from our model's projection of per capita GNP from the previous year.

17. U.S. Bureau of the Census, "Projections of the Population of the United States by Age, Sex, and Race: 1983–2080," *Current Population Reports*, series P-25, no. 952 (Washington, D.C.: USGPO, 1984).

18. GNP can be calculated in two ways: as the sum of value added to raw materials, or as the value of final demand. The first counts fuel use directly. Fuel use also appears indirectly in the cost of products sold for final demand. Producers pass the costs of labor, fuel, and capital on to their customers, who pass them on to *their* customers, and so on down to the consumer. Both methods yield the same result.

19. Indeed, the real gap would be even bigger than this calculation suggests because we spread the energy costs of fuels evenly over time. In fact, however, most of the energy costs of fuels are paid up front when the necessary capital is built. The gap between GNP and the nonfuel national product would therefore be much greater when the alternative fuels are first being developed.

20. R. Jungk, *The New Tyranny* (New York: Grosset & Dunlap, 1979).

CHAPTER 5

Except where noted otherwise, figures for crop production and consumption, agricultural inputs, food exports, farm employment and income, and consumer expenditures for food came from Bureau of the Census, U.S. Department of Commerce, *Statistical Abstract of the United States* (Washington, D.C.: USGPO, 1982–83 and 1984), and USDA, *Agricultural Statistics* (Washington, D.C.: USGPO, various years).

1. R. Caro, *The Path to Power* (New York: Knopf, 1983).
2. Speech by Richard Bell at the National Farm Broadcasters Association Meeting, Kansas City, Kansas, November 15, 1975.
3. Moreover, data relating to on-farm issues are far more abundant than for off-farm issues, and our analysis reflects that fact.
4. The Center for Agriculture and Rural Development has published numerous reports on these matters, the latest being conducted under the aegis of the Resource Conservation Act (RCA) Appraisals. See B.C. English, K.F. Alt, and E.O. Heady, *A Documentation of the Resources Conservation Act's Assessment Model of Regional Agricultural Production, Land and Water Use, and Soil Loss* (CARD Report 107T) (Ames: Center for Agriculture and Rural Development, Iowa State University, 1982); USDA, *Soil and Water Resource Conservation Act: 1980 Appraisal*, pts. I and II (Washington, D.C.: USGPO, 1981) (widely known simply as the "RCA Appraisal"), Table 8, p. 59. Generally, the CARD models use a range in the estimates of future productivity. These estimates are derived from information and assumptions concerning the amount of technology (such as fertilizers, machinery, pesticides, and so forth) that will be used by farmers in the future. During the past 50 years, productivity grew at an average rate of 1.6 percent per year but has declined from 2.1 percent per year between 1940 and 1965 to 1.7 percent per year from 1965 to 1977. The CARD models provide a range of productivity growth to 2030 of from 0.6 percent per year to 1.6 percent per year. Their base model, which is used for most of their assessments, assumes a 1.1 percent per year growth in 1980, which declines to 0.8 percent per year growth by 2030. Crop yields follow these trends exactly; the CARD model and the USDA RCA Appraisal both assume that yields per acre will grow at 1.0 percent per year. It must be noted that this growth is due to both technology and an increased use of fossil fuel-based inputs like fertilizers. For specific crops, yields per acre will be as follows (at 1.1 percent) in 2030:

Corn	137 Bu. per acre
Wheat	42 Bu. per acre
Soybeans	46 Bu. per acre

Note further that the term *productivity* is often vague and confusing. Productivity is variously measured as "crop production per unit of cropland," "farm output per hour of labor," "crop output per unit of nitrogen fertilizer," "farm output per unit of all inputs," and more. We chose to rely on land productivity (crop output per unit of land, or yield per acre), as well as on our own measure of energy yield per unit of energy used. Moreover, the data often conflict concerning a measure of productivity from year to year. A 1975 National Academy of Sciences report, *Agricultural Production Efficiency* (Washington, D.C.: NAS, 1975), showed that when a time series of output per input from 1950 to 1970 was constructed first with data compiled in 1970 and then with 1972 data, the plots look different. The line labeled 1970 indicates that efficiency was increasing quite consistently from 1950 through 1963, then remained generally unchanged until 1970—the last year of that series. . . . However, the 1972 line exhibits a rather steady growth in efficiency from 1950 through 1971. The period of stagnation in efficiency exhibited in the [1970 line] was largely eliminated by the revisions made in 1972.

5.   B.C. English et al., *RCA Symposium: Future Agricultural Technology and Resource Conservation* (Ames: Center for Agricultural and Rural Development, Iowa State University, 1983). At this symposium a number of experts from various disciplines of agricultural research and development gathered to discuss future developments in technology, yields, and other issues. They predicted that feed grains and wheat could increase from 50 to 200 percent by 2030 (20 to 100 by 2000) with a most probable increase of around 100 percent (40 to 50 by 2000). Soybean yields could increase from 60 to 300 percent by 2030 (50 to 150 by 2000) with increases most probably being around 120 percent by 2030 (60 by 2000).

6.   K.M. Menz and C.F. Neumeyer, "Evaluation of Five Emerging Bio-Technologies for Maize," *Bioscience* 32 (1982):675–76. The 1 to 2 percent figure is based on a 5 tonne/ha yield figure, given in K.R. Keller, "Generating Technology," in J.W. Rosenblum, ed., *Agriculture in the Twenty-First Century* (New York: John Wiley & Sons, 1983), pp. 242–48.

7.   V.W. Ruttan, "Agricultural Research and the Future of American Agriculture," in S.S. Batie and R.G. Healy, eds., *The Future of American Agriculture as a Strategic Resource* (Washington, D.C.: Conservation Foundation, 1980), pp. 117–55. Table 1 is the

source of this information, under the heading "Land Productivity."

8. The RCA Appraisal itself suggests that

> while changes in agricultural technology have greatly increased the ability of farmers to produce more and better crops, technological advances have also masked conservation problems, and even contributed to them. For example, through the use of fertilizer and hybrid grains, yield per acre has continued to increase on soils that have lost a significant portion of the original fertile topsoil. . . . Some changes in production technology have adversely affected conservation practices. For example, some field windbreaks and terraces have been removed and the use of contour farming has been reduced to accommodate larger machinery.

9. H.T. Odum, *Environment, Power, and Society* (New York: John Wiley & Sons, 1971).

10. W.E. Larson, F.J. Pierce, and R.H. Dowdy, "The Threat of Soil Erosion to Long-Term Crop Production," *Science* 219 (1983):458–65.

11. W.H. Schlesinger, "Soil Organic Matter: A Source of Atmospheric Carbon Dioxide," in G. Woodwell, ed., *The Role of Terrestrial Vegetation in the Global Carbon Cycle*, SCOPE 23 (New York: John Wiley & Sons, 1984); R.P. Voroney, "Decomposition of Crop Residues," doctoral dissertation, University of Saskatchewan, 1983.

12. G. Leach, *Energy and Food Production* (Guilford, Surrey, U.K.: IPC Science and Technology Press, International Institute for Environment and Development, 1976); M.J.T. Norman, "Energy Inputs and Outputs of Subsistence Cropping Systems in the Tropics," *Agro-Ecosystems* 4 (1978):355–66. R. Rappaport, "Energy Flow in an Agricultural System," *Scientific American* 225 (1971):117–32.

13. The status of the Amish as archetypical organic farmers is now in some jeopardy. In recent years the number of Amish families has grown in areas of long-time settlement, such as Pennsylvania's Lancaster County. Originally farming on some of the nation's best soils, they now find themselves under pressure (due both to economic conditions and poorer soil fertility) to use commercial fertilizers, pesticides, and other industrial inputs. Some younger farmers are adopting these methods of industrial agriculture.

14. FONE, *Summary Report on Farming Operations* (Emmaus, Penn.: Regenerative Agriculture Association, 1985). This report summarizes a survey of 631 farms employing various conservation practices. In the first year of adopting conservation practices, 82 percent reported an increase or no change in net income.

15. Soil Conservation Service, "Conservation Tillage Systems" (Madison: SCS/USDA, June 1980); R.E. Phillips et al., "No-Tillage Agriculture," *Science* 208 (1980):1108–13; W.H. Wischmeier and D.D. Smith, *Predicting Rainfall Erosion Losses*, USDA Agricultural Handbook 537, (Washington, D.C.: USGPO, 1978). Phillips et al. suggest that no-till reduces soil erosion almost to zero, citing individual cases where erosion was reduced by as much as 99.5 percent. Wischmeier and Smith report less dramatic reductions, more in keeping with an 80 percent figure.

16. *Nova*, "Down on the Farm," transcript 1106 of television program broadcast on March 20, 1984 (Boston: WGBH Educational Foundation, 1984).

17. "Our Thinning Soil," *Land Resource Use and Protection*, Report 38 (Ames: Iowa State University, 1975). This reference given in The Cornucopia Project, *Empty Breadbasket?* (Emmaus, Penn.: Rodale Press, 1981), p. 32.

18. USDA, *Basic Statistics: National Resource Inventory*, USDA Stat. Bull. 686 (Washington, D.C.: USGPO, 1982). Also, the RCA Appraisal. The concept of erosion tolerance has been very controversial. Arguments have arisen as to whether any soil loss is tolerable; see K. Cook, "Soil Loss: A Question of Values," *Journal of Soil and Water Conservation* 37(2) (1982):89–92 and S. Ebenreck, "A Partnership Farmland Ethic," *Environmental Ethics* 5(1) (1983):33–45. For reviews of the historical development of soil loss tolerance theory, see D.L. Shertz, "The Basis for Soil Loss Tolerance," *Journal of Soil and Water Conservation* 38(1) (1983):10–14, and C. Elfring, "Land Productivity and Agricultural Technology," *Journal of Soil and Water Conservation* 38(1) (1983):7–9.

19. Martin Alexander, *Introduction to Soil Microbiology*, 2d ed. (New York: John Wiley & Sons, 1977), pp. 134–37.

20. High Plains Study Council, "A Summary of Results of the Ogallala Aquifer Regional Study, with Recommendations to the Secretary of Commerce and Congress" (1982); also, H.O. Banks, "Six-State High Plains Ogallala Aquifer Area Regional Study," in *Western Water Resources: Coming Problems and the Policy*

Alternatives, a symposium sponsored by the Federal Reserve Bank of Kansas City, 1980, pp. 199–220.

21. U.S. Water Resources Council, *The Nation's Water Resources 1975–2000: 2nd National Water Assessment* (Washington, D.C.: USGPO, 1978).

22. U.S. Water Resources Council, *The Nation's Water Resources 1975–2000: 2nd National Water Assessment*, volume 1 (Washington, D.C.: USGPO, 1978).

23. High Plains Study Council, "A Summary of Results of the Ogallala Aquifer Regional Study"; Banks, "Six-State High Plains Ogallala Aquifer Regional Study."

24. D. Pimentel et al., "Environmental Quality and Natural Biota," *Bioscience* 30(11) (1980):750–55. Estimates of annual pesticide use vary widely, because few hard data are available. *Agricultural Statistics* reports that pesticide use in 1980 may have approached 700,000 tons, while the National Academy of Sciences estimated in 1982 that it may have been as little as 257,000 tons ("Impacts of Emerging Agricultural Trends on Fish and Wildlife Habitat," Washington, D.C.: NAS, 1982), though the NAS figure did not include all pesticides. And in 1979, the Council on Environmental Quality ("Environmental Quality: The Tenth Annual Report of the CEQ," Washington, D.C.: USGPO, 1979) gave a figure of 480,000 tons that it derived from data given by the International Trade Commission.

25. National Academy of Sciences, "Impacts of Emerging Agricultural Trends on Fish and Wildlife Habitat."

26. C.B. Huffaker "Life against Life—Nature's Pest Control Scheme," *Environmental Research* 3 (1970):162–75.

27. USDA, "Food Consumption, Prices, and Expenditures 1962–82," ERS Stat. Bull. 702 (Washington, D.C.: USGPO, 1983).

28. This was taken from unpublished tables supplied to us by the USDA in 1984. These tables update the USDA publication *Livestock-Feed Relationships*, Statistical Bulletin 530 and supplements. The 40/60 split between forage- and crop-fed animals is based on the assumption that the meat kcal finding their way into the diet are proportional to those kcal found in forage and crop feeds (in "corn feeding equivalents") for all meat products. A calculation performed on a commodity-by-commodity basis would show a somewhat different split: 30/70.

29. U.S. Forest Service, *An Assessment of the Forest and Range Land Situation in the United States* (Washington, D.C.: USDA, 1980), part 1, section on "Range."

30. Feed consumed by animals was given in an unpublished table sent to us by USDA in January 1984. The tables standardize different feed sources by expressing them as equivalent feeding weights of corn grain. To convert to crop energy output, we used the value of 3.48 million kcal per metric ton of feed using information supplied in Table 1 of USDA, *Composition of Foods: Raw, Processed, Prepared*, Agricultural Handbook 8 (Washington, D.C.: USGPO, 1963). We compared total feed kcal inputs to animal-derived kcal in the U.S. diet. This dietary estimate was based on U.S. population, the caloric content of the average per capita diet and the proportion of animal-derived kcal in the diet. USDA, *Food Consumption, Prices, and Expenditures*, USDA Statistical Bulletin 672 (Washington, D.C.: USGPO, 1981) gives the per capita kcal consumption and the fractionation of animal and nonanimal-derived kcal in the diet. By looking at total kcal inputs and outputs in this way we get an overall system efficiency of 15.1:1 in 1979. These statistics are weighted in recognition of the fact that many animals are fed on pasture for some part of their lives and on crops for the rest (final fattening, for example).

31. Based on carcass weights for the three commodities (English, Alt, and Heady, *Documentation of the Resource Conservation Act's Assessment Model*; USDA, *Food Consumption, Prices, and Expenditures*), dressed weight percentage, the edible energy content of each retail cut (USDA, *Composition of Foods*, Agriculture Handbook 8 (Washington, D.C.: USGPO, 1963)), and the energy content of feed, 1,580 kcal/lb of corn grain.

32. This estimate includes energy used in restaurants, energy used in cars on food-related errands, energy used to construct and maintain food-related buildings, energy used at home to cook food, and energy used in waste disposal, as well as energy used in food processing, packaging, and transportation industries. There are many other estimates, which vary widely due to differing definitions of food-related activities and differing estimates of fuel use for a given activity. See M.B. Green, *Eating Oil: Energy Use in Food Production* (Boulder: Westview Press, 1978); J.S. Steinhart and C.E. Steinhart, "Energy Use in the U.S. Food System." *Science* 184 (1974):307–16; Federal Energy Administration, *Energy Use in the Food System* (Washington, D.C.: USGPO, 1976); J.D. Buffington and J.H. Zar, "Realistic and Unrealistic Energy Conservation Potential in Agriculture," in W. Lockeretz, ed., *Agriculture and Energy* (New York: Academic Press, 1977), p. 696.

CHAPTER 6

1. Energy inputs for 1940 to 1970 based on data in J.S. Steinhart and C.E. Steinhart, "Energy Use in the U.S. Food System," *Science* 184 (1974):307–16. The Steinharts' data for fuel used in irrigation and to make agricultural steel were left out of our analysis because irrigation fuel use is almost certainly already accounted for in the category "direct fuel use" and the data for agricultural steel are small and unreliable. Direct energy use on farms in 1974 and 1978 came from David Torgerson and Harold Cooper, *Energy and U.S. Agriculture 1974 and 1978*, USDA Statistical Bulletin 632 (Washington, D.C.: USGPO, 1980) Direct energy use on farms in 1979 came from the 1978 *Census of Agriculture*, vol. 5, 1979 Farm Energy Survey, Special Reports pt. 9 (Washington, D.C.: USGPO, 1979). These sources report various types of fuels used in agriculture. To maintain consistency, we used the same fuel/energy conversion factors as Steinhart and Steinhart. Data for energy embodied in agricultural chemicals and farm machinery for 1974, 1978, and 1979 were taken from the *Annual Survey of Manufacturers*, various years, and were corrected for exports.

   Data for domestic food energy output were derived from per capita caloric intake and the fraction of that intake assignable to crop-fed animal foods, vegetables, fruits, grains. Feed consumed by animals that eventually became part of the diet was given in a USDA unpublished table sent to us in January 1984. We also made corrections for the energetic value of exports, crop failure, fallow, area in cotton and tobacco, and feeds consumed by draft animals.

2. B.C. English et al., *RCA Symposium: Future Agricultural Technology and Resource Conservation* (Ames: Center for Agricultural and Rural Development, Iowa State University, 1983); S.H. Wittwer, "The New Agriculture: A View of the Twenty-First Century," and R.L. Mitchell, "Implications for Plant Agriculture," in J.W. Rosenblum, ed., *Agriculture in the Twenty-First Century* (New York: John Wiley & Sons, 1983); K.M. Menz and C.F. Neumeyer, "Evaluation of Five Emerging Biotechnologies for Maize," *Bioscience* 32 (1982):675–76; Food and Agriculture Organization, *Agriculture: Toward 2000* (Rome: FAO, 1981); E.O. Heady, "The Adequacy of Agricultural Land: A Demand-Supply Perspective," in P.R. Crosson, ed., *The Cropland Crisis* (Baltimore: Johns Hop-

kins University Press, 1982); "Feeding a Hungry World," *Resources* 76 (1984):1–20; National Academy of Sciences, *Agricultural Production Efficiency*, (Washington, D.C.: NAS, 1975); Office of Technology Assessment, *Global Models, World Futures, and Public Policy* (Washington, D.C.: USGPO, 1982).

3. P. Crosson and A.T. Stout, *Productivity Effects of Cropland Erosion* (Washington, D.C.: Resources for the Future, 1984); USDA, *RCA 1980 Appraisal Part II* (Washington, D.C.: USGPO, 1981).

4. This assumption is probably unrealistic. Most of this land is forest, wetland, or grazing land, the conversion of which would remove land from an important existing use and entail an energy cost. Moreover, USDA's 1977 National Resources Inventory suggests that much of this land will be of poorer quality than existing cropland—35 percent of the potential cropland is in the USDA's top two quality classes, compared to 54 percent of active cropland—so that the energy cost of a unit of food grown on it will be higher than average. However, data is not available on how much higher, so we made the extremely conservative assumption that the land is of average quality. As a consequence, the model *overestimates* on-farm energy efficiency.

5. R.I. Dideriksen, A.R. Hidlebaugh, and K.O. Schmude, *Potential Cropland Study*, USDA, Soil Conservation Service, Statistical Bulletin 578 (Washington, D.C.: USGPO, 1977); K.O. Schmude, "A Perspective on Prime Farmland," *Journal of Soil and Water Conservation* (September/October 1977).

6. B.C. English, K.F. Alt, and E.O. Heady, *A Documentation of the Resource Conservation Act's Assessment Model of Regional Agricultural Production, Land and Water Use, and Soil Loss* (CARD Report 107T) (Ames: Center for Agricultural and Rural Development, Iowa State University, 1982).

7. Future estimates of commodity weight consumption given by English, Alt, and Heady, *A Documentation* (Appendix B), converted to kcal equivalents using information in USDA, *Composition of Foods*, Agricultural Handbook 8 (Washington, D.C.: USDA, 1963).

8. The 35 percent animal-derived kcal in the typical U.S. diet came from a USDA series entitled *Food Consumption, Prices and Expenditures* (Washington, D.C.: USGPO, various years) and updates. The crop-fed/forage-fed fractionation is based on the proportional contribution of each type of feed consumed by the animals that are eventually consumed by humans. This information was taken from unpublished tables prepared by USDA.

9. English, Alt, and Heady, *A Documentation*.
10. USDA, *RCA 1980 Appraisal*; English, Alt, and Heady, *A Documentation*. This assumed rate of increase, incidentally, is even faster than the anticipated increase in oil imports.
11. See note 2 for sources. The 1975 NAS study offers a discussion regarding the semantic difficulties encountered in analyzing such data, and it was evident from our reading that the vagueness has persisted into the 1980s. We assumed that half of the projected yield increases could be assigned to true efficiency gains like those from genetic improvement of crop strains (see Mitchell, note 2).
12. P.R. Crosson and S. Brubaker, *Resource and Environmental Effects of U.S. Agriculture*, (Washington, D.C.: Resources for the Future, 1982); V.W. Ruttan, "Agricultural Research and the Future of American Agriculture," in S. Batie and R.G. Healy, eds., *The Future of American Agriculture as a Strategic Resource* (Washington, D.C.: Conservation Foundation, 1980).
13. See note 3.
14. The timeseries should not be interpreted as a validation of our model, *per se*, for a true test would require use of an independent dataset. Since there is no such additional energy-related data, we can only state that the model is operating correctly within the bounds of our knowledge and that it is valid to base our analysis on a single aggregate regression.
15. D. Dvoskin and E.O. Heady, "Economic and Environmental Impacts of the Energy Crisis on Agricultural Production," in W. Lockeretz, ed., *Agriculture and Energy* (New York: Academic Press, 1977). See also review in R.C. Fluck and C.D. Baird, *Agricultural Energetics* (Westport, Conn.: Avi Publishing Co., 1980).
16. P. M. Raup, "Competition for Land and the Future of American Agriculture," in Batie and Healy, *The Future of American Agriculture as a Strategic Resource*.
17. The per-acre yield curve approaches the absolute maximum output asymptotically; so, strictly speaking, additional energy inputs will always give some increase, though increasingly tiny, in output. Thus, the model stops adding energy and starts adding land when output reaches 96 percent of the asymptotic limit.
18. See note 2.
19. A.F. Turhollow, C. Short, and E.O. Heady, *Potential Impacts of Future Energy Price Increases on U.S. Agricultural Production*, CARD Report 116 (Ames: Center for Agricultural and Rural Development, Iowa State University, 1983). Note that the aggregate figure masks the fact that certain elements of energy use

are especially hard hit, such as groundwater irrigation, which is projected to fall by more than 75 percent with a doubling of energy prices and moderate food demand.

20. National Academy of Sciences, *Agricultural Production Efficiency*, pp. 79–83.

21. W. Lockeretz, G. Shearer, and D.H. Kohl, "Organic Farming in the Corn Belt," *Science* 211 (1981):540–46.

CHAPTER 7

1. Bose Anderson, "Impact of New Technologies on Generation Scheduling," *IEEE TPAS* 1(3) (Jan. 1984).

2. P.G. Lebel, *Energy, Economics, and Technology* (Baltimore: Johns Hopkins University Press, 1982).

3. A. Lovins, *Soft Energy Paths: Towards a Durable Peace* (Cambridge, Mass.: Ballinger, 1977).

4. J. T. Edsall, "Toxicity of Plutonium and Some Other Actinides," *Bulletin of the Atomic Scientists* 32 (1976):26–37.

5. R. Jungk, *The New Tyranny* (New York: Grossett & Dunlap, 1979).

6. U.S. General Accounting Office, "Net Energy Analysis: Little Progress and Many Problems," GAO 1.13 EMD-77-57 (Washington, D.C.: USGPO, August 1977).

7. R. Aster, "Progress Report 18," DOE-JPL 1012-58 (Washington, D.C.: USGPO, July 1981).

8. Atomic Industrial Forum, quoted in the *Boston Globe*, March 31, 1984.

9. The U.S. government has spent about $15.9 billion (1972 dollars) on research and development of commercial nuclear power (U.S. Department of Energy, "Federal Support for Nuclear Power: Reactor Design and the Fuel Cycle," DOE/EIA-0201/13 (Washington, D.C.: USGPO, Feb. 1981)). Another $8.5 billion has been invested in cancelled nuclear power plants (U.S. Department of Energy, Energy Information Administration, *Nuclear Plant Cancellations: Causes, Costs, and Consequences*, DOE/EIA-0392 (Washington, D.C.: USGPO, April 1983)). A rough calculation of the relationship of dollar costs to energy costs indicates that this $24.4 billion is equivalent to about 283 trillion kcal, which, in addition to the 1,890 trillion kcal invested by the corporations that built the plants (based on an energy profit ratio of 4 for the plants alone), makes a total

investment in nuclear power of 2,170 trillion kcal. On the other side, we will ultimately receive a total of about 7,500 trillion kcal of electricity from existing plants and others still under construction (assuming that none of them is cancelled or closed early). Thus, the energy profit ratio of the U.S. nuclear system, without counting decommissioning and permanent waste storage costs, will be about 3.4.

10. The five-year lag is extremely optimistic. It may take nearly ten years to build a nuclear fission plant and fifteen for an oil shale retort. Individual solar panels and other tools of the soft path may be built much more quickly, but years could pass before a significant number are built and distributed.

11. U.S. Department of Energy, "Residential Energy Consumption Survey: Consumption and Expenditures", DOE/EIA-0321/1 (Washington, D.C.: USGPO, 1982).

12. R.G. Lillard, *The Great Forest* (New York: Alfred A. Knopf, 1947), p. 85.

13. L. Brown et al., *The State of the World 1984* (New York: W.W. Norton, 1984).

14. J. Darmstadter et al., *How Industrial Societies Use Energy: A Comparative Analysis* (Baltimore: Johns Hopkins University Press, 1977).

15. D.B. Goldstein, "Refrigerator Reform: Guidelines for Energy Gluttons," *Technology Review* 86(2) (1983):36–46.

16. B.J. Friedan and K. Baker, "The Market Needs Help: The Disappointing Record of Home Energy Conservation," *Journal of Policy Analysis and Management* 2 (1983):432–48.

17. P.M. Boffey, "Rational Decisions' Prove Not To Be," *New York Times* (Dec. 6, 1983), p. C1.

18. A.H. Rosenfeld, *Progress in Energy Efficient Buildings* (Berkeley: Lawrence Berkeley Laboratory, Nov. 12, 1981), p. 22.

19. E. Hirst, *Evaluation of Utility Home Energy Audit (RCS) Programs* (Oak Ridge, Tenn.: Oak Ridge National Laboratory, Feb. 1984).

20. See note 32.

21. For details, see C. Flavin, *Energy and Architecture: The Solar and Conservation Potential*, Worldwatch Paper 40 (Washington, D.C.: Worldwatch Institute, 1980).

22. J.A. Hausman, "Individual Discount Rates and the Purchase and Utilization of Energy Using Durables," *Bell Journal of Economics* 10 (1979):33–54.

23. W.H. Cunningham and S.C. Loprento, *Energy Use and Conservation Incentives: A Study of the Southwestern United States* (New York: Praeger, 1977), pp. 84–86.

24. H.H. Landsberg and J.M. Dukert, *High Energy Costs: Uneven, Unfair, Unavoidable* (Baltimore: Johns Hopkins University Press, 1981).

25. R. Perlman and R.L. Warren, *Families in the Energy Crisis* (Cambridge, Mass.: Ballinger, 1977).

26. D.A. Stockman, "The Wrong War? The Case against a National Energy Policy", *The Public Interest* 53 (1978):3–44.

27. D.B. Goldstein, "Refrigerator Reform."

28. B. Harrison and B. Bluestone, "More Jobs, Lower Wages," *New York Times*, June 19, 1984, p. A27.

29. T. Page, *Conservation and Economic Efficiency: An Approach to Materials Policy* (Baltimore: Johns Hopkins University Press, 1977).

30. M. Conte and A. Tannenbaum, "Employee-Owned Companies: Is the Difference Measurable?," *Monthly Labor Review* 101(7) (1978):23–28; K. Bradley and A. Gelb, *Worker Capitalism: The New Industrial Relations* (Cambridge, Mass.: MIT Press, 1983); K. Rosenberg, "Promoting Employee-Run Firms," book review, *Technology Review* 88(3) (1985):20–21.

31. Council for Agricultural Science and Technology, *Energy Use and Production in Agriculture*, report 99 (Ames: CAST, February 1984), pp. 50–51.

32. See note 20.

AFTERWORD

1. J. Russell Smith, *Tree Crops* (New York: Harper & Row, 1950).

2. President's Materials Policy Commission, *Resources for Freedom*, vol. 4: *Promise of Technology*, by William S. Paley, Chairman (Washington, D.C.: Government Printing Office, 1952), pp. 213–20.

3. Christopher Flavin, *Renewable Energy at the Crossroads* (Washington, D.C.: Center for Renewable Resources, 1985), p. 2.

GLOSSARY

Agricultural technology: biotechnology and crop hybridization as well as the development of machinery, fertilizers, insecticides, herbicides, and other means of increasing crop production on the same amount of land.

Biotechnology: the future development of improved crop strains through genetic engineering, cell or tissue culture, the use of synthetic or natural growth regulators, and enhancement of photosynthesis and nitrogen fixation.

Calorie: a measure of heat energy; the amount of energy that will heat a gram of water by one degree centigrade. One thousand calories (one kcal) equal one food Calorie (usually distinguished by being spelled with a capital "C").

Carrying capacity: a biological term that refers to the number of individuals of a species that can be supported in a sustainable way in a particular region. A field, for example, has a carrying capacity for cattle, a maximum number that can graze there without overgrazing it. Carrying capacity depends on numerous factors, some of which are: the number of predators, the climate, the availability of food, and the recovery rate of the species and of its food sources.

Conservation: reducing the amount of energy that is used to produce a given good or service without reducing the consumption of that good or service. For example, heating a house to the same tempera-

289

ture while using less fuel through installing a more efficient boiler or insulation. Cf. *curtailment.*

Conservation tillage: methods of planting or conditioning soil that leave residues from previous crops on the field to protect the soil from wind- and rain-induced erosion. This may also be called low-till or no-till farming.

Constant dollars: see *real dollars.*

Cornucopianism: the belief that the world's resources are now and always will be abundant, regardless of the size of human population, and that human living standards on earth will continually improve. This is associated particularly with Julian Simon and Herman Kahn.

Crop-fed animal products: that portion of the human diet composed of meat, poultry, eggs, dairy products, and animal fats that were derived from animals that were fed crops (including harvested forage) rather than grazed.

Curtailment: reducing the amount of energy consumed through reducing the amount of goods or services consumed. For example, reducing the amount of fuel used to heat a house by lowering the temperature in the house. Cf. *conservation.*

Energy: the capacity to do work, to oppose the natural tendency of things toward disorder; one of the two fundamental constituents of the universe (the other is matter; energy may be converted to matter and vice versa through the Einstein equation, $E = mc^2$).

Energy cost: the amount of energy needed to extract a given quantity of a resource from the environment and to refine it for human use. Also, the cost of any process or economic activity in terms of the total amount of energy required to provide or maintain it.

Energy efficiency: a measurement of the amount of energy required to produce a given amount of a good or service, or all goods and services. This concept is usually used to compare different methods of producing a good or service. It is distinguished from fuel efficiency.

Energy profit ratio: the ratio of heat energy contained in a fuel divided by the energy used to extract the fuel from the environment, refine it to a socially useful state, and deliver it to consumers.

Erosion: the loss of soil from agricultural land, particularly through water run-off or wind.

Existing market: the current system of producing and distributing goods and services in the United States, including private enterprise, government incentives and disincentives, and information available to consumers. This system determines the current and future make-up of the economy.

Export capacity: as it applies to food, the difference between total food production and domestic demand. Because of the potential foreign consumers' lack of willingness or ability to pay, not all of the export capacity of food need actually be exported.

Fuel: a form of energy usable by humans to produce goods and services. This can include solar energy insofar as it can be used directly; for example, to heat homes.

Fuel efficiency: an index of the amount of economic output that can be obtained from a kilocalorie of a particular fuel; for example, for most applications a kilocalorie of oil can generate more output than a kilocalorie of coal. Oil is therefore a more efficient fuel than coal. This is distinct from energy efficiency.

Fuel quality: resource quality as it applies to fuels; an index of the amount of energy required to obtain fuels from the environment.

Gross national product (GNP): the total market dollar value of all final goods and services produced by a nation during a year, or the sum of all value added to resources.

Hard path: fuel alternatives to oil and gas that are based on nonrenewable energy sources such as nuclear fission and fusion, liquified and gassified coal, and oil shale. This term was coined by Amory Lovins; cf. *soft path.*

Household fuel consumption: fuel that is not used to produce goods and services for sale but that is consumed directly by individuals in homes or private transportation.

Hubbert curve: a bell-shaped curve describing the rate of oil production over time. Named for geologist M.K. Hubbert, who introduced the concept in 1956.

Human carrying capacity: the number of humans who can live in a given territory indefinitely. This is difficult to quantify because human beings differ from other species in that we trade goods and natural resources, our standard of living can vary widely, and we are able to change the materials we use as resources and to transform natural resources substantially. But the population of human beings is limited by the resources available to us at any given time. Because our current standard of living is much higher than necessary for basic survival, a more useful concept is the limits placed by natural systems on our ability to produce enough goods and services to sustain our current standard of living.

Kilocalorie (kcal): one thousand calories or one food Calorie.

National energy efficiency: a measure of the amount of energy needed to produce all goods and services, usually expressed as the ratio of gross national product (GNP) in real dollars to total national fuel use.

Neoclassical economics: the conventional view of the economic world, which sees the production of goods and services as a closed, self-regulating cycle of money and goods between households and firms.

Net energy: the heat energy contained in a fuel minus the energy used to extract the fuel from the environment, refine it to a socially useful state, and deliver it to consumers. Also, the amount of energy available to produce nonfuel goods and services.

Nonrenewable resources: a resource that is not replenished after its use by humans or that replenishes too slowly for human use; for example, minerals and fossil fuels. Nonrenewable resources are generally geological in origin. Cf. *renewable resources.*

Off-farm: the portion of the agricultural sector that refines, transports, stores, and cooks food products for human consumption.

On-farm: the portion of the agricultural sector that plants, raises, and harvests raw food products. This includes the production of inputs (machinery and chemicals) that are used by farmers.

Production curve (also yield curve): a graph of the mathematical relation between crop production per acre on the vertical axis and energy input per acre on the horizontal axis.

Productivity: the amount of economic output, in dollars, produced per worker-hour of labor.

Real dollars (also constant dollars): dollars corrected for inflation to a standard year.

Renewable resource: a resource that may be fully replenished (over a relatively short time scale, usually years but possibly centuries) after its use by humans; for example, fish, most groundwater, trees, and solar energy. In general, the replenishment cycles of renewable resouces are powered by solar energy. However, a renewable resource can be used at a fast enough rate that it is fully depleted and unable to renew itself; for example, some fisheries and groundwater deposits. Cf. *nonrenewable resource.*

Reserves: the amount of a resource that is known to exist in a form that can be economically exploited with existing technolgy.

Resource: a naturally occurring material that can be used to produce a good or service for humans or that is in itself useful to humans.

Resource quality: the energy needed to obtain a unit of some resource. Resources vary in accessibility and concentration and therefore require varying amounts of effort to extract them from the environment and make them useful to the economy. Resource quality is an index of this variation.

Soft path: fuel alternatives to oil and gas that are based on renewable, particularly solar, energy sources such as photovoltaics, passive and active solar thermal energy, wind, and hydroelectricity. This term was created by Amory Lovins. Cf. *hard path*.

Yield curve: see *production curve*.

INDEX

ABOUT THE AUTHORS

JOHN GEVER has been the staff writer/editor at CSRC since 1982. He holds a B.S. in astronomy and physics from the University of Michigan, which he received in 1977, and a 1981 M.S. in science journalism from Boston University. He has written about environmental issues, biotechnology, and medicine for a number of regional and national publications.

ROBERT KAUFMANN was a research scientist at CSRC from 1979 to 1984; he is now obtaining a doctorate from the University of Pennsylvania's Energy Management and Policy program. He graduated with honors from Cornell University in 1979 with a B.S. in biology and received an M.A. in economics from the University of New Hampshire in 1984. He is co-author (with Charles Hall and Cutler Cleveland) of a book on energy-based economic analysis, *Energy and Economics: The Ecology of Industrial Systems*, to be published in 1985 by John Wiley & Sons. He has also co-authored several scientific papers in biology and economics, including an article in *Science* titled "Energy and the U.S. Economy: A Biophysical Perspective."

DAVID SKOLE has been a research scientist at CSRC since 1980. He has two degrees from Indiana University, an A.B. in biology (1977) and an M.S. in environmental science (1979). He has worked extensively with computer modeling in environmental science, publishing several papers on tropical land use and the role of terrestrial life in the global carbon budget.

CHARLES VÖRÖSMARTY is a research scientist at CSRC, where he has been since its founding in 1978. He received a B.S. in biology from Cornell University in 1977 and an M.S. in civil engineering from the University of New Hampshire in 1983, where he is now obtaining a doctorate. A specialist in ecological modeling, he has authored numerous papers dealing with estuarine water quality. He has developed a special interest in how nutrients are processed within drainage basins disturbed by humans.

COMPLEX SYSTEMS
RESEARCH CENTER

The COMPLEX SYSTEMS RESEARCH CENTER of the University of New Hampshire, founded in 1978, investigates problems stemming from interactions between humans and their environment. These problems—the global buildup of atmospheric carbon dioxide, pollution of coastal environments, and faltering industrial economies, to name a few—are manifestations of *complex systems* involving the interplay of biological, physical, and economic systems.

Center research cuts across the boundaries of traditional scientific disciplines and embraces the social sciences and humanities as well. Rather than break down national and global problems into isolated pieces and then studying each piece separately, the Center uses mathematical modeling and policy analysis to study them as systems. Within this framework, the Complex Systems Research Center uses three criteria in choosing its research projects: CSRC projects must be related to the human use of resources; they need a strong natural science component; and, most importantly, their study must yield results

305

which will influence industrial and governmental policy judgments.

In addition to the study that led to this book, current CSRC investigations include models of global biogeochemical cycles; studies of estuarine nutrient dynamics; examinations of the use of science in policymaking; assessment of local water quality controls and the institutions available to implement them; joint use of the resources of the Gulf of Maine and Georges Bank by the United States and Canada; models for closed life support systems for use in outer space; and management of databases relating to New Hampshire's economy, demographics, and physical infrastructure.

The Center's funding has grown enormously since its founding, increasing from $30,000 in 1978 to $812,000 in grants, contracts, and awards in fiscal 1984. Sources of current funding include the National Science Foundation, the National Aeronautics and Space Administration, the Department of Energy, the National Oceanic and Atmospheric Administration, and the State of New Hampshire's Office of State Planning.